JOURNAL OF MORAL THEOLOGY

VOLUME 14, SPECIAL ISSUE 1
APRIL 2025

VERITATIS SPLENDOR
THREE DECADES ON:
ITS LEGACY FOR OUR TIMES

EDITED BY
JANA BENNETT
and
ALESSANDRO ROVATI

JOURNAL · OF
M · O · R · A · L
THEOLOGY

Journal of Moral Theology is published semiannually, with regular issues in January and July. Our mission is to publish scholarly articles in the field of Catholic moral theology, as well as theological treatments of related topics in philosophy, economics, political philosophy, and psychology.

Articles published in the *Journal of Moral Theology* undergo at least two double blind peer reviews. To submit an article for the journal, please visit the "For Authors" page on our website at jmt.scholasticahq.com/for-authors.

Journal of Moral Theology is available full text in the *ATLA Religion Database with ATLASerials®* (RDB®), a product of the American Theological Library Association.
Email: atla@atla.com, www.atla.com.
ISSN 2166-2851 (print)
ISSN 2166-2118 (online)

Journal of Moral Theology is published by The Journal of Moral Theology, Inc.

Copyright © 2025 individual authors and The Journal of Moral Theology, Inc. All rights reserved.

Pickwick Publications, An Imprint of Wipf and Stock Publishers, 199 W. 8th Ave., Suite 3, Eugene, OR 97401
www.wipfandstock.com. ISBN: 979-8-3852-5223-7

JOURNAL · OF
M·O·R·A·L
THEOLOGY

EDITOR EMERITUS
Jason King, *St. Mary's University, San Antonio, TX*

EDITOR
M. Therese Lysaught, *Loyola University Chicago Stritch School of Medicine*

SENIOR EDITOR
William J. Collinge, *Mount St. Mary's University*

ASSOCIATE EDITORS
Mari Rapela Heidt, *Notre Dame of Maryland University*
Alexandre A. Martins, *Marquette University*
Mary M. Doyle Roche, *College of the Holy Cross*
Matthew Shadle, *Window Light*
Kate Ward, *Marquette University*

MANAGING EDITOR
Jean-Pierre Fortin, *St. Michael's College, University of Toronto*

EDITORIAL ASSISANT
Aaron Weisel, *Ave Maria University*

EDITORIAL BOARD

Christina Astorga, *University of Portland*
Jana M. Bennett, *University of Dayton*
James Caccamo, *St. Joseph's University*
Victor Carmona, *University of San Diego*
Carolyn A. Chau, *King's University College at Western University, Ontario*
Stan Chu Ilo, *DePaul University*
Meghan Clark, *St. John's University*
Dana Dillon, *Providence College*
Jorge Jose Ferrer, SJ, *Pontifical Catholic University of Puerto Rico*
Daniel Fleming, *St. Vincent's Health Australia/University of Notre Dame Australia*
Julia A. Fleming, *Creighton University*
Joseph Flipper, *University of Dayton*
Nichole M. Flores, *University of Virginia*
Craig A. Ford, Jr., *St. Norbert College*
Matthew J. Gaudet, *Santa Clara University*
Leo Guardado, *Fordham University*
Andrew Kim, *Marquette University*
Cory Labrecque, *Université Laval*
Amy Levad, *University of St. Thomas, MN*
Leocadie Lushombo, *Santa Clara University*
Christina G. McRorie, *Boston College*
Cory D. Mitchell, *PeaceHealth*
Suzanne Mulligan, *Institute for Social Concerns, University of Notre Dame*
Sheryl Overmyer, *DePaul University*
Anna Perkins, *University of the West Indies/St. Michael's Theological College, Jamaica*
Bernard G. Prusak, *John Carroll University*
Emily Reimer-Barry, *University of San Diego*
Alessandro Rovati, *Belmont Abbey College*
Tobias Winright, *St. Patrick's Pontifical University, Ireland*

JOURNAL OF MORAL THEOLOGY
VOLUME 14, SPECIAL ISSUE 1
APRIL 2025

CONTENTS

Veritatis Splendor Three Decades On: Shared Principles and Hidden Conflicts
    Jana Bennett and Alessandro Rovati 1

A *Ressourcement* Encyclical: *Veritatis Splendor* and the Recovery of Christocentric Moral Theology
    Michael A. Wahl 13

Seeds for an Encounter Ethics: The Fruit of Reading *Veritatis Splendor* Beyond a Post-Conciliar Binary Narrative
    Catherine Moon 38

Veritatis Splendor and the Persistence of the Law-Conscience Binary in Catholic Moral Theology
    Nicholas Ogle 62

The Pastoral Conversion of Moral Theology and "The Perspective of the Acting Person" in *Veritatis Splendor*
    Matthew Kuhner 85

Amoris Laetitia Develops the Subjective Conscience from *Veritatis Splendor*
    Matthew P. Schneider 106

Moral Law and Pastoral Praxis from *Veritatis Splendor* to the Magisterium of Francis
    Gustavo Irrazábal 132

The Splendor of Freedom in Theory and Practice: The Complementary Moral Theologies of John Paul II and Francis
    Conor Kelly 156

Divine Authority and Absolute Moral Norms
    Anthony Hollowell 182

Veritatis Splendor After Thirty Years: Exposition and Critique
    Todd A. Salzman and Michael G. Lawler............................ 202

"He Himself Becomes a Living and Personal Law": *Veritatis Splendor*, Eating Disorders, and Misguided Moralism
    Megan Heeder.. 222

Veritatis Splendor Three Decades On: Shared Principles and Hidden Conflicts

Jana Bennett and Alessandro Rovati

Abstract: *Veritatis Splendor* marked a pivotal moment in contemporary moral theology and its teaching addresses many topics that remain at the center of current theological debates. The encyclical invites scholars to continue its work by extending, integrating, and pursuing new questions with it. Thus, two years after the thirtieth anniversary of its publication, the time is ripe for a theological appraisal of and engagement with the legacy of *Veritatis Splendor* that seeks to bring its biblical, dogmatic, and pastoral claims into conversation with contemporary moral theology and the challenges it strives to address. Such a project is especially urgent in light of the request to moral theologians advanced by Francis and the Synod of Bishops to reflect more on the relationship between love and truth, on the one hand, and pastoral care and doctrine, on the other. Furthermore, the question of how to think about the relationship between the magisterium of John Paul II and Francis has been at the center of scholarly and popular debates for quite some time. Addressing these two crucial issues and many others necessitates that we come to terms with the legacy of *Veritatis Splendor* and its doctrinal commitments. The current special issue of the *Journal of Moral Theology* makes a valuable contribution to this task by including essays that closely engage with John Paul II's moral theology from various standpoints. Thus, we hope it might help moral theologians identify elements of consensus, name the remaining tensions, and engage in productive disagreements that help the church move forward in its attempt to give a loving witness to the light of truth amidst contemporary challenges.

THE PUBLICATION OF THE ENCYCLICAL LETTER *VERITATIS Splendor* on August 6, 1993, marked a pivotal moment in moral theology. The encyclical combined a thoroughly Christocentric and scriptural approach to ethics, a deeply personalist perspective, and the reaffirmation of the centrality of natural law and universal unchanging moral norms for human flourishing. *Veritatis Splendor* also reflected on the interconnections between freedom and law, conscience and truth, and grace and moral actions. At the same time, the encyclical spurred intense debates among moral theologians and caused some seemingly intractable disagreements to emerge.¹

Clearly, *Veritatis Splendor* addresses many topics moral theologians continue to reflect on, and it simultaneously invites contemporary scholars to continue its work by extending, integrating, and pursuing new questions with it.² Two years after the thirtieth anniversary of its publication, the time is ripe for a theological appraisal of and engagement with the legacy of *Veritatis Splendor* that seeks to bring its biblical, dogmatic, and pastoral claims into conversation with contemporary moral theology and the challenges it strives to address. Such a project is especially urgent in light of the request to moral theologians advanced by Francis and the Synod of Bishops to reflect more on the relationship between love and truth, on the one hand, and

---

¹ For a very thorough bibliography of the theological engagements with *Veritatis Splendor* see Michael Dauphinais, "The Splendor and Gift of the Christian Moral Life: *Veritatis Splendor* at Twenty-Five," *Nova et Vetera* 16, no. 4 (2018): 1303–1312. Some examples include: John Wilkins, ed., *Considering* Veritatis Splendor (Pilgrim, 1994); Michael E. Allsopp and John J. O'Keefe, eds., Veritatis Splendor*: American Responses* (Sheed & Ward, 1995); Charles E. Curran and Richard A. McCormick, eds., *John Paul II and Moral Theology: Readings in Moral Theology No. 10* (Paulist, 1998); J. A. DiNoia and Romanus Cessario, eds., Veritatis Splendor *and the Renewal of Moral Theology* (Scepter, 1999); Livio Melina, *Sharing in Christ's Virtues: For a Renewal of Moral Theology in Light of* Veritatis Splendor (The Catholic University of America Press, 2002); Charles E. Curran, *The Moral Theology of Pope John Paul II* (Georgetown University Press, 2005); Christopher Kaczor, *Proportionalism and the Natural Law Tradition* (The Catholic University of America Press, 2010); Janet E. Smith, *Self-Gift: Essays on* Humanae Vitae *and the Thought of John Paul II* (Emmaus Academic, 2018); Nenad Polgar and Joseph A. Selling, *The Concept of Intrinsic Evil and Catholic Theological Ethics* (Lexington, 2023); David S. Crawford, ed., *The Body as Anticipatory Sign: Commemorating the Anniversaries of* Humanae Vitae *and* Veritatis Splendor (Humanum Academic, 2025).

² Examples of the ongoing scholarly debate on the themes at the center of John Paul II's encyclical abound. Just as an illustration, we can point readers to a few recent publications: Beth Zagrobelny Lofgren, *Intersexual Persons and Theology of the Body: A Limit Case for John Paul II's Theological Anthropology* (The Catholic University of America Press, 2025); Ryan Connors, *Rethinking Cooperation with Evil: A Virtue-Based Approach* (The Catholic University of America Press, 2024); Angela McKay Knobel, *Aquinas and the Infused Moral Virtues* (University of Notre Dame Press, 2024); Cristina L. H. Traina, *Finitude, Feminism, and Flourishing: On Being Mortal Like Everyone Else* (Paulist, 2024); William C. Mattison III, *Growing in Virtue: Aquinas on Habit* (Georgetown University Press, 2023); Karen Peterson-Iyer, *Reenvisioning Sexual Ethics: A Feminist Christian Account* (Georgetown University Press 2022); D. C. Schindler, *Retrieving Freedom: The Christian Appropriation of Classical Tradition* (University of Notre Dame Press, 2022); Ryan J. Brady, *Conforming to Right Reason: On the Ends of the Moral Virtues and the Roles of Prudence and Synderesis* (Emmaus Academic, 2022).

pastoral care and doctrine, on the other.[3] Furthermore, the question of how to think about the relationship between the magisterium of John Paul II and Francis has been at the center of scholarly and popular debates for quite some time. Addressing these two crucial issues and many others necessitates that we come to terms with the legacy of *Veritatis Splendor* and its doctrinal commitments.[4] The current special issue of the *Journal of Moral Theology* makes a valuable contribution to this task by including essays that closely engage with John Paul II's moral theology from various standpoints. Thus, we hope it might help moral theologians identify elements of consensus, name the remaining tensions, and engage in productive disagreements that help the church move forward in its attempt to give a loving witness to the light of truth amidst contemporary challenges.[5] Furthermore, we think that such a path is the synodal work to which Pope Francis has called us, in the context of our field.

NAMING CONSENSUS: *VERITATIS SPLENDOR*'S LEGACY OF SHARED PRINCIPLES IN MORAL THEOLOGY

It seems fitting to begin considering *Veritatis Splendor*'s enduring legacy by naming the shared principles in moral theology the

---

[3] To pursue such reflection, Francis set up a study group of international experts tasked with devising a framework for "shared discernment of controversial doctrinal, pastoral, and ethical issues" (General Secretariat of the Synod, "Study Groups for Questions Raised in the First Session of the XVI Ordinary General Assembly of the Synod of Bishops to Be Explored in Collaboration with the Dicasteries of the Roman Curia," March 14, 2024).

[4] For some examples of the critical appraisal of the relationship between the moral theology of John Paul II and the emphases of Francis's pontificate, see Robert L. Fastiggi and Matthew Levering, eds., Humanae Vitae *and Catholic Sexual Morality: A Response to the Pontifical Academy for Life's* Etica teologica della vita (Sapientia, 2024); Conor M. Kelly and Kristin E. Heyer, eds., *The Moral Vision of Pope Francis: Expanding the US Reception of the First Jesuit Pope* (Georgetown University Press, 2024); Todd A. Salzman and Michael G. Lawler, *Pope Francis and the Transformation of Health Care Ethics* (Georgetown University Press, 2022); Pedro Gabriel, *The Orthodoxy of* Amoris Laetitia (Wipf and Stock, 2021); Walter Kasper, *The Message of* Amoris Laetitia*: Finding Common Ground* (Paulist, 2019); Matthew Levering, *The Indissolubility of Marriage:* Amoris Laetitia *in Context* (Ignatius, 2019); Stephen Walford, *Pope Francis, the Family, and Divorce: In Defense of Truth and Mercy* (Paulist, 2018); José Granados, Stephan Kampowski, and Juan José Pérez-Soba, *Accompanying, Discerning, Integrating: A Handbook for the Pastoral Care of the Family According to* Amoris Laetitia (Emmaus Road, 2017).

[5] We understand such an undertaking as an embodiment of the synodal path the ordinary magisterium is encouraging all members of the church, theologians included, to take, namely, to search "for the widest possible consensus which will emerge when our hearts burn within us (cf. Luke 24:32), without hiding conflicts or searching for the lowest common denominator" (XVI Ordinary General Assembly of the Synod of Bishops, *Final Document*, no. 84).

encyclical identifies and recommends as the starting point for further analysis and deliberation. We argue that such foundational claims spelled out in the document's first chapter reflect a synthesis of the Catholic moral tradition broadly understood and, as such, constitute a point of consensus among most moral theologians working today, no matter their particular commitments. For example, as professors of moral theology at Catholic institutions, we often teach classes in which we draw resources from various moral theology textbooks. Despite the stark difference in their authors' theological perspectives, the common themes and principles we identify below are present in all of them in one form or another.[6] Thus, notwithstanding the abundance of disagreements among moral theologians, there still appears to be some shared but often unstated consensus that may allow us to take a step toward overcoming the field's increasing siloing and polarization. Granted that the overall agreement is limited to the most general articulation of such principles, we find it nonetheless important to highlight them. At the very least, going through this exercise can invite others to disagree with us regarding the common ground we have identified and encourage different scholars to spell out how they would describe the implications of the broad principles we identify.

First, Christian morality is the response to the human longing for happiness. "Teacher, what good deed must I do to have eternal life?" (Matthew 19:16). John Paul II chose this question to frame the rest of *Veritatis Splendor* to point us to the aspiration present in the heart of every human being (no. 7). The question about what gives life meaning, purpose, certainty, and worth is essential and unavoidable for every person (no. 8). It is so fundamental that we all answer it, at least implicitly. As *Veritatis Splendor* reminds us, in fact, to ask about the good and happiness is to ask a religious question (no. 9). It is to find oneself oriented towards the reality of God, who alone is

---

[6] For examples that would substantiate our claims, see Paul J. Wadell, *Happiness and the Christian Moral Life: An Introduction to Christian Ethics* (Rowman & Littlefield, 2024); James F. Keenan, *The Moral Life: Lectures at the Martin Marty Center* (Georgetown University Press, 2023); David Matzko McCarthy and James M. Donohue, *Moral Vision: Seeing the World with Love and Justice* (Eerdmans, 2018); David Matzko McCarthy and M. Therese Lysaught, eds., *Gathered for the Journey: Moral Theology in Catholic Perspective* (Eerdmans, 2007); John Rziha, *The Christian Moral Life: Directions for the Journey to Happiness* (University of Notre Dame Press, 2017); Joseph A. Selling, *Reframing Catholic Theological Ethics* (Oxford University Press, 2016); Cataldo Zuccaro, *Fundamental Moral Theology* (Urbaniana University Press, 2015); Romanus Cessario, *Introduction to Moral Theology* (The Catholic University of America Press, 2013); Todd A. Salzman and Michael G. Lawler, *Virtue and Theological Ethics: Toward a Renewed Ethical Method* (Georgetown University Press, 2012); William C. Mattison III, *Introducing Moral Theology: True Happiness and the Virtues* (Brazos, 2008).

goodness, the fullness of life, the final end of human activity, and perfect happiness. In light of this, one of moral theology's essential tasks is to show that Christ is the only response fully capable of satisfying the human heart's desire (no. 7). In fact, the very attractiveness of Jesus clarifies and prompts the authentic human question regarding life's destiny. As the passage from *Gaudium et Spes* John Paul II often quoted teaches us, it is only in the mystery of the Word incarnate that light is shed on the mystery of what it means to be a human being. To find ourselves, we need to find Jesus (*Gaudium et Spes*, no. 22).

Second and related, Christian morality is rooted in the encounter with Christ. "Jesus, looking at him, loved him" (Mark 10:21): Christian morality is a response prompted by the loving and merciful gaze that has touched our lives (*Veritatis Splendor*, no. 10). We are Christians, Benedict XVI reminded us, not because of our lofty ideas, but because of an encounter with a presence that gives life new horizon and meaning (*Deus Caritas Est*, no. 1). It is because of the many gratuitous initiatives taken by God out of love for human beings that we find our lives transformed and called to a new mode of existence. "For God so loved the world that he gave his only Son, so that everyone who believes in him may not perish but may have eternal life" (John 3:16).

Third, Christian morality is built upon the primacy of grace. Given that it depends primarily on a spontaneous act of God, Christian morality is not the titanic effort to be righteous the individual engages in by himself or herself. Morality is a gift from God; to be good is to belong to God, obey God, and walk with God (*Veritatis Splendor*, no. 11). "This teaching is difficult; who can accept it?" (John 6:60) asked the disciples to Jesus, a question we often ask when confronted by the radical demands of the Gospel. Who can? Only the one who has discovered that Christ will accompany and abide in him or her, that Christ is the love of one's life, and that in him we find the satisfaction of everything we desire. Such a discovery that completely transforms our lives is an effect of grace, of the active presence of the Holy Spirit in us. It is Christ himself who enters into our hearts through the Holy Spirit and transforms us from within. Through the sacrament of Baptism and the Eucharist, we receive new life: "We have become not only Christians, but Christ," John Paul II beautifully says, quoting from Saint Augustine (*Veritatis Splendor*, no. 21).

Fourth, Christian morality is following Christ. Jesus himself takes the initiative and calls people to follow him. Thus, Christian morality is not only a matter of disposing oneself to hear a teaching and obediently accepting a commandment. More radically, it involves holding fast to the very person of Jesus, partaking of his life and destiny, and sharing in his free and loving obedience to the will of the

Father (no. 19). Accordingly, Jesus's way of acting, his words, deeds, and precepts constitute the moral rule of the Christian life (no. 20). "I give you a new commandment: . . . as I have loved you, you also should love one another" (John 13:34). Obviously, we immediately feel the utter disproportion between our ability and the call to discipleship because imitating and living out Christ's love is impossible for human beings by their strength alone. Yet "for God all things are possible" (Matthew 19:26).

Fifth, Christian morality is grounded in creation and revelation. God's first gratuitous gift in our lives is that we exist. We do not give life to ourselves. Instead, we are creatures, which means that every day, at every moment, the Lord renews his initiative by giving us the gift of existence. Not only does God create us and constantly keep us in existence, but God makes us in such a way that we are drawn towards, ordered to, our final end, complete happiness, that is, God himself. The created order and finality we find in ourselves is the natural law, a light infused in us by God to direct our lives (*Veritatis Splendor*, no. 12). God did not leave us alone, though, having to discover and abide by such a light by ourselves, but took a second, even more decisive initiative instead. God reached out to us by revealing himself and manifesting his will. "And the Word became flesh and lived among us, and we have seen his glory . . . full of grace and truth" (John 1:14).

The power of natural reason is not the only way we can know God and his will anymore. Instead, "Through divine revelation, God chose to show forth and communicate himself" (*Dei Verbum*, no. 6) and thus show himself in history. With the coming of Jesus, God takes his definitive initiative and gives us the New Law, an interior law that coincides with the Holy Spirit's indwelling into our hearts and that finds its most powerful written expression in the Sermon on the Mount (no. 12). In what *Veritatis Splendor* calls the *magna carta* of Christian morality, Jesus proclaims the Beatitudes, the basic attitudes and dispositions in life that will lead us to enjoy full communion with God (no. 15). They are promises, but most of all, they are a self-portrait of Christ himself; for this very reason, they are a call to discipleship and communion of life with him (no. 16). What in the natural law is simply a summons to seek truth and goodness and live by them becomes, in the New Law, a relationship of friendship with the Lord: "I do not call you servants any longer, . . . but I have called you friends, because I have made known to you everything that I have heard from my Father" (John 15:15).

Sixth, Christian morality is an invitation to each person's freedom. The Christian vocation is not in opposition to human freedom and not a denial or violence against it. For this reason, Jesus prefaces the radical proposal of embarking on a life entirely devoted to being a disciple with the clause "If you wish to be perfect" (Matthew 19:21). Christ is patient, meek, and humble (Matthew 11:29) and never breaks down the doors of our hearts with violence. Christ loves us and waits for a response (*Veritatis Splendor*, nos. 17–18). We can clearly see this method of Christ at work in the Gospels. The disciples came to believe because their relationship with Jesus filled them with such wonder that they started asking themselves, "But who is this man? We know his mother; we know his father; but who is he? Where does he really come from?" (see Mark 6:2–3 and Luke 8:25). The encounter with his exceptional presence filled them with wonder and led people, aided by the Holy Spirit, to finally recognize Jesus for who he truly was, the Word incarnate, "You are the Messiah, the Son of the living God" (Matthew 16:16). The grace of the divine intervention that makes Christian morality possible goes hand in hand with the reality of human freedom (*Veritatis Splendor*, no. 34).

Seventh, Christian morality is essentially connected to the church. The church, the Mystical Body of Christ and the Temple of the Holy Spirit constituted by divine and human elements (*Lumen Gentium*, nos. 8 and 17), is the place where God remains present. Through the church, Christ communicates his grace to contemporary men and women through Word, sacraments, and the community of the baptized, the holy and faithful People of God, in whose hearts the Holy Spirit dwells (no. 9). God, in fact, does not save us as individuals, but as "a people which acknowledges Him in truth and serves Him in holiness" (no. 9) so as to become "in Christ like a sacrament or as a sign and instrument both of a very closely knit union with God and of the unity of the whole human race" (no. 1). It is by belonging to such a people that we allow Christ to take his initiative and communicate his grace in our lives today (*Veritatis Splendor*, no. 6). In fact, just as the community of the disciples was progressively formed by listening, following, and acting with Jesus, so too do we come to be transformed by the life of the church (no. 88). There, we do not simply do certain things but are transformed from within and become a certain kind of person, namely, individuals who live out the virtues embodied by Jesus and start to shape the world according to his will: "It is no longer I who live, but it is Christ who lives in me. And the life I now live in the flesh I live by faith in the Son of God, who loved me and gave himself for me" (Galatians 2:19–20). Accordingly, by affirming Christian morality's fundamental ecclesial dimension, we are also highlighting its structural connection with the reality of moral formation and the related themes of practices and virtues, on the one hand, and the call to mission, on the other (*Veritatis Splendor*, no. 106).

VERITATIS SPLENDOR'S LEGACY TODAY: RETRIEVAL, EXTENSION, OR DEPARTURE?

Starting from naming the shared principles *Veritatis Splendor* articulates that can serve to discover the consensus necessary to allow moral theologians to engage in further investigations and debates together, reflecting on the encyclical's legacy requires us to discern to what extent we should retrieve, extend, or depart from its proposal. In this volume's essays, contributors take on that important discernment in ways we find illuminating.

The authors responded to our request to reflect on *"Veritatis Splendor* Three Decades On" by describing and assessing John Paul II's proposed moral doctrine. Thus, Catherine Moon, Michael A. Wahl, and Megan Heeder unpack and reflect on the implications of the Christocentric morality espoused in the first chapter of *Veritatis Splendor* and undergirding the rest of the encyclical's teachings. Matthew Kuhner considers the object of the moral act and the perspective of the acting person, while Todd Salzman and Michael Lawler focus on John Paul II's account of the natural law. Matthew P. Schneider studies the link between conscience and the objective moral order, and Conor Kelly examines the connection between freedom and truth. Finally, Nicholas Ogle, Gustavo Irrazábal, and Anthony Hollowell appraise the encyclical's claims on objective moral standards, moral absolutes, and intrinsically evil actions.

Along with the careful analysis of specific elements of *Veritatis Splendor*, the authors also explore the encyclical's impact on three interconnected issues. First, Wahl, Moon, and Ogle argue that the teachings of John Paul II remain relevant to understanding and responding to some of the unresolved debates in moral theology, the question regarding the so-called law-conscience binary, on the one hand, and the reception of the Second Vatican Council's instructions regarding moral theology, on the other. Second, there are those who mine the resources contained in John Paul II's moral proposal to extend them to new ethical problems and questions. Such a project is perfectly exemplified by Heeder, who uses aspects of *Veritatis Splendor* to address the challenge of eating disorders in the age of social media. Third, there are contributors who carefully analyze the relationship between *Veritatis Splendor* and the magisterium of Francis. On this topic, the assessment of the scholars featured in the special issue varies a great deal. There are those who emphasize the need to extend and integrate the teachings of John Paul II with those of Francis. Among them, Kuhner and Schneider stress the fundamental continuity between the two popes, Irrazábal and Kelly adopt a hermeneutic of reform that points out elements of continuity and discontinuity at different levels,[7] while Hollowell underscores the unresolved tensions between John Paul II's and Francis's approaches. At the same time, there are also authors, like Salzman and Lawler, who call for a more radical discontinuity and consider the overall approach of *Veritatis Splendor* surpassed by Francis's teaching.

As this simple map of its articles shows, there's a substantive diversity of perspectives concerning John Paul II's influence on moral theology represented in this special issue. As such, we have the sincere desire that it might serve as a conversation starter to help moral theologians engage one another and understand the reasons of those who hold different positions. Not only would such an interaction allow scholars to make their disagreements more precise and constructive, it would also allow us to find convergences that might help us move beyond the current dead end among moral theologians with divergent formations and outlooks.

HIDDEN CONFLICTS OR HOW TO DISAGREE MORE AND BETTER

One final element that allows us to reflect on *Veritatis Splendor* and its relationship with today's moral theological landscape is to turn to the contemporary field's unresolved tensions. This special issue's authors clarify several tensions with great precision and skill, but many underlying disputes remain hidden. Thus, we wish to conclude by attempting to make some of them explicit. It is our hope that such an exercise will encourage theologians to reframe their opposing arguments in ways that reach to their foundation, allow for a clearer statement of the principles at stake, enable the discovery of unexpected convergences, and give the church a greater chance to adjudicate or bring competing claims into a synthesis.

Of course, invisible conflicts abound, and this is not the place to try to analyze and settle all of them. Nevertheless, it needs to be done eventually if we want to move beyond some of the current impasses, as we see them. Take the disagreements regarding natural law, the authority of absolute norms, and the relationship between conscience and truth that emerge in the essays, for example. The authors assist us in identifying the terms of the debate and the issues at stake, and readers will have the opportunity to judge for themselves which

---

[7] In making their claims, Irrazábal and Kelly draw upon Benedict XVI's famous address to the Roman Curia considering the competing theories about how to properly receive the Second Vatican Council. See Benedict XVI, "Address to the Roman Curia," December 22, 2005, www.vatican.va/content/benedict-xvi/en/speeches/2005/december/documents/hf_ben_xvi_spe_20051222_roman-curia.html. It is worth noting that Schneider appeals to that same address but without stressing the elements of reform and discontinuity as much as Irrazabal and Kelly.

perspective they find more convincing. However, the disputes about those topics are rooted in more foundational, and by and large unnamed, conflicts. Just as an illustration, think about how presuppositions regarding original sin, its effects, and the reliability of Scripture and the magisterium ground how a theologian ends up thinking about the trustworthiness of the church's moral teachings. Being mindful that such a simplification does not do justice to the complex terms and nuances of the debate that needs to be had, we can sketch two alternatives.

If human nature is fundamentally wounded by original sin in ways that darken reason and will and mar the integrity of human life with concupiscence, on the one hand, and Scripture is the inspired and infallible Word of God, on the other, then the moral teachings of revelation as received and taught by the church's magisterium serve as reliable tools for moral discernment that rescue people from the deceptions of sin. Consider a theological position whose starting point is a different account of sin and a greater emphasis on the contextually dependent character of natural law, the teachings of the church, and some of the moral absolutes contained in Scripture instead. Starting from these premises, theologians will look at moral norms with a critical eye and will give greater precedence to the person's experience and conscience as the proper locus to discern the moral path to which God calls her. Furthermore, such a position would justify the presence of ineradicable moral pluralism and moral life's ultimate indeterminacy as constitutive elements of our status as historical creatures rather than as consequences of the confusion introduced by sin.

Again, we are simplifying for the sake of exemplification, and there are certainly alternative accounts we did not mention, variations on the ones we pointed to, and perspectives that would qualify and mix elements contained in both—this third path is certainly walked by many scholars, ourselves included. Still, the illustration above shows us that, first, at the root of many disagreements among moral theologians, there are implicit conflicts regarding the reality of sin. In particular, how a theologian understands and articulates the implications of the traditional doctrine of original sin has far-reaching consequences for how the rest of the Christian moral proposal is developed. In fact, some of the debates in the field hinge on the very foundational question about whether the doctrine of original sin as it is currently articulated by the official magisterium adequately represents the reality of sin. The related issues of the darkening of reason, weakness of the will, and wound of concupiscence, on the one hand, and of the devil's existence and his role in the moral life, on the other, are all connected with these often-unnamed disputes and thus linger under the surface—not to mention the questions about the proper theology and effects of the sacraments, the Sacrament of Penance and Reconciliation and the Eucharist in particular.

Second, contemporary moral theologians are split regarding the nature and scope of authority in the life of the church. The frequently unnamed conflicts extend to arguments regarding the very source of Christian theology, namely, revelation. On this front, foundational disagreements exist regarding the reliability of Scripture, how Scripture should be interpreted and received, the integration of different approaches to biblical interpretation, and the very doctrine of divine inspiration and the related issue of the inerrancy of Scripture. Furthermore, theologians contest the authority and scope of the Catholic tradition, in general, and the church's teaching office, in particular. Seemingly intractable and hidden disagreements exist regarding what counts as an authentic development of doctrine, the levels of authority of different magisterial pronouncements, the notion of infallibility, and the relationship between the Church's hierarchical structure, the *sensus fidei*, and people's experiences, of Christians and non-Christians alike. When we add the dissensions regarding epistemology, metaphysics, the relationship between theology and other disciplines, and the relative contribution of each to the attainment of truths regarding the moral life to the mix, we have the kind of impasse that usually characterizes conversations across theological divides of which the siloing and polarization of the field of moral theology are both a symptom and a cause.

FOR A SYNODAL RECEPTION OF *VERITATIS SPLENDOR*

Hidden conflicts such as these must be brought to the surface in explicit and systematic ways if we want to respond to some of the urgent moral questions the church faces in the contemporary situation. Accordingly, we have highlighted the shared principles articulated by *Veritatis Splendor* that can offer opportunities for dialogue while also naming the unresolved tensions that mark the essays and require further discussion and study. In this endeavor, we believe we are doing moral theology in a synodal way, just as the *Final Document* of the XVI Ordinary General Assembly of the Synod of Bishops asked us to. "Synodality is the walking together of Christians with Christ and towards God's Kingdom, in union with all humanity. Orientated towards mission, synodality involves gathering at all levels of the Church for mutual listening, dialogue, and community discernment. It also involves reaching consensus as an expression of Christ rendering Himself present, He who is alive in the Spirit."[8] Amidst the fractures,

---

[8] XVI Ordinary General Assembly of the Synod of Bishops, *Final Document*, no. 28.

polarizations, and siloing that mark moral theology, such synodal commitments should become the method for debates among theologians. If they do, we will become more capable of carrying out our specific service to the church, namely, to "help the People of God to develop an understanding of reality enlightened by Revelation and to develop suitable responses and the appropriate language for mission."[9] Such a service, in fact, requires us to increase our capacity "to listen to each other, to dialogue, to discern, and to harmonize [our] many and varied approaches and contributions."[10] Pursuing such a demanding project necessitates engaging across the divides that mark contemporary moral theology in ways that are committed, sustained, and charitable.[11] That, after thirty years, a special issue considering *Veritatis Splendor* might give us an occasion to begin this much needed work is a sign of the encyclical's enduring legacy and gift to the church. M

Jana Bennett, PhD, is department chair and professor of moral theology at the University of Dayton. Her current research relates the theology of Teresa of Avila to moral concerns.

Alessandro Rovati, PhD, is department chair and associate professor of theology at Belmont Abbey College, where he also serves as director of the diaconal formation program. He is the Synod coordinator for the Diocese of Charlotte and has recently led the association for early-career moral theologians New Wine New Wineskins.

---

[9] XVI Ordinary General Assembly of the Synod of Bishops, *Final Document*, no. 67.
[10] International Theological Commission, *Synodality in the Life and Mission of the Church*, no. 75.
[11] XVI Ordinary General Assembly of the Synod of Bishops, *Final Document*, no. 67.

A *Ressourcement* Encyclical: *Veritatis Splendor* and the Recovery of Christocentric Moral Theology

Michael A. Wahl

Abstract: This article proposes that Pope John Paul II's *Veritatis Splendor* is a *ressourcement* encyclical that creatively retrieves insights from a movement to renew moral theology in a Christocentric mode which had flourished in the decades immediately preceding Vatican II but dissipated soon after the Council. Although most clearly expressed in its often-neglected first chapter, in fact *Veritatis Splendor*'s Christocentric vision permeates the entire encyclical, including those portions often presumed to be purely philosophical, and lends the encyclical an internal coherence frequently overlooked. Reading *Veritatis Splendor* as a work of *ressourcement* and attending to its first chapter as a constructive proposal for moral theology rather than a mere prologue to an analysis of disputed questions offers promising new pathways for receiving the encyclical three decades later.

IN RECENT SCHOLARSHIP, A COMMON CRITIQUE OF JOHN PAUL II's 1993 encyclical *Veritatis Splendor* is that the encyclical embodies, or at least desires, a return to the tradition of the moral manuals that dominated Catholic moral theology prior to the Second Vatican Council. For example, in his history of twentieth-century Catholic moral theology, James Keenan describes *Veritatis Splendor* as "a contemporary expression of neo-manualism."[1] While acknowledging that the encyclical is "not a manual *per se*," Keenan maintains that it reflects key elements of a neo-manualist approach including a belief "that moral truth [is] found primarily in norms and principles."[2] Such an approach, he argues, stands in contrast to contemporary historicist approaches to moral theology, making the encyclical decidedly nostalgic. Joseph Selling laments that *Veritatis Splendor* merely "reiterated the theory of the moral textbooks with

---

[1] James F. Keenan, SJ, *A History of Catholic Moral Theology in the Twentieth Century: From Confessing Sins to Liberating Consciences* (Continuum, 2010), 128.
[2] Keenan, *A History of Catholic Moral Theology*, 128, 118.

regard to the primacy of behavior in ethical decision-making."[3] Similarly, James Bretzke argues that the encyclical "seems to be arguing strongly for a return to the *status quo ante* of the pre-Vatican II understanding of moral theology, rather than mapping a route to move with the challenges of the new millennium."[4]

Supporters of the encyclical, on the other hand, have argued that *Veritatis Splendor* is innovative and forward-looking precisely because it rejects the legalistic casuistry of the manuals and promotes a renewed vision of the moral life inspired by and aligned with the desire of the Second Vatican Council. For example, Romanus Cessario declares that "*Veritatis Splendor* inaugurates a new moment for Catholic moral theology, one that officially brings a close to the period of casuistry."[5] Servais Pinckaers, too, begins his lengthy commentary on the encyclical by asserting that *Veritatis Splendor* "is far more innovative than first appears."[6] He suggests that this innovation is largely due to its eschewal of the morality of obligation espoused by the manuals and its desire to reconnect Christian morality to the Gospel and the person of Christ. Indeed, Pinckaers goes so far as to suggest that, in undertaking this project, the encyclical "launches a kind of discreet revolution in the concept of Christian morality, down to its very foundations."[7]

Both narratives about the encyclical are oversimplified, however. *Veritatis Splendor* is neither a nostalgic return to the manuals nor a novel reframing of the moral life. Rather, I submit that the encyclical can be more profitably read as a work of *ressourcement*. Specifically,

---

[3] Joseph A. Selling, *Reframing Catholic Theological Ethics* (Oxford University Press, 2016), 186.
[4] James T. Bretzke, SJ, "Moral Theology and the Paradigm Shift of Vatican II," in *Oxford Handbook of Vatican II*, ed. Catherine E. Clifford and Massimo Faggioli (Oxford University Press, 2023), 418–431, at 425. See also Charles Curran, "*Veritatis Splendor*: A Revisionist Perspective," in Veritatis Splendor*: American Responses*, ed. Michael E. Allsopp and James J. O'Keefe (Sheed & Ward, 1995), 224–243, at 230: "John Paul II understands morality primarily on the basis of a legal model. Such an approach, which characterized the manuals of moral theology in vogue until very recent times, sees morality primarily in terms of obedience to the law or the commandments of God." See also Daniel J. Daly, *The Structures of Virtue and Vice* (Georgetown University Press, 2021), 107: "A lasting vestige of the manuals has been the continued presence of a norm-centered moral theology in papal writings. *Veritatis Splendor*, John Paul II's encyclical on moral theology, focuses more on the natural law, norms, and obedience than on virtue."
[5] Romanus Cessario, OP, "From Casuistry to Virtue-Ethics," *Ethics & Medics* 19, no. 10 (1994): 1.
[6] Servais Pinckaers, OP, "An Encyclical for the Future: *Veritatis Splendor*," trans. Mary Thomas Noble, OP, in Veritatis Splendor *and the Renewal of Moral Theology*, ed. J. A. DiNoia, OP, and Romanus Cessario, OP (Midwest Theological Forum, 1999), 11–12.
[7] Pinckaers, "An Encyclical for the Future," 12.

Veritatis Splendor succeeds in recovering the insights of a Christocentric renewal of moral theology that flourished in the decades immediately preceding the Council. In the mid-twentieth century, several prominent Catholic moral theologians sought to reorient the discipline around the person of Christ, moving away from the legalistic casuistry of the manuals. Figures such as Fritz Tillmann, Louis-Bertrand Gillon, and the early Bernard Häring emphasized discipleship and interior conformity to Christ as the foundation of the moral life. While this Christocentric renewal gained initial traction, it was largely eclipsed in the post-conciliar period. In what follows, I argue that *Veritatis Splendor* represents a significant retrieval of this earlier Christocentric impulse and thus offers a promising vision for the ongoing renewal of moral theology.

To this end, the article is divided into two main parts. The first section presents the case for reading *Veritatis Splendor* as a *ressourcement* encyclical. It begins by offering a brief survey of three moral theologians working before the Council who endeavored to renew moral theology along decidedly Christocentric lines. It then examines the sudden eclipse of this Christocentric renewal in the decades following the Council and concludes with an analysis of the opening chapter of *Veritatis Splendor*, highlighting the Christocentrism of John Paul II's encyclical and demonstrating its creative retrieval of, and continuity with, the pre-conciliar Christocentric renewal movement. In the second part of the essay, I consider two objections to the claim that *Veritatis Splendor* advances a genuinely Christocentric morality: first, the alleged subordination of its Christocentrism to a morality of law and obligation within chapter one and, second, the apparent methodological discontinuity between chapters one and two. In response to these concerns, the second section underscores John Paul II's insistence on Christ as the fulfillment of the moral law and demonstrates how his Christocentric vision informs at a fundamental, albeit less visible, level even the seemingly philosophical elements of the encyclical's second chapter.

CHRISTOCENTRISM AND THE RENEWAL OF MORAL THEOLOGY

The Pre-Conciliar Christocentric Renewal Movement

Most narratives of twentieth-century Catholic moral theology rightly highlight the hegemony of the moral manuals prior to the Second Vatican Council.[8] Prefaced by theoretical treatments of law,

---

[8] Keenan, *A History of Catholic Moral Theology*, 9–34; Servais Pinckaers, OP, *The Sources of Christian Ethics*, trans. Mary Thomas Noble, OP (The Catholic University of America Press, 1995), 254–279, 298–300; John Mahoney, *The Making of Moral*

human action, conscience, and sin, the heart of the manuals was their treatment of specific cases of conscience, typically organized around the precepts of the Decalogue. As handbooks designed to assist priests in the confessional, the manuals were intended to be practical aids in assessing the extent of the penitent's obligations under law, the gravity of particular sins, and the assignment of suitable penance. Contemporary critics of the manuals frequently decry their voluntaristic conception of moral obligation, their rationalistic and deductive approach to law, and their minimalist conception of the moral life as concerning merely the satisfaction of the most essential duties.[9] Yet, even amid the predominance of the moral manuals, seeds of renewal were being sown during the decades preceding the Second Vatican Council as some moral theologians sought to escape the rationalistic and legalistic casuistry that dominated the discipline and instead organized their treatments of the moral life around more decidedly theological themes, including around the person of Christ.[10] Although a comprehensive examination lies beyond the scope of this article, it is possible to get a sense of this movement for the renewal of moral theology by considering three moral theologians who sought to frame the moral life in explicitly Christocentric terms.[11]

The figure most widely regarded as the pioneer of a Christocentric approach to ethics in the middle of the twentieth century is Fritz Tillmann (1874–1953), a German biblical scholar turned moral theologian who brought his significant scriptural expertise to bear in moral theology. In his four-volume *Handbuch der katholischen Sittenlehre* and the later, more popular *Der Meister Ruft*, Tillmann champions a vision of the moral life permeated by the themes of discipleship and the following of Christ.[12] So central to his thought are

---

Theology: A Study of the Roman Catholic Tradition (Clarendon, 1987), 224–258; John A. Gallagher, *Time Past, Time Future: An Historical Study of Catholic Moral Theology* (Paulist, 1990), 29–122; Matthew Levering, *The Abuse of Conscience: A Century of Catholic Moral Theology* (Eerdmans, 2021), 50–124.

[9] See Pinckaers, *The Sources of Christian Ethics*, 277–279; Keenan, *A History of Catholic Moral Theology*, 29–30.

[10] In addition to the examples of Christocentric renewal considered below, other noteworthy efforts to renew moral theology include Gérard Gilleman, SJ, *The Primacy of Charity in Moral Theology*, trans. William F. Ryan, SJ, and André Vachon, SJ (Newman Press, 1959 [1954]); Emile Mersch, SJ, *Morality and the Mystical Body*, trans. Daniel F. Ryan, SJ (P. J. Kenedy & Sons, 1939 [1937]).

[11] For more thorough treatments of the pre-conciliar Christocentric renewal movement in moral theology, see Vincent MacNamara, *Faith and Ethics: Recent Roman Catholicism* (Gill and Macmillan, 1985), 14–36; Livio Melina, "Christ and the Dynamism of Action: Outlook and Overview of Christocentrism in Moral Theology," *Communio* 28 (2001): 112–139.

[12] Although there is relatively recent scholarly literature on Tillmann, Keenan nevertheless describes Tillmann's work as a "breakthrough" for his scriptural

these ideas that Tillmann defines moral theology as "the scientific presentation of the following of Christ in individual and communal life."[13] Drawing deeply on Scripture, Tillmann develops a rich and textured portrait of Jesus, who stands as the fundamental norm of the moral life, model to imitate, and master to follow.

As Stuart Chalmers observes, "Tillmann frames discipleship and the imitation of Christ in the light of love and in the context of relationship."[14] He begins *Der Meister Ruft* with a reflection on Jesus's invitation to the disciples, "Come, follow me" (Matt 4:19). Inspired by the personalist philosophy of Max Scheler, Tillmann explains that *to follow*

> means to choose someone as a model and to form and transform one's own life according to his example. The fundamental prerequisite is to find a person whom we wish to imitate, because it will be in his conception and manner of life that we recognize a great good, the ideal. Love of the ideal opens the way for this recognition. Only in the light of love does the model appear to us in all his unique Splendor. Because of the irresistible attraction he exerts, the determination to become like the idea grows in us. Hence to follow someone means to choose him as a model, because one has been captivated by love of him.[15]

For Tillmann, Jesus is not a mere historical figure or an abstract ideal. Rather, he is a living, personal model whom the disciple follows only because of an intimate encounter, a personal invitation, and the captivation of love.

Moreover, Tillmann insists that following Christ does not consist only in outward imitation but in an ontological transformation through which one becomes a child of God, conformed to the image of the Son.[16] The sacrament of baptism thus features prominently in Tillmann's work as the foundation of the moral life, for it not only demonstrates the gratuity of the invitation to follow Christ, but also bestows the spiritual resources necessary to embark on the path of discipleship and enjoins a new way of life upon those who form a new

---

orientation, turn to the virtues, and pastoral sense (*A Brief History of Catholic Moral Theology*, 69).

[13] Fritz Tillmann, *Handbuch der katholischen Sittenlehre*, vol. 3: *Die Idee der Nachfolge Christi* (Druck and L. Schwann, 1934), 5.

[14] Stuart Patrick Chalmers, "Fritz Tillmann, Discipleship, and the Renewal of Moral Theology," *Irish Theological Quarterly* 86, no. 4 (2021): 367.

[15] Fritz Tillmann, *The Master Calls: A Handbook of Christian Living*, trans. Gregory J. Roettger, OSB (Helicon, 1960), 3. This is, as far as I am aware, the only work of Tillmann's moral theology translated into English.

[16] Tillmann, *The Master Calls*, 4–5.

creation.[17] Tillmann's moral theology is marked by a dynamism of growth and progress. He stresses that the Christian's assimilation to Christ begins with baptism but is oriented toward subsequent advancement as one matures as Jesus's disciple. Tillmann's moral theology therefore does not foreground categories of obligation as if these were the hallmark of the disciple. Such an approach would be too static and inconsistent with Scripture's attestation to the organic abiding and mutual indwelling of Christ in the disciple. Instead, Tillmann notes that "Christ very fundamentally and decisively shifts attention from the external action to its origin" in one's interior dispositions, and he consequently adopts the language of virtue not only to highlight the salient features of Christ's person and action but also to underscore the inherently developmental character of following Jesus.[18]

Tillmann's ethic of discipleship is clearly an ethic of Christian perfection. In contrast to the minimalism of the manuals, which trade on the distinction between precepts and counsels as an essential feature of moral theology, Tillmann stresses the universality of Christ's summons to discipleship:

> Christian perfection is the duty of every one of Christ's followers. No distinctions are made; it is not just the goal of a few especially endowed Christians . . . . [Jesus] clearly indicates its universal character and its obligatory force for all. Perfection applies to the whole of the Christian life and hence is based on the fundamental relationship of the child of God to his Father in heaven.[19]

Tillman understands this universal call to holiness to be rooted in baptism, for the pursuit of Christian perfection is simply the unfolding of the identity of the children of God. Tillmann has rightly been hailed as a "true innovator" for his efforts to reframe moral theology not as the acceptance of a set of abstract ethical principles but rather as the following of Christ, "the absolute personality," so that "whoever professes to be a follower of [Christ] . . . must therefore also be of the same mind as he was, and act as he acted, and do what he demanded."[20]

Tillmann's influence is readily perceptible in the work of a second figure, the French Dominican Louis-Bertrand Gillon (1901–1987), whose 1961 book *Cristo e la teologia morale* aims to complement the dominant "Alphonsian" approach of the moral manuals with a

---

[17] Tillmann, *The Master Calls*, 15–23.
[18] Tillmann, *The Master Calls*, 36.
[19] Tillmann, *The Master Calls*, 45.
[20] Tillmann, *Die Idee der Nachfolge Christi*, 12.

Thomistic approach emphasizing the beatific vision as the ultimate end of human life and the role of distinctly theological accounts of virtue, sin, law, and grace in the pursuit of that end. Most significantly, however, Gillon argues for the centrality of Christ in moral theology. Citing Tillmann, Gillon argues that

> the moral life is the consequence of a "decision," of a total choice, by which a personal subject takes up a position with regard to another person. . . . Either the subject decides to take this other person as model and as pattern of his own life, willing in that case to become a disciple, to "follow" in all things the person who makes an urgent appeal to him: come, follow me; or, on the contrary the subject remains in an attitude of refusal, it rejects the call that is made to him.[21]

For Gillon, the moral life is centered around a personal model and in the case of Christian ethics, that exemplar is none other than Christ. He recognizes that this requires a reframing of moral theology, arguing that it is necessary to "do away with that mass of casuistical solutions, with theoretical considerations, which lead the faithful to think that their moral existence is governed by quite another principle than the only valid one: *esse in Christo Jesu*."[22] To be clear, Gillon does not argue for the abrogation of moral norms nor does he think that moral theology should cease to reflect on practical questions. Rather, he argues these matters need to be integrated within a broader theological context. He explains that "the moral teaching of 'personal exemplarity' does not claim to suppress the norms of morality, moral and juridical laws. But these are abstract and general in character. They are meant to be placed and understood in the context of the personal exemplar which gives to them concrete vitality: the *Vorbild* [person-model] gives to the norms the life they lack."[23] Gillon maintains that in Christ, the person-model of the Christian life, the precepts of the moral law cease to be impersonal abstractions but become the lived response to Christ's personal invitation to follow him.

Although Gillon deploys the vocabulary of Scheler's personalist philosophy and its theological appropriation by Tillmann when he develops his account of exemplarism, the burden of Gillon's project is to demonstrate that such an approach is deeply resonant with the Thomistic tradition of moral theology. Against the common complaint that Christ is absent from Aquinas's moral theology, Gillon insists that "Christ is everywhere present in the moral theology of St. Thomas,

---

[21] Louis Bertrand Gillon, OP, *Christ and Moral Theology*, trans. Cornelius Williams, OP (Alba House, 1967), 13.
[22] Gillon, *Christ and Moral Theology*, 23–24.
[23] Gillon, *Christ and Moral Theology*, 14–15.

because the sacred humanity of Christ and the mysteries of his life exercise a universal instrumental causality on each and every one of the structures of the supernatural life."[24] This Christological mediation produces in human beings their adoption as children of God and their reception of the infused virtues and gifts of the Holy Spirit. Aquinas's scholastic understanding of *sacra doctrina* as a unified whole enables him to integrate moral theology and Christology seamlessly. Gillon aims to advance that integration by more explicitly highlighting Christ's role as the fundamental and personal norm of the moral life and more clearly casting the Christian moral life as the imitation of Christ.

A third figure who, at least early in his career, aimed to emphasize more vigorously the centrality of Christ for the moral life was the Redemptorist Bernard Häring (1912–1998), whose 3-volume *Das Gesetz Christi* was first published in 1954.[25] According to John Gallagher, with the publication of this early work "a process was set in motion that would result in the gradual removal of the neo-Thomist manuals of moral theology from the seminaries of Europe and the United States."[26] Although the book's basic structure still conforms to that of the manuals, *The Law of Christ* aims to reorient traditional categories of moral theology around Christ as the center of the moral life. Moreover, Häring, whose doctoral dissertation focused on the thought of Max Scheler and Rudolf Otto, consistently deploys personalist philosophical categories, often in place of more traditional scholastic terminology.[27]

In this vein, *The Law of Christ* opens with the bold declaration that "the principle, the norm, the center, and the goal of Christian Moral Theology is Christ."[28] This claim, formulated in language similar to Tillmann's, provides the framework for the rest of Häring's program and constitutes a notable departure from the methodology of the manuals. Rather than grounding his moral doctrine on philosophical principles about human nature, Häring insists that Christology rather than anthropology is the proper starting point for moral theology:

---

[24] Gillon, *Christ and Moral Theology*, 139.
[25] I emphasize Häring's early work as a contribution to this renewal movement because there is a notable shift in his perspective and approach after Vatican II. For example, his 1978 trilogy *Free and Faithful in Christ*, despite its title, lacks the robust Christocentrism that characterizes his earlier work and opts instead for an approach to moral theology centered on the interplay of freedom and conscience. Indeed, some have even criticized *The Law of Christ* as excessively conscience-centered. See Levering, *The Abuse of Conscience*, 174–184.
[26] Gallagher, *Time Past, Time Future*, 169.
[27] Levering, *The Abuse of Conscience*, 174–176.
[28] Bernard Häring, CSsR, *The Law of Christ: Moral Theology for Priests and Laity*, vol. 1, trans. Edwin G. Kaiser, CPPS (Newman, 1966), vii.

> Christ stands before us as the perfect man, fully spiritual and devoted to the Father, entirely human and open to His brethren, to all the joys and sorrows of the world, absorbed in the majesty of the Father and filled with wonder over the lilies of the field. He also calls to us with all our powers. He appeals to all that is in man: intellect and will, heart and spirit. Christ who lives on in history, Christ who is the Church mystically does the same. . . . There is no surer way to the full perfection of the whole man than the perfect following of Christ in the communal life of the church.[29]

Although he does not include any lengthy treatment of Christology proper, the primacy of Christ informs Häring's presentation of the human person as one called by Christ and whose life and actions constitute a response to that invitation. *The Law of Christ* still includes treatments of traditional moral categories typical of the manuals like freedom, conscience, human action, and sin. At the same time, these categories are often couched in the language of personalism rather than scholasticism, and they are integrated into a larger vision of the moral life as the human response to the invitation offered in Christ. Hence, conversion toward Christ and growth in likeness to Christ through the theological and cardinal virtues provide the culmination of Häring's treatment of general moral theology. Moreover, Häring attempts to reconfigure even these moral categories around the person of Christ as the focal point of moral theology. Thus, he describes the virtues as those traits of character "which make us like to Christ" and the moral law as "those limits beyond which our conduct becomes a contradiction to the life in Christ and a hazard to the imitation of Christ."[30] In short, for Häring in *The Law of Christ*, moral theology is quite simply "the doctrine of the imitation of Christ," and the theoretical elaboration of any other moral categories is at the service of elucidating this fundamental truth.[31]

Taken together, the work of Tillmann, Gillon, and the early Häring helpfully illustrates the main contours of the trend toward a more Christocentric moral theology during the decades that preceded the Second Vatican Council. They reflect a decidedly different methodological approach than the casuistry of the manuals. Indeed, they are, to quote the Council's own desiderata for moral theology as articulated in *Optatam Totius*, "renewed through a more living contact with the mystery of Christ," they were "deeply nourished by Sacred Scripture," and "shed light on the loftiness of the calling of the faithful in Christ and the obligation that is theirs of bearing fruit in charity for the life of the world" (no. 16).

---

[29] Häring, *The Law of Christ*, 72.
[30] Häring, *The Law of Christ*, viii.
[31] Häring, *The Law of Christ*, 61.

The Postconciliar Eclipse of Christocentric Moral Theology

Nevertheless, this enthusiasm for Christocentric moral theology did not have staying power in mainstream post-conciliar moral theology. In the years immediately following the Council, there was still an eagerness to emphasize the centrality of Christ for moral theology. For example, in a lengthy 1966 article entitled "Moral Theology According to Vatican II," Josef Fuchs takes *Optatam Totius* to be the charter for moral theology's renewal, and in elaborating its vision, he reiterates themes central to the Christocentric renewal of the preceding decades. He argues, for instance, that the "Christian life is misconceived if it is not seen as an imitation of the example of Christ," and he adopts Tillmann's category of discipleship as the most fitting description of the moral life.[32] Moreover, for Fuchs, as for his teacher Häring, Christology has important implications for anthropology, and thus the starting point for Christian ethics is not "man in the raw" but rather "Christian man . . . man, called by God 'in Christ.'"[33] As a result, Fuchs underscores the distinctiveness of Christian ethics, insisting that "we are not meant to live merely as man, but as man baptized into Christ, into his death and into his resurrection."[34]

Only a few years later, however, one can detect a shift in Fuchs's approach both to the interpretation of the conciliar call for renewal and the most adequate approach to moral theology itself. In a 1970 article on "conciliar morality," Fuchs submits that

> It would be a grave mistake to think that *Optatam Totius* was the last or only word on the subject of the renewal of moral theology. The Council was not satisfied to adopt the Christocentric approach in moral theology and leave it at that. In the Constitution *Gaudium et Spes*, it had already begun to advance toward a position *vis-à-vis* problems that were facing the Council then and in which we are engaged today. Thus, in *Gaudium et spes*—though in a preliminary and fragmented fashion—the Council began to grapple with questions that have become most important to Christians living in the world.[35]

---

[32] Josef Fuchs, SJ, "Moral Theology According to Vatican II," in *Human Values and Christian Morality* (Georgetown University Press, 1983), 1–55 [original: "'Theologia moralis perficienda; votum Concilii Vaticani II," *Periodica de re morali, canonica, liturgica* 55 (1966): 499–548].

[33] Fuchs, SJ, "Moral Theology According to Vatican II," 8.

[34] Fuchs, SJ, "Moral Theology According to Vatican II," 5.

[35] Josef Fuchs, SJ, "Vocation and Hope: Conciliar Orientations for a Christian Morality," in *Personal Responsibility and Christian Morality* (Georgetown University Press, 1983), 32–49 [original: "Vocazione e Speranza: indicazioni conciliari per una morale christiana," *Seminarium* 23 NS 11 (1971): 491–510]. One can detect a developmental shift in Fuchs's thought on these issues between 1965 and 1971. For an intermediate position between the two articles cited here, see his 1967 address

As Fuchs's remarks suggest, the reception of *Gaudium et Spes* would become a significant factor in the development of post-conciliar moral theology. While the history of the document's composition and reception is too circuitous to rehearse in detail, it suffices to say that *Gaudium et Spes* is a complex document which has been read through various theological lenses, and different aspects of the document itself lend textual support to each of these interpretations.[36]

Some theologians—especially those associated with the journal *Communio*—adopted a strongly Christocentric reading of *Gaudium et Spes* based on its assertion that "only in the mystery of the incarnate Word does the mystery of man take on light" (no. 22). This interpretation did not exert a significant influence among mainstream moral theologians, however. They tended instead to highlight the anthropological and social-ethical dimensions of *Gaudium et Spes* as the most essential ingredients for the renewal of moral theology and often downplayed the document's Christocentric thrust, either by ignoring or subordinating it to the document's anthropological claims. On this view, the pastoral constitution's significance consists primarily in its articulation of an anthropology rooted in human dignity, relationality, freedom, and conscience, its respect for the "autonomy of earthly affairs," and its summons to a robust engagement with the world characterized by attending to the "urgent needs characterizing the present age . . . in the light of the Gospel and of human experience" (nos. 36, 46).

Inspired by this reading of *Gaudium et Spes*, many moral theologians aimed to articulate Christian ethics in a manner that could engage cooperatively and constructively with non-Christian modes of ethical thinking in order to address the myriad problems confronting the modern world. This desire for dialogue, collaboration, and common ground encouraged moral theologians to abandon strategies that seemed excessively particular to instead promote approaches rationally accessible and universalizable. Among other things, this entailed a marginalization of the person of Christ in moral theology. Thus, Livio Melina laments that in the dominant strains of moral theology, the Christocentric renewal that characterized the immediate pre-conciliar period was "succeeded . . . by drastic calls to abandon

---

published as "The Christian Morality of Vatican II," in *Human Values and Christian Morality*, 56–75.

[36] On the drafting and reception of *Gaudium et Spes*, see Joseph A. Komonchak, "Le valutazioni sulla *Gaudium et Spes*: Chenu, Dossetti, Ratzinger," in *Volti di fine concilio: Studi di storia e teologia sulla conclusion del Vaticano II*, ed. Joseph Dore and Alberto Melloni (Il Mulino, 2000), 115–153; Brandon Peterson, "Critical Voices: The Reactions of Rahner and Ratzinger to 'Schema XIII' (*Gaudium et Spes*)," *Modern Theology* 31, no. 1 (2015): 1–26.

this road in light of the demands of rational autonomy and the universality of ethics."[37]

The Swiss moral theologian Franz Böckle exemplifies this abandonment of a Christocentric perspective in a 1977 book when he suggests that the Christocentric renewal movement preceding the Council ultimately failed because "it soon became clear . . . that it would not be possible to formulate a universally valid normative theory on the basis of such slogans as the 'imitation of Christ,' the 'kingdom of God,' or 'sacramental conformity with Christ.' It also emerged quite soon from Karl Barth's idea of Christological concentration that the figure of Christ as the *Universale Concretum* had to be in opposition to a normative generalization."[38] Given the desire for a universally accessible ethic that could promote dialogue and cooperation in addressing contemporary social issues, Böckle maintains that grounding moral theology in the person of Christ is a non-starter.

Böckle's position is representative of the 1970s movement in moral theology known as autonomous ethics—a position most notably espoused by Fuchs, Alfons Auer, and Bruno Schüller—in which "emphasis is . . . not on the specific morality of Christians but on the common morality of all people."[39] Although there exist a variety of perspectives within this school, proponents of autonomous ethics generally agree there is no substantive difference, at least in terms of material content, between Christian morality and human morality.[40] Fuchs is representative of this position when he submits that "the principles and commands of moral conduct are the same for a truly human morality as for Christian morality."[41] These principles and commands, he argues, are accessible to human reason. The Gospel neither adds to nor detracts from the precepts of the natural law. According to Fuchs, the unique claims of Christian theology only enter moral analysis at the level of transcendental motivation and intentionality rather than at the level of categorical conduct.[42] Although some moral theologians, known as the *Glaubensethik* school, responded to this movement toward autonomy by developing

---

[37] Livio Melina, "Christ and the Dynamism of Action," 113.
[38] Franz Böckle, *Fundamental Moral Theology*, trans. N. D. Smith (Pueblo, 1980), 3–4. [Original: *Fundamentalmoral* (Kösel, 1977).]
[39] MacNamara, *Faith and Ethics*, 38.
[40] MacNamara, *Faith and Ethics*, 37–54; Paulinus Ikechukwu Odozor, CSSp, *Moral Theology in an Age of Renewal: A Study of the Catholic Tradition Since Vatican II* (University of Notre Dame Press, 2003), 101–134.
[41] Josef Fuchs, SJ, "Human, Humanist, and Christian Morality," in *Human Values and Christian Ethics*, 121–122.
[42] Josef Fuchs, SJ, "Is There a Normative Non-Christian Morality?," in *Personal Responsibility and Christian Ethics*, 76.

a distinctively theological account of morality rooted in a Christocentric faith, these efforts had a relatively modest influence in mainstream academic moral theology.[43] Thus, the Christocentric impulse in moral theology, although not entirely stifled, was nonetheless marginalized in the decades after Vatican II.

Veritatis Splendor *and the Recovery of Christocentric Morality*

The extent to which the Christocentric impulse was eclipsed is perhaps most evident when one considers the initial reception of *Veritatis Splendor*. In the earliest analyses of the encyclical, nearly all the attention of Catholic moral theologians—critics and supporters alike—was trained on what Richard McCormick described as "its key second chapter."[44] Revisionists focused on responding to and critiquing its treatments of issues like fundamental option and proportionalism.[45] At the same time, many supporters of the encyclical dedicated their energy to buttressing the pope's teaching on intrinsically evil actions, demonstrating the flaws of proportionalist reasoning, and advocating magisterial intervention against dissent.[46]

An unfortunate consequence of the overwhelming amount of scholarly attention devoted to the controversial material in the second chapter of *Veritatis Splendor* is the comparative neglect of its first

---

[43] See Heinz Schürmann, Joseph Ratzinger, and Hans Urs von Balthasar, *Principles of Christian Morality*, trans. Graham Harrison (Ignatius, 1986 [1975]); Carlo Caffara, *Living in Christ: Fundamental Principles of Catholic Moral Teaching*, trans. Christopher Ruff (Ignatius, 1987 [1981]). For a helpful overview of the *Glaubensethik* approach, see MacNamara, *Faith and Ethics*, 55–66.

[44] Richard A. McCormick, SJ, "Killing the Patient," in *Considering* Veritatis Splendor, ed. John Wilkins (Pilgrim, 1994), 17. For early reviews of the literature on *Veritatis Splendor*, see Richard A. McCormick, SJ, "Some Early Reactions to *Veritatis Splendor*," *Theological Studies* 55, no. 3 (1994): 481–506; Raphael Gallagher, "The Reception of *Veritatis Splendor* within the Theological Community," *Studia Moralia* 33 (1995): 415–435.

[45] Charles E. Curran, "*Veritatis Splendor*: A Revisionist Perspective," in Veritatis Splendor*: American Responses*, 224–243; Bernard Häring, "A Distrust that Wounds," in *Considering* Veritatis Splendor, 9–13; Joseph Selling, "The Context and Arguments of *Veritatis Splendor*," in *The Splendor of Accuracy: An Examination of the Assertions Made by* Veritatis Splendor, ed. Joseph Selling and Jan Jans (Eerdmans, 1994), 22–70.

[46] German Grisez, "Revelation and Dissent," in *Considering* Veritatis Splendor, 1-8; Martin Rhonheimer, "Intrinsically Evil Acts and the Moral Viewpoint: Clarifying a Central Teaching of *Veritatis Splendor*," *The Thomist* 55 (1994): 481–506; William E. May, "John Paul II, Moral Theology, and Moral Theologians," in Veritatis Splendor *and the Renewal of Moral Theology*, 211–239. More recently, see John Finnis, "Grounds and Preparations for the Main Thesis of *Veritatis Splendor*," *Studia Philosophiae Christianae* 51, no. 2 (2015): 7–26.

chapter.[47] Moral theologians typically offered a few passing words of praise for the opening chapter before quickly moving on to a careful examination of chapter two. For example, although critical of the encyclical's second chapter, McCormick declares that "all Catholic moral theologians should and will welcome the beautiful Christ-centered presentation unfolded in chapter one," but he devotes no further analysis to that presentation.[48] Despite positioning himself as a staunch supporter of the encyclical, Germain Grisez treats the first chapter perhaps even more dismissively when he asserts that "while the encyclical's first chapter provides an inspiring articulation of the Gospel's teaching about following Jesus, its second chapter takes up and criticizes four ways in which various dissenters have tried to soften received moral teaching about intrinsically evil acts."[49] Grisez's words suggest that he views the opening chapter as a mere (inspiring) prologue to the real substance of the encyclical contained in chapter two.

A minority of theologians, however, did recognize the significance of the encyclical's first chapter. For example, Pinckaers argues that, while chapter two fulfills a much-needed polemical purpose, "the first chapter of *Veritatis Splendor* is every bit as important as the second, because it traces the broad lines of a renewal of Catholic moral theology through a return to its chief source—the Gospel—which means bridging the gap which has been created between morality and spirituality."[50] Indeed, he maintains that the first chapter is a truly "constructive" exercise in moral theology. Pinckaers connects the constructive project in chapter one to the Council's call for the renewal of moral theology and argues that John Paul II undertakes this work of renewal specifically through "the reestablishment of a profound and sustained contact with that primary source of inspiration for Christian life and theology that is the Word and Person of Christ."[51]

---

[47] One might argue that there exists an even more profound neglect of chapter three, and indeed this chapter will remain largely beyond the purview of the present article. For analysis of this chapter, see John Berkman, "Truth and Martyrdom: The Structure of Discipleship in *Veritatis Splendor*," *New Blackfriars* 75 (1994): 533–541.

[48] McCormick, "Killing the Patient," 17.

[49] Grisez, "Revelation and Dissent," 3.

[50] Pinckaers, "An Encyclical for the Future," 19. See also Livio Melina, *Sharing in Christ's Virtues: For a Renewal of Moral Theology in Light of* Veritatis Splendor, trans. William E. May (The Catholic University of America Press, 2001); Patrick M. Clark, "The Case for an Exemplarist Approach to Virtue in Catholic Moral Theology," *Journal of Moral Theology* 3, no. 1 (2014): 54–82; Ryan Connors, "The Incarnate Word in Catholic Moral Theology: The Christocentric Visions of John Paul II and Robert Imbelli," in *The Center is Jesus Christ Himself: Essays on Revelation, Salvation, and Evangelization in Honor of Robert P. Imbelli*, ed. Andrew Meszaros (The Catholic University of America Press, 2021), 189–204.

[51] Pinckaers, "An Encyclical for the Future," 13.

The Christocentrism of *Veritatis Splendor* is evident from the very beginning of the encyclical. The opening line's reference to the "Splendor of truth," which "shines forth in the works of the Creator" and "enlightens man's intelligence and shapes his freedom," establishes light as the driving image of the introduction (no. 1). This sets the stage for John Paul II's affirmation that "the light of God's face shines in all its beauty on the countenance of Jesus Christ, 'the image of the invisible God' (Col 1:15), the 'reflection of God's glory' (Heb 1:3), 'full of grace and truth' (John 1:14)" (no. 2). He then applies this bold Christological claim to the situation of contemporary human beings, insisting that

> The decisive answer to every one of man's questions, his religious and moral questions in particular, is given by Jesus Christ, or rather is Jesus Christ himself, as the Second Vatican Council recalls: "In fact, *it is only in the mystery of the Word incarnate that light is shed on the mystery of man.* For Adam, the first man, was a figure of the future man, namely of Christ the Lord. It is Christ, the last Adam, who fully discloses man to himself and unfolds his noble calling by revealing the mystery of the Father and the Father's love" (no. 2).[52]

Consequently, John Paul II proposes that the encounter with Christ offers a new perspective on the moral life. He urges Christians "to turn to Christ once again in order to receive from him the answer to their questions about what is good and what is evil. . . . It is he who . . . by fully revealing the Father's will, teaches the truth about moral action" (no. 8). As the one who most fully reveals humanity to itself, Jesus is the consummate teacher of what is good for human beings.

John Paul II cautions, however, that to learn from Jesus about the human good is "not a matter only of disposing oneself to hear a teaching and obediently accepting a commandment" (no. 19)—a point

---

[52] The quote refers to *Gaudium et Spes*, no. 22, which is instructive, for it both situates the encyclical as a response to the Council's call for the renewal of moral theology—a call to which he explicitly connects *Veritatis Splendor* in subsequent paragraphs—and proposes that a Christological hermeneutic is the appropriate method for pursuing that renewal. For a critique of John Paul II's use of *Gaudium et Spes*, see Mary Elsbernd, "The Reinterpretation of *Gaudium et Spes* in *Veritatis Splendor*," *Horizons* 29, no. 2 (2002): 225–239. Elsbernd argues that John Paul II's consistent citation of *Gaudium et Spes* does not *ipso facto* indicate theological continuity and in fact argues that in *Veritatis Splendor* "the theological anthropology of *Gaudium et Spes* has been recast in a dualistic and individualistic concept" and "re-contextualized *Gaudium et Spes* quotations on change, conscience, dialogue with modern culture, human autonomy, and social institutions by placing them into paragraphs stressing law and precepts" (226). However, Elsbernd operates out of a presumption that the "signs of the times" reading of *Gaudium et Spes* is the only legitimate interpretation of the document and gives no consideration to the type of Christocentric reading John Paul II espouses.

to which we shall return in the next section. "More radically," the pope insists, "it involves holding fast to the very person of Jesus" (no. 19). This is demonstrated most clearly when, "conscious of the young man's yearning for something greater, which would transcend a legalistic interpretation of the commandments, the Good Teacher invites him to enter upon the path of perfection" (no. 16). That path of perfection entails the radical and bracing call of Jesus to "come, follow me" (Matt 19:21). For John Paul II, this is the very heart of Christian ethics. Indeed, he asserts that "following Christ is . . . the essential and primordial foundation of Christian morality" (no. 19).

For John Paul II, holding fast to the person of Christ involves both outward imitation and interior conformity. He posits that "Jesus's way of acting and his words, his deeds and his precepts, constitute the moral rule of the Christian life" (no. 20). Nevertheless, such a claim faces challenges with respect to discerning precisely what features of Jesus's life are most central and therefore worthy of imitation. Therefore, John Paul II offers an interpretive key to guide this process: "[Jesus's] actions, and in particular his Passion and Death on the Cross, are the living revelation of his love for the Father and for others. This is exactly the love that Jesus wishes to be imitated by all who follow him" (no. 20). To imitate Jesus is thus not just to replicate this or that particular action but primarily to embody his self-giving love. The pope emphasizes the point: "As he calls the young man to follow him along the way of perfection, Jesus asks him to be perfect in the command of love, in "his" commandment: to become part of the unfolding of his complete giving, to imitate and rekindle the very love of the 'Good' Teacher, the one who loved 'to the end'" (no. 20). Although the pope employs the language of a commandment of love, this is not a precept that can be exhaustively codified. Rather, his point is that the law of love is Jesus himself in his very person. "*He himself becomes a living and personal law*," the pope explains, "who invites people to follow him; through the Spirit, he gives the grace to share his own life and love and provides the strength to bear witness to that love in personal choices and actions" (no. 15).

At the same time, John Paul II asserts that "following Christ is not an outward imitation, since it touches man at the very depths of his being. Being a follower of Christ means becoming conformed to him who became a servant even to giving himself on the Cross" (no. 21). The capacity to live like Christ morally depends on having first been likened to him ontologically. By grace (especially the grace of baptism), the human person is conformed to the pattern of Christ and made a member of his Body and sharer in his power. The emphasis on interior conformity to Christ, an assimilation that occurs at the very core of the person and not merely a process of reprogramming one's habits, underscores the necessity of grace for the moral life. "To imitate and live out the love of Christ is not possible for man by his own strength alone," John Paul II writes. "He becomes capable of this love only by virtue of a gift received" (no. 22).

Near the end of chapter one, John Paul II neatly summarizes his Christocentric vision of the moral life and reasserts the enduring relevance of this encounter for the present moment: "Jesus's conversation with the rich young man continues, in a sense, in every period of history, including our own. The question: 'Teacher, what good must I do to have eternal life?' arises in the heart of every individual, and it is Christ alone who is capable of giving the full and definitive answer. The Teacher who expounds God's commandments, who invites others to follow him and gives the grace for a new life, is always present and at work in our midst" (no. 25). For John Paul II, the Christian moral life is Christocentric not merely because Christ is a moral teacher but more fundamentally because Christ is the principle of the moral life as both its pattern and source. As the pattern and exemplar of the moral life, he "sheds light on man's condition and his integral vocation," manifesting concretely the pattern of life to which human beings are called (no. 2). As source of the moral life, he communicates a share in his own life to human beings by grace, empowering them to follow him not simply by the repetition of his actions but the conformity of their very selves.

Echoes of the Christocentric movement from a half-century earlier are readily perceptible in the first chapter of *Veritatis Splendor*. The notions of Christ being a model and exemplar of the moral life and of that life consisting principally in following Christ through outward imitation and interior conformity align with central themes in the works of moral theologians like Tillmann, Gillon, and the early Häring and suggest that the pope seeks to recover, albeit in his own way, the insights of the movement to which these figures belong. Although *Veritatis Splendor* does not cite any of these theologians explicitly— indeed, the encyclical studiously avoids direct references to any theologians after Alphonsus Liguori—there are good, albeit indirect, reasons to think that John Paul II was familiar with their thought.[53]

---

[53] With respect to Tillmann, one finds in Karol Wojtyla's habilitation thesis on Max Scheler two citations of *Die Idee der Nachfolge Christi* as an attempt to appropriate Scheler's personalist philosophy and emphasis on imitation as a framework for Christian ethics. See Karol Wojtyla, *The Lublin Lectures and Works on Max Scheler*, trans. Grzegorz Ignatik (The Catholic University of America Press, 2023), 505, 561. Concerning Gillon's influence, the evidence is less direct. However, Gillon served on the faculty of the Angelicum while Wojtyla was completing his doctorate there. Finally, with respect to Häring, Wojtyla clearly knew him personally from their common work on the drafting committee for *Gaudium et Spes* during the Second Vatican Council. See John Sikorski, "Towards a Conjugal Spirituality: Karol Wojtyla's Vision of Marriage Before, During, and After Vatican II," *Journal of Moral*

Building upon their insights in the service of a more Christocentric moral theology, the opening chapter of *Veritatis Splendor* does not merely aim to correct certain contemporary theories about human action, conscience, and freedom, but proposes a fundamentally different, *ressourcement* approach to moral theology by beginning with the person of Christ and his irreducible centrality to the moral life.

THE CHRISTOCENTRIC UNITY OF *VERITATIS SPLENDOR*

Among the relatively few moral theologians who give sustained attention to the first chapter of *Veritatis Splendor*, one typically finds enthusiasm for the pope's desire to put the person of Christ and the life of discipleship at the forefront of moral theology.[54] Nevertheless, some of them, although generally amenable to its effort to root moral theology in Scripture and the person of Christ, contend that the encyclical ultimately undermines its own Christocentric impulses. Thus, to show that *Veritatis Splendor* does in fact present a thoroughly and consistently Christocentric moral theology, it is necessary to consider and respond to two objections.

Christ and the Moral Law

The first objection, advanced most prominently by Charles Curran, argues that the Christocentrism of chapter one is subordinated—in that very chapter—to a morality of law and obligation. Although Curran, like many revisionists, devotes most of his attention to the contentious issues of the encyclical's second chapter, he is nonetheless appreciative of John Paul II's substantive engagement with Scripture and emphasis on the centrality of Christ. Curran argues, however, that the encyclical's references to Jesus are ultimately futile because they remain trapped within an overarching legal approach to the moral life. He alleges that

> The encyclical has distorted the meaning of Christian morality by putting primary emphasis on obedience to the Ten Commandments. . . . In fairness, however, the encyclical tries to put the commandments of the

---

Theology 6, no. 2 (2017): 103–129. Moreover, as noted above, *The Law of Christ* was perhaps the most well-known moral textbook in circulation in the years preceding the Council, so it is likely that Wojtyla would have had at least some familiarity with its central claims and methods.

[54] A notable exception is to be found in scholars who criticize the pope's exegesis of the rich young man pericope in chapter one. See, for example, Gareth Moore, "Some Remarks on the Use of Scripture in *Veritatis Splendor*," in *The Splendor of Accuracy*, 71–98.

Decalogue into a bigger picture. The pope mentions the invitation to be perfect, the following of Jesus, commitment to the very person of Jesus, and the new law of love proposed by St. Paul. But the encyclical proposes all these as illustrations of obedience to God's will and law.[55]

According to Curran, even the theological, personalist elements of the encyclical that might be hailed as evidence of a renewal of moral theology are deprived of their force because they are framed within a legal paradigm. Indeed, Curran maintains that even the opening chapter's presentation of the call to perfection is reduced to a species of law-following insofar as "the call to holiness is based on a command to love one another as God has loved us and involves a free and loving obedience to the will of the Father."[56]

Curran's criticism reflects the dominant trend of treating chapter two as the true heart of *Veritatis Splendor* and then interpreting chapter one in light of chapter two. As Curran reads it, the second chapter enforces a legal paradigm concerned with insisting that certain acts are always and everywhere impermissible, and he views the first chapter as a biblical preamble put at the service of this higher goal. Yet, if one attends carefully to the first chapter's articulation of the relationship between the commandments and the following of Christ, one finds precisely the opposite of what Curran alleges.

Law is an essential element of Christian ethics, and it cannot merely be jettisoned. Rather, the challenge is to understand and appreciate the importance of law and its role within the broader context of the Christian moral life, and this is precisely what *Veritatis Splendor* aims to do. John Paul II seizes on Jesus's initial answer to the rich young man's question as an opportunity to emphasize the indispensability of the commandments, to be sure.[57] Yet, the young man's reply that he has observed all the commandments and still lacks something also provides an occasion for the pope to illustrate how the commandments are not ends in themselves. As John Paul II explains, "The young man's commitment to respect all the moral demands of the commandments represents the absolutely essential ground in which the desire for perfection can take root and mature, the desire, that is, for the meaning of the commandments to be completely fulfilled in following Christ" (no. 17). Here, one can see clearly how the commandments are ordered to the following of Christ. Again, he insists, "Jesus shows that the commandments must not be understood

---

[55] Charles E. Curran, *The Moral Theology of John Paul II* (Georgetown University Press, 2005), 53.
[56] Curran, *The Moral Theology of John Paul II*, 105.
[57] See *Veritatis Splendor*, no. 12: "From the very lips of Jesus, the new Moses, man is once again given the commandments of the Decalogue. Jesus himself definitively confirms them and proposes them to us as the way and condition of salvation."

as a minimum limit not to be gone beyond, but rather as a path involving a moral and spiritual journey toward perfection, at the heart of which is love" (no. 15). The summons to perfection, in other words, is not reducible to obeying the commandments, but at the same time the call to perfection does not leave the commandments behind. Rather, John Paul II suggests that the freedom coming from following Jesus transforms the commandments into invitations to deeper and more perfect love.[58]

Thus, even as *Veritatis Splendor* upholds the inviolability of the commandments, it recognizes that the commandments are not the only vocabulary—or even the best vocabulary—for describing the Christian life. John Paul II affirms that "love and life according to the Gospel cannot be thought of first and foremost as a kind of precept" but only as the graced response to Jesus's call to follow him (no. 23). Again, the pope insists that this way of discipleship "is not a matter only of disposing oneself to hear a teaching and obediently accepting a commandment. More radically, it involves holding fast to the very person of Jesus, partaking of his life and his destiny, sharing in his free and loving obedience to the will of the Father" (no. 19). Far from reducing Jesus's summons to perfection to mere obedience to precepts, the first chapter of *Veritatis Splendor* clearly views the moral law as being at the service of a decidedly Christocentric vision of the moral life.[59]

The Theo-Logical Coherence of Veritatis Splendor

The second—and, in my view, more potent—line of criticism alleges that the Christological overture in *Veritatis Splendor*'s first chapter is ultimately incompatible with the methodology that governs its second chapter. Thus, William Spohn contends that *Veritatis Splendor* "opens up the possibility of a Christocentric ethics, at least initially. It subordinates a realist epistemology and the natural law to the religious realities of discipleship and the cross, which are the moral core of Christian discipleship. . . . However, the encyclical does not sustain this Christological ethics into the remainder of the text."[60] Unlike Curran, Spohn recognizes the Christocentric integrity of

---

[58] See, for example, *Veritatis Splendor*, no. 15: "Thus the commandment 'You shall not murder' becomes a call to an attentive love which protects and promotes the life of one's neighbor. The precept prohibiting adultery becomes an invitation to a pure way of looking at others, capable of respecting the spousal meaning of the body."

[59] Livio Melina, "The Desire for Happiness and the Commandments in the First Chapter of *Veritatis Splendor*," trans. Margaret H. McCarthy, in Veritatis Splendor *and the Renewal of Moral Theology*, 143–160.

[60] William C. Spohn, "Morality on the Way of Discipleship: The Use of Scripture in *Veritatis Splendor*," in Veritatis Splendor: *American Responses*, 94.

chapter one. However, the problem he detects is a fundamental inconsistency between the purportedly Christocentric aims expressed in chapter one and the theological concepts on which the rest of the document relies. He laments that while "the encyclical promises a Christonomous ethics of discipleship . . . it cannot deliver because it reduces morality to a matter of rules and principles. The ethics of discipleship gets quickly transformed into a theonomous naturalism which enshrines the natural law realism of the recent tradition."[61] For Spohn, *Veritatis Splendor* is, at best, an incoherent encyclical. Its theologically rich, biblically inspired, and Christocentric opening chapter offers a vision of the moral life undermined and contradicted by the act-based, rule-focused philosophical ethics presented in chapter two.[62] This is a serious charge and one worthy of careful consideration, for if *Veritatis Splendor* is to have value for Catholic moral theology, it must be internally coherent. It is therefore necessary to determine the extent to which the encyclical possesses intrinsic unity and, accordingly, understand how the seemingly disparate emphases of its first two chapters fit together.

It is true that explicit mention of the person of Christ all but disappears in the second chapter. On the one hand, one might account for this shift in terms of the encyclical's twofold aim as Pinckaers articulates it. Thus, one could argue that while chapter one articulates a constructive vision for a Christocentric moral theology, that vision can only be developed if certain technical errors are first corrected. Thus, chapter two undertakes its polemical work for the sake of a fuller implementation of the Christocentric vision outlined but not fleshed out in the opening chapter. While this is certainly a plausible rationale for the encyclical's structure, it does not adequately resolve the issue at hand, because it does not explain how clarifying technical questions about human action and natural law is at the service of advancing a Christocentric moral theology. A more promising approach to discerning the conceptual unity of *Veritatis Splendor* requires engaging the substance of its treatment of these technical questions in order to recognize a Christocentric perspective even there. A prime candidate for such examination is its treatment of natural law, the foundation for its account of human action.

---

[61] Spohn, "Morality on the Way of Discipleship," 102. See also Karl P. Donfried, "The Use of Scripture in *Veritatis Splendor*," in *Ecumenical Ventures in Ethics: Protestants Engage John Paul II's Moral Encyclicals*, ed. Reinhard Hütter and Theodor Dieter (Eerdmans, 1998), 46.

[62] See also Nicholas Lash, "Crisis and Tradition in *Veritatis Splendor*," in *Considering Veritatis Splendor*, 23.

Veritatis Splendor emphasizes the natural law as an expression of divine wisdom.[63] John Paul II expresses this conviction in his very first reference to the natural law in chapter one where he submits that God instructs humanity about what is good first of all "by creating man and ordering him with wisdom and love to his final end through the law which is inscribed in his heart, the 'natural law.'" (no. 12). He elaborates on this with greater precision in chapter two, where he situates the natural law within the broader context of the eternal law. Following Augustine and Aquinas, he posits that the eternal law is nothing other than God's providential governance of creation, an expression of divine wisdom by which God leads all created things to their proper acts and ends. This providence, he notes, extends in a unique manner to human beings whom God cares for "'from within,' through reason, which by its natural knowledge of God's eternal law, is consequently able to show man the right direction to take in his free actions" (no. 43). Thus, John Paul II concludes that the natural law, discerned by reason, "enters here as the human expression of God's eternal law" (no. 43).

By all accounts, John Paul II here rehearses a very traditional view of the natural law which underscores its source in God's wisdom, congruency with human nature, and accessibility to human reason. At the same time, he seeks to highlight the theological character of the natural law by connecting it specifically to the person of Christ. In an insightful essay, Lawrence Welch links the pope's observations about the eternal law in *Veritatis Splendor* to an even more direct claim he makes in his 1986 encyclical on the Holy Spirit, *Dominum et Vivificantem*. Reflecting on the nature of sin as embodying "a rejection, or at least a turning away from the truth contained in the Word of God," John Paul II attests that "this Word is the same Word who was 'in the beginning with God,' who 'was God,' and without whom 'nothing has been made of all that is,' since 'the world was made through him.' He is the Word who is also the eternal law, the source of every law which regulates the world and especially human acts" (no. 33).[64] Here, John Paul II explicitly equates the eternal law with the Person of the Word, who becomes incarnate in Christ. Such an identification further entails that the natural law is the human person's rational participation in the Word. It is, in other words, to assert the fundamentally Christological character of the natural law.

In *Veritatis Splendor* itself, John Paul II emphasizes the unity of the moral law in the wisdom of God and, by extension, the

---

[63] Russell Hittinger, "*Veritatis Splendor* and the Theology of Natural Law," in Veritatis Splendor *and the Renewal of Moral Theology*, 97–128.

[64] Quoted in Lawrence J. Welch, "Christ, the Moral Law, and the Teaching Authority of the Magisterium," *Irish Theological Quarterly* 64 (1999): 24.

Christological foundation of the moral law. In one particularly illustrative passage, he submits that

> Even if moral-theological reflection usually distinguishes between the positive or revealed law of God and the natural law, and, within the economy of salvation, between the "old" and the "new" law, it must not be forgotten that these and other useful distinctions always refer to that law whose author is the one and the same God and which is always meant for man. The different ways in which God, acting in history, cares for the world and for mankind are not mutually exclusive; on the contrary, they support each other and intersect. They have their origin and goal in the eternal, wise and loving counsel whereby God predestines men and women "to be conformed to the image of his Son" (Rom 8:29). (no. 45)

Here, John Paul II does not merely situate natural law and divine law together under the broader heading of the eternal law as an expression of divine providence, he identifies their origin and goal as the conformity of human beings to Christ as their ontological exemplar. Human beings are not merely redeemed by the person of the Son, they are also *created* in, through, and after the pattern of the Son. As Welch observes, "What the Pope takes very seriously is Christ, the head and the Alpha by whom the human race is redeemed and in whom we are created. . . . Just as creation and redemption are distinct but find their unity in Christ, so the natural law and the positive law find their unity in Christ the Word, who is the eternal law."[65]

Similarly, when he reflects on the challenges posed to the universality and immutability of the natural law by variations among cultural and historical particularities, John Paul II appeals to a metaphysical account of human nature to argue that human beings, although existing within and shaped by a particular culture, nevertheless are "not exhaustively defined by that same culture" (*Veritatis Splendor*, no. 53). Yet, this appeal to human nature and its intrinsic dignity as morally normative is further buttressed by a Christological appeal. He contends that

> To call into question the permanent structural elements of man . . . would render meaningless Jesus's reference to the "beginning," precisely where the social and cultural context of the time had distorted the primordial meaning and the role of certain moral norms. This is the reason why "the Church affirms that underlying so many changes there are some things which do not change and are ultimately founded upon Christ, who is the same yesterday and today and

---

[65] Welch, "Christ, the Moral Law, and the Teaching Authority of the Magisterium," 26.

forever." Christ is the "Beginning" who, having taken on human nature, definitively illumines it in its constitutive elements and in its dynamism of charity towards God and neighbor. (no. 53)[66]

Here again one sees at work John Paul II's Christocentric anthropology, drawn from *Gaudium et Spes* as the foundation for a Christocentric view of the moral law, both natural and revealed. In short, if human nature provides the norm for human action, and human nature is ultimately patterned after the person of Christ as its exemplar, then even the natural law itself is inherently Christological.

Commenting on *Veritatis Splendor* ten years after its promulgation, Joseph Ratzinger offers a hermeneutical key to discerning the encyclical's internal unity and coherence. He argues that it presents a "magnificent renewed vision that is at once Christological and rational, because Christ is the *Logos*. . . . Recognition of the centrality of the figure of Christ implies the true reconciliation between history and reason, between supernatural revelation and reason, because . . . Christ is the *Logos* made flesh, that is, the fullness of creative reason itself, who speaks to us and opens our eyes to see anew . . . the presence of a creative truth that lies at the foundation of being."[67] The person of Christ is not only the *Logos* who gives logical consistency to John Paul II's encyclical but, more importantly, He is the *Logos* who grants coherence to the entire moral order, both natural and revealed.

CONCLUSION

This essay has argued that the Christocentric moral vision that John Paul II proposes in *Veritatis Splendor* is not altogether novel but involves a creative retrieval of an earlier Christocentric renaissance in moral theology during the decades preceding Vatican II. Without seeking to marginalize the encyclical's crucial interventions in technical debates in moral theology, I have argued that, more than a philosophical treatise or a brute exercise of magisterial power, *Veritatis Splendor* is a work of *ressourcement* whose first chapter must be taken seriously as a positive proposal for the ongoing renewal of Catholic moral theology. Its thoroughly and coherently Christocentric approach opens promising new avenues for, among other things, integrating traditional understandings of the moral law with the

---

[66] This passage quotes *Gaudium et Spes*, no. 10, another Christocentric text, which asserts that Christ "can through His Spirit offer man the light and the strength to measure up to his supreme destiny" and that "in her most benign Lord and Master can be found the key, the focal point, and the goal of man."

[67] Joseph Cardinal Ratzinger, "The Renewal of Moral Theology: Perspectives of Vatican II and *Veritatis Splendor*," *Communio* 32, no. 2 (2005): 365.

evangelical summons to life in Christ, highlighting the centrality of ecclesial discipleship to the moral life, and overcoming the artificial barriers often set between moral theology and other aspects of Christian theology and practice.

When *Veritatis Splendor* was first released, the Anglican ethicist Oliver O'Donovan remarked that "everyone has had a nice word to say about this first section, [but] not everyone has appreciated its innovative strength as a program for moral theology. Future generations may find the Splendor of *Veritatis Splendor* here in these pages which shape the moral discourse of the church as an evangelical proclamation."[68] The task of continuing to receive the wisdom of *Veritatis Splendor* three decades later only stands to benefit from such an exhortation to a more robust theological engagement with its constructive first chapter's—and, indeed, the entire encyclical's—Christocentric moral vision and the *ressourcement* that undergirds it. ∎

Michael A. Wahl, PhD, is assistant professor of theology at Providence College, where his research focuses on Catholic fundamental moral theology, Thomistic ethics, virtue theory, and moral development. His recent publications include articles in *The Thomist*, *Nova et Vetera*, and *The Heythrop Journal*.

---

[68] Oliver O'Donovan, "A Summons to Reality," in *Considering* Veritatis Splendor, 42.

Seeds for an Encounter Ethics: The Fruit of Reading *Veritatis Splendor* Beyond a Post-Conciliar Binary Narrative

Catherine Moon

Abstract: Two of the more recent methodological narratives about twentieth-century moral theology, written by James Keenan and Matthew Levering, argue that an intractable methodological division over law and conscience emerges in the wake of Vatican II. Within these narratives, *Veritatis Splendor* is situated as authoritatively taking sides amidst this division, leaving *Veritatis Splendor*'s key methodological insights out of view. While (re)turning to a more spiritual approach to moral theology, the Second Vatican Council does not set out a clear *method* for the discipline but instead leaves post-conciliar moral theology with the task of figuring out *how to do moral theology according* to this new paradigm. *Veritatis Splendor* ought to be read as a continuation and deepening of this post-conciliar moral methodological project set in motion by Vatican II. Through the concept of "encounter with Christ" and its emphasis on the lives of the saints, *Veritatis Splendor* plants seeds for the development of a post-conciliar moral theological method consistent with the methodological task set out by the Second Vatican Council, a foundational point of methodological continuity between "revisionists" and "traditionalists," and responsive to unresolved methodological concerns from the Council.

THERE HAS BEEN WIDESPREAD DISAGREEMENT ABOUT *Veritatis Splendor*'s true purpose since the time of its promulgation.[1] For example, *Veritatis Splendor* has been interpreted as attempting "to endorse total assent and submission to all utterance of the Pope,"[2] and yet it also has been inter-

---

NB: In this article, the author often preferred to use the plural "criteria" instead of the singular "criterion."—Ed.

[1] See Richard A. McCormick, "Some Early Reactions to *Veritatis Splendor*," *Theological Studies* 55, no. 3 (1994): 481–506 and "*Veritatis Splendor*," *Commonweal* 120, no. 18 (1993): 11–18.
[2] Bernard Häring, "A Distrust that Wounds," in *John Paul II and Moral Theology: Readings in Moral Theology No. 10*, ed. Charles E. Curran and Richard A. McCormick (Paulist, 1998), 42.

preted as attempting to reaffirm "that the exceptionlessness of ... norms is a revealed truth."[3] Since *Veritatis Splendor* is a post-conciliar encyclical on moral theology, questions about how to interpret the purpose of *Veritatis Splendor* are ultimately inseparable from questions about how to interpret the meaning of the Second Vatican Council's call to renew moral theology. Yet, there has also been widespread disagreement about how to interpret *Veritatis Splendor*'s relationship to the Second Vatican Council and the moral methodological developments it set in motion. *Veritatis Splendor* has been interpreted as "a retreat from the reforms of the Council and retrenchment of older pre-conciliar ideas."[4] As a result, some theologians argue that the encyclical is an "attempt to put the lid on what has been a lively debate for more than 30 years."[5] In contrast, *Veritatis Splendor* has also been interpreted as "a critical discernment and purification of the Council's vision which had been clouded,"[6] leading some theologians to argue that the encyclical "represents a significant step on the road to rehabilitating and communicating the tradition."[7]

These conflicting interpretations are embedded within larger narratives that view *Veritatis Splendor* as an authoritative intervention in methodological disputes in the field of moral theology.[8] James Keenan and Matthew Levering have written two of the more popular narratives about methodological developments in twentieth-century

---

[3] Germain Grisez, "Revelation vs. Dissent," in *John Paul II and Moral Theology*, 40.

[4] John S. Grabowski, "The Luminous Excess of the Acting Person: Assessing the Impact of Pope John Paul II on American Catholic Moral Theology," in *Journal of Moral Theology* 1, no. 1 (2012): 118. See also Mary Elsbernd, "The Reinterpretation of *Gaudium et Spes* in *Veritatis Splendor*," *Horizons* 29 no. 2 (2002): 225–39; Charles Curran, *Catholic Moral Theology in the United States: A History* (Georgetown University Press, 2008), 98.

[5] William Uren, "Think of the Consequences," *Eureka Street* 3, no. 9 (1993): 6–7, at 6. See also Lawrence S. Cunningham, "*Veritatis Splendor*," *Commonweal* 120, no. 18, (1993): 11–18.

[6] Grabowski, "The Luminous Excess of the Acting Person," 118. See also Tracey Rowland, "Pope John Paul II: Authentic Interpreter of Vatican II," in *John Paul the Great: Maker of the Post Conciliar Church* (Ignatius, 2005), 27–48.

[7] Russell Hittinger, "The Splendor of Truth: A Symposium," *First Things* 39 (January 1994): 17. See also Richard John Neuhaus, "The Splendor of Truth: A Symposium" *First Things* 39 (January 1994): 15.

[8] For additional "revisionist" narratives see Charles Curran, *Diverse Voices in Modern US Moral Theology* (Georgetown University Press, 2018); Klaus Demmer, MSC, *Shaping the Moral Life: An Approach to Moral Theology*, ed. James F. Keenan, SJ, trans. Roberto Dell'Oro (Georgetown University Press, 2000). For additional "traditionalist" narratives see Servais Pinckaers, OP, *Morality: The Catholic View*, trans. Michael Sherwin, OP (St. Augustine's Press, 2001); Romanus Cesario, OP, *The Moral Virtues and Theological Ethics*, 2nd ed. (University of Notre Dame Press, 2009).

Catholic moral theology. In their own ways, Keenan and Levering argue that an intractable methodological division over law and conscience emerging in moral theology between so-called "revisionist" and "traditionalist" theologians over the course of the twentieth century becomes solidified in the wake of the Second Vatican Council. Both narratives situate *Veritatis Splendor* as authoritatively taking sides amidst this intractable division. Although these narratives rightly recognize that post-conciliar moral theology suffers from methodological divisions and that *Veritatis Splendor* seeks to speak authoritatively on method in moral theology, they wrongly understand the nature of post-conciliar division, incorrectly situate *Veritatis Splendor* as taking sides amidst this division, and fail to seriously recognize *Veritatis Splendor*'s key methodological contributions to post-conciliar moral theology.

I propose to situate and read *Veritatis Splendor* within an alternative twentieth-century and post-conciliar methodological narrative. *Veritatis Splendor* ought to be read as a continuation and deepening of the post-conciliar moral methodological project set in motion by Vatican II: "to return to a substantially biblical and Christological ethics, inspired by the *encounter with Christ*, an ethics conceived not as a series of precepts, but as the event of encounter of a love that then also knows how to create corresponding actions."[9] In order to make this case, I begin by outlining Keenan's and Levering's recent narratives about method in twentieth-century Catholic moral theology. Following this, I clarify the meaning of the term "method" and describe what to suffer from methodological divisions means for the discipline of Catholic moral theology. I contend that these methodological narratives suffer from a law-conscience binary framework that cannot make sense of or accurately recognize the underlying methodological unity at work in post-conciliar moral theology.

In order to retrieve a coherent narrative by which to make sense of post-conciliar moral theology's underlying methodological unity and express divisions, I return to the Second Vatican Council to seek a new horizon in which to situate and interpret *Veritatis Splendor*. While turning to a spiritual, moral framework in *Optatam Totius*, I argue that the Second Vatican Council does not set out a clear method for this new framework and leaves difficulties about it unresolved. I conclude that when read beyond a post-conciliar methodological binary

---

[9] Joseph Cardinal Ratzinger, "The Renewal of Moral Theology: Perspectives of Vatican II and *Veritatis Splendor*," in *Communio* 32 (Summer 2005): 359. In this view, I follow Joseph Ratzinger and John S. Grabowski. See Grabowski, "The Luminous Excess of the Acting Person," and Grabowski, "Catechesis and Moral Theology: Toward a Renewed Understanding of Christian Experience," *Nova et Vetera* 13, no. 2 (2015): 459–487.

narrative, *Veritatis Splendor* plants seeds for the development of a post-conciliar moral theological method consistent with the methodological task set out by the Second Vatican Council, a foundational point of methodological continuity between "revisionists" and "traditionalists," and responsive to unresolved methodological concerns from the Council as manifest in the contention over *De Ordine Morali*. Through its approach to Scripture, attention to the saints, and epistemological turn to "encounter with Christ," *Veritatis Splendor* teaches that the heart of moral method and light of faith is Christ's call to "Come, follow me!" (no. 14).

A House Divided: Popular Narratives on Post-Conciliar Method

In this section, I outline Keenan's and Levering's narratives about the developmental shifts in moral theological method prior to and in the wake of the Second Vatican Council. I delineate the way Keenan and Levering situate and interpret *Veritatis Splendor* within the context of their methodological narratives. Following these outlines, I then evaluate Keenan's and Levering's accounts of the nature and source of methodological division in post-conciliar moral theology. I argue that Keenan's and Levering's narratives invoke more or less the same law-conscience binary methodological narrative where each methodological track is defined against the other by means of law or conscience. I conclude that as a result of their binary frameworks, Keenan's and Levering's narratives of post-conciliar method cannot recognize, let alone account for the fact that the "revisionist" track and the "traditionalist" track have the same formal criteria and both expressly understand themselves to be in continuity with the Second Vatican Council. I deduce that a methodological narrative of post-conciliar moral theology that can make sense of and account for these phenomena is necessary.

Post-Conciliar Methodological Divisions over Law and Conscience

Like most theologians, Keenan and Levering agree on the distinctive features of conciliar and, thus, post-conciliar moral theology. They agree that the Second Vatican Council turns away from the more legalist framework of the moral manuals to the more spiritual framework of Sacred Scripture. They agree that the Council sets out clear features for moral theological method given this paradigmatic shift away from legalism: (1) turn to the subject or person, (2) incorporation of virtue, (3) recognition of the social and historical dimensions of human life, (4) basis in Scripture, and (5) Christ-centered approach.[10] Despite this agreement, as both Levering and Keenan narrate, disagreement begins to emerge over what constitutes an authentic instantiation of post-conciliar moral theology in the wake of the Council.

According to Levering's narrative, "Most moral theologians and most bishops found themselves operating out of two very different and distinctive methodologies that responded to very different presuppositions" following the Second Vatican Council.[11] Moral theology bifurcated into "a minority of moral theologians" who "carried forward" this conciliar vision and into a majority of "mainstream" moral theologians who advanced "a conscience-centered morality resituated within a transcendental anthropology" that distorts the conciliar vision.[12] Levering argues that this conscience-centered method "slides inevitably into sovereign subjectivity"[13] because the individual person's conscience is made the formal criteria for evaluating truth claims and is no longer "focused upon receptivity to eternal law and universal norms."[14] To Levering, the other method, which he identifies as faithful to the conciliar project, pursues truth "in obedience to the God who is both love and lawgiver," and "offers us beatitude, but on the path of cruciform love."[15] This method has "Christ and the grace of the Holy Spirit at the center" as its formal criteria for evaluating truth claims, "healing and elevating the powers of human nature in accord with God's law."[16]

Keenan's narrative also notes a methodological bifurcation, writing that moral theology began "taking place and developing on two different tracks" with "conscience" as "the point of departure for" one track[17] and "God's law" as the point of departure for the other.[18] For Keenan, however, this bifurcation is understood not so much as a split between those who distort the Council and those who carry it forward but between those who reject the Council and those who carry it forward.[19] Keenan argues that the law-centered track pursues moral truth "in specific and (possibly) long-held propositional utterances" such that law as interpreted or promulgated by magisterial authority is

---

[10] See Levering, *The Abuse of Conscience*, 195; Keenan, *A History of Catholic Moral Theology*, 35–36.
[11] Keenan, *A History of Catholic Moral Theology*, 1.
[12] Levering, *The Abuse of Conscience*, 196.
[13] Levering, *The Abuse of Conscience*, 195. See also 205–206.
[14] Levering, *The Abuse of Conscience*, 127–128.
[15] Levering, *The Abuse of Conscience*, 205.
[16] Levering, *The Abuse of Conscience*, 206.
[17] Keenan, *A History of Catholic Moral Theology*, 97.
[18] Keenan, *A History of Catholic Moral Theology*, 112.
[19] Keenan, *A History of Catholic Moral Theology*, 118 and 123.

its formal criteria for evaluating truth claims.[20] Parallel to Levering, Keenan asserts that the conscience-centered track, the one he identifies as faithful to the Conciliar project, "pursues truth in the person of Christ and the realization of that truth in the very human lives of Christians."[21] For Keenan, this method has Christ—not self-will—as its formal criteria for evaluating truth claims.[22]

The Place of Veritatis Splendor *Within These Methodological Narratives*

Where is *Veritatis Splendor*, the only encyclical on Catholic moral theology, situated in these twentieth-century narratives about moral theology? Although Keenan recognizes that *Veritatis Splendor* "is in tone and substance innovative in its use of Scripture,"[23] he sees the encyclical as "for the most part a very lengthy philosophical document, written it seems by mostly philosophers," who do not accurately understand and thereby, "[write] erroneously about the writing of moral theologians."[24] Within his narrative framework, Keenan interprets *Veritatis Splendor* as a work of "neo-manualism" that admonishes revisionist moral theologians without fully or accurately grasping their arguments.[25] By neo-manualist, Keenan means that *Veritatis Splendor* is teaching morals through "propositional utterances" rather than "through the person of Christ and the realization of that truth" in the lives of Christians.[26] Keenan situates *Veritatis Splendor* within his post-conciliar methodological bifurcation narrative as authoritatively taking sides—the side of the law-centered track, which he argues wants to return to pre-conciliar moral theology. From this vantage point, whatever innovative use of Scripture or other methodological insights *Veritatis Splendor* might offer, they would ultimately serve a law-centered methodology that seeks to reject the Council, making further development of those recognized insights inherently nonsensical.

Within Levering's narrative framework, *Veritatis Splendor* is interpreted as "[ensuring] that the commandments are not misunderstood

---

[20] Keenan, *A History of Catholic Moral Theology*, 120.
[21] Keenan, *A History of Catholic Moral Theology*, 120.
[22] Keenan, *A History of Catholic Moral Theology*, 120.
[23] Keenan, *A History of Catholic Moral Theology*, 128. For other analyses of *Veritatis Splendor* and its reception by Keenan, see James F. Keenan, SJ, and Thomas R. Kopfensteiner, "Moral Theology out of Western Europe," *Theological Studies* 59, no. 1 (1998): 107–135; James F. Keenan, SJ, "Fundamental Moral Theology at the Beginning of the New Millennium: Looking Back, Looking Forward," *Theological Studies* 65, no. 1 (2004): 119–140.
[24] Keenan, *A History of Catholic Moral Theology*, 133.
[25] Keenan, *A History of Catholic Moral Theology*, 133.
[26] Keenan, *A History of Catholic Moral Theology*, 120.

as external or arbitrary laws of an aloof God"[27] but as a personal gift through its "biblical and existentialist emphases."[28] Unlike Keenan, Levering devotes very little time to *Veritatis Splendor* or Karol Wojtyla/John Paul II in his narrative of twentieth-century moral theology. *Veritatis Splendor* shows up twice in Levering's narrative: once in his survey of the thought of Servais Pinckaers and once in his critique of Keenan. Levering responds to Keenan's charge of neo-manualism against the encyclical, retorting "Perhaps by this statement, Keenan means simply that *Veritatis Splendor* defends universal moral norms as well as the ability of the magisterium to authoritatively teach these norms, and it also contains teachings on the structure of human action, natural law, conscience, and sin."[29] Levering finds Keenan's charge not simply wrong but unintelligible. Within Levering's narrative, *Veritatis Splendor* is ultimately interpreted as a work of renewal, taking the side of the Christ-centered track over and against the conscience-centered track. From this vantage point, as evident in his retort to Keenan, *Veritatis Splendor* is viewed more as an authoritative corrective than a work rich with its own methodological insights. It is not simply an odd choice for Levering's book on twentieth-century moral theology to not robustly address the unique twentieth-century encyclical on moral theology. It is a telling choice.

EVALUATING METHODOLOGICAL DIVISION AND BINARY NARRATIVES

Keenan and Levering tell similar narratives about twentieth-century moral theology and *Veritatis Splendor*'s place within it: the "good guys" and the "bad guys" happen to be a bit different, but the narrative arc and contour of events are just about the same. Do these similar narratives get the story right? To what extent are Keenan's and Levering's descriptions of post-conciliar methodological division coherent and accurate? What does it mean for Catholic moral theology to suffer methodological division? Over what precisely does this division occur? In the section to follow, I evaluate the methodological bifurcation narratives Keenan and Levering tell by investigating what it means for a field like Catholic moral theology to suffer methodological division. I do this by clarifying what a methodological division is, what the sources of methodological division are, and how, if at all, methodological division can be overcome and adjudicated. I turn to Bernard Lonergan for some basic conceptual distinctions

---

[27] Levering, *The Abuse of Conscience*, 119.
[28] Levering, *The Abuse of Conscience*, 197.
[29] Levering, *The Abuse of Conscience*, 197.

regarding method and methodological division.³⁰ I do not presume to exhaustively treat method and its implications for theology or the church.

Methodological Division Not over Content

The term "method" derives from the Ancient Greek word "μέθοδος" meaning "following after," "pursuit of knowledge," or "mode of prosecuting such inquiry."³¹ Method is not a content. Method is an activity; it is a being-at-work.³² Method is not the *outcome* or *result* of a study, investigation, or inquiry in a given field (e.g., don't run red lights!). Method rather is the activity by which outcomes in a given field are properly achieved (e.g., how we determine proper driving etiquette). Therefore, for a discipline to undergo a change or shift in method is not about a change or shift in its content or outcomes. A field's content or outcomes could very well stay the same even if its method changes. It is about how to properly achieve insights in a field. Reflection on methodological division is thus reflection on the formal criteria and "operations by which those [contents] are reached."³³

Having clarified that method is an activity, we can then say that Keenan and Levering rightly identify that the methodological division in post-conciliar moral theology is not division over content but operations and criteria. Keenan and Levering identify that the methodological division is division over the operations of law and conscience. Neither Keenan nor Levering, for example, attributes the post-conciliar methodological division to disagreements over the permissibility of married couples using artificial contraception. Different contents or outcomes like this can only be adjudicated on the level of how the field *arrived at* those outcomes, not on the level of the outcomes themselves. Conflating method and content can lead to intractable divisions in a field because results do not possess a way out of methodological conflict since methodological conflict is criteriological conflict.

---

³⁰ For the purpose of this article, I am only taking up Lonergan's *description* of method to clarify the concept and meaning of the term. It is beyond the scope of this present investigation to give an account of or evaluate Lonergan's thought.
³¹ Henry George Liddell and Robert A. Scott, *Greek-English Lexicon*, 9th ed. (Clarendon, 1940), s.v. "μέθοδος."
³² Bernard Lonergan, *Collected Works*, vol. 14, *Method in Theology,* ed. Robert M. Doran and John D. Dadosky (University of Toronto Press, 1972), 8–10.
³³ See Jeremy D. Wilkins, *Before Truth: Lonergan, Aquinas, and the Problem of Wisdom* (The Catholic University of America Press, 2018), 185. See Lonergan, *Method in Theology*, 345.

Methodological Division as Criteriological

A method is the formal criteria or "normative pattern of recurrent and related operations yielding cumulative and progressive results" by which a field achieves its insights.[34] Method is not a rule or set of rules and procedures for performing operations (e.g., if you catch on fire, stop, drop, and roll!). Method is also not an operation (e.g., stopping, dropping, rolling) or set of operations and their ordering (e.g., [1] stop, [2] drop, [3] roll). Method is the criteriological pattern *by which* operations are determined, operate, and stand in relation to one another. Methodological divisions over operations and the ordering of operations always have their basis in a more original division over the formal criteria of a field's method. The formal criteria by which a field determines that it has properly performed its operations depends on how a field conceives of the way a knower comes to know an object in truth. For instance, the *operations* of stopping, dropping, and rolling are not random but have their basis in *what* fire *is,* how we *know* what fire is, and our understanding that it is physically harmful for human persons to be on fire. Likewise, the *ordering* of the operations is not random but has its basis in *what* the activities of stopping, dropping, and rolling *are* and how these activities relate to one another within the context of something being on fire. If the formal criteria (e.g., fire injury prevention) changes such that what is understood by "fire," "injury," or "prevention" is no longer the same, then what is determining the operations and their ordering would no longer be the same.

To experience methodological division in theology is to have a theology unclear or in dispute about its proper criteria. Both Keenan and Levering argue that moral theology splits into two methodological tracks following the Council because one side rejects or distorts and the other preserves and carries on the Council in some way. Levering's methodological division is born of "revisionist" conceptions of transcendental subjectivity that do not sufficiently consider the stable character of reality and the divine ground of human knowing. According to Levering, "revisionists" have conscience as their formal criterion, causing their method to err in its determination and ordering of operations, whereas "traditionalists" more rightly have encounter with Christ as their formal criterion for moral theology. For Keenan, methodological division is born of "traditionalist" conceptions of magisterial authority and law that do not sufficiently consider the historical character of reality and human knowing. According to Keenan, "traditionalists" have law as interpreted by the Magisterium

---

[34] Lonergan, *Method in Theology*, 8, emphasis added.

for their formal criterion, causing their method to err in its determination and ordering of operations, whereas "revisionists" more rightly have encounter with Christ as their formal criterion for moral theology.

One of the major problems with their conceptions of methodological division is that it is simply inaccurate. Both narratives designate Christ and the human person's encounter with Christ—not law or conscience—as the formal criteria of operations for evaluating truth claims for the track they recognize as consistent with Vatican II. Neither Keenan nor Levering incorporates this fact into his narrative understanding of post-conciliar moral theology. Here, we begin to see potential sources for intractability and division. Suppose moral method bifurcates and continues on two different tracks after the Second Vatican Council. How is it possible that these two tracks have the same formal criteria and claim to be consistent with the Council?

Overcoming and Adjudicating Methodological Division

Methodological divisions are ultimately ontological, epistemological, or anthropological in nature. The ultimate ground upon which to fully adjudicate methodological division is at the level of *what* can be known and *how* what is knowable can come to be known by the knower.[35] Without differentiating formal criteria from a foundational framework, there is no ground upon which to fully assess whether a field's formal criteria rightly reflects its ontology, epistemology, or anthropology. In order to be fully adjudicated, reflection on methodological division cannot stay at the level of operation or the ordering of operation but must move to the level of reflecting on foundations and formal criteria. Even formal criteria, especially when in dispute, must return to a field's foundations for understanding; it must return to what is held in common to be true. By definition, the "revisionist" track from Levering's view is defined as revisionist because its method is distinct from and incompatible with traditionalist methodology. Likewise, from Keenan's perspective, the "traditionalist" track is defined as traditionalist because its method is distinct from and incompatible with revisionist methodology. Keenan's and Levering's narratives of method in post-conciliar moral theology thus appear to be law-conscience binary narratives and more or less the same law-conscience binary narrative from different sides of the binary.

By law-conscience binary narrative, I mean a narrative framework in which "conscience's and law's self-understandings depend in part on defining themselves in opposition to each other and on each

---

[35] See Bernard Lonergan, *Insight: A Study of Human Understanding*, ed. Frederick E. Crowe and Robert M. Doran, 5th ed. (University of Toronto Press, 1992), 5.

conceiving itself as the corrective alternative to the other" such that one or the other must lose and lose in a way where it is not simply incorrect but anathema.[36] Keenan's and Levering's post-conciliar methodological narratives fit this description insofar as they define the methodological differences they see in post-conciliar moral method against one another, do so using law and conscience, and regard the alternative as contrary to the spirit of Vatican II and the church as a whole.[37] Since they are defined against one another, there is no ground upon which to recognize that they both claim to have the same method.

The source of post-conciliar methodological division cannot be post-conciliar methodological division itself. What is uniquely problematic about a law-conscience binary narrative is that when the two sides define themselves against one another, the true source of their methodological division becomes occluded because the existence of the method itself is set forth as the source of the division. Even though this is distinct from a division over content, it takes on the character of a division over content because the ground on which to investigate what is going wrong is defined out of view. Methodological division in this kind of binary narrative cannot be mediated or overcome because it precludes the possibility of investigation or adjudication. This has a direct bearing on *Veritatis Splendor*. When read within a methodological binary framework it, by definition, cannot offer any insights or amelioration between the two tracks because to be on the side of one track is to be against and working toward eradicating the other.

RETRIEVING A METHODOLOGICAL NARRATIVE BEYOND THE BINARY

Returning to what most, if not all, post-conciliar moral theologians methodologically share in common—personalist, Christ-centered formal criteria—is the proper next step for trying to find a more accurate narrative framework for post-conciliar moral theology in which to situate *Veritatis Splendor*. I turn to *De Ordine Morali*, the draft conciliar document on morality, and *Optatam Totius*, the Council's most explicit statement on moral theological method as such. I first argue that there is moral methodological division at the Second Vatican Council, as evidenced in the fate of *De Ordine Morali*. I then argue that although the Council turns to a spiritual, moral framework as evidenced in *Optatam Totius,* the Council does not set out a clear method in light of this turn and leaves methodological difficulties unresolved. I conclude that post-conciliar moral theology's

---

[36] David Cloutier and Robert Koerpel, "Beyond the Law-Conscience Binary in Catholic Moral Thought," *Journal of Moral Theology* 10, no. 2 (2021): 177.
[37] Cloutier and Koerpel, "Beyond the Law-Conscience Binary," 160–161.

methodological narrative is more rightly conceived of as a methodological project set out by the Council for moral theology to develop a coherent spiritual method.

Methodological Division in Moral Theology at the Council

In the 1960 Motu Proprio *Superno Dei*, John XXIII established a preparatory commission for theological matters known as the Theological Commission, specifically tasked with thinking through and thoroughly investigating questions regarding Scripture, Tradition, faith, and *morals* (no. 7a, emphasis added). A subcommission drafted a document on morality, *Schema Constitutionis Dogmaticae de Ordine Morali Christiano*, also known as Schema III or *De Ordine Morali*. The history of Schema III is fraught pretty much from start to finish. While still being revised in committee, *De Ordine Morali* received fairly harsh critiques for being overly negative, not biblical enough, and "neglect[ing] or even downplay[ing] the central and formal role of charity in the Christian life."[38] Some of this negative feedback came from the pope himself.[39] The schema used a fairly legalistic framework, which the term "moral order" accurately conveys. According to Joseph Komonchak, the text presents moral decisions as "simply matters of deducing particular applications of general laws or principles" and views "the observation of the positive and negative laws laid down by God" as the essence of the moral order.[40] In its moral methodology, *De Ordine Morali* primarily advocates for applying principles to particular cases, with law acting as the formal criteria for determining and ordering the application of universals to particulars.

De Ordine Morali was sent with six other schemata to the Council Fathers the summer before the official opening of the Council. It was never formally debated, put to a vote, revised, or redrafted.[41] Schema I, *De Fontibus Revelationis,* met with massive criticism from figures as theologically diverse as Karl Rahner, Joseph Ratzinger, Edward Schillebeeckx, and Karol Wojtyla when it was formally debated.[42]

---

[38] Joseph A. Komonchak, "The Struggle for the Council During the Preparation of Vatican II (1960–1962)," in *History of Vatican II*, vol. 1: *Announcing and Preparing Vatican Council II toward a New Era in Catholicism,* ed. Giuseppe Alberigo and Joseph A. Komonchak (Orbis Books, 1995), 248.

[39] Komonchak, "The Struggle for the Council," 352.

[40] Komonchak, "The Struggle for the Council," 249.

[41] Klaus Wittstadt, "On the Eve of the Second Vatican Council (July 1–October 10, 1962)," in *History of Vatican II*, vol. 1, 410.

[42] John W. O'Malley, SJ, *What Happened at Vatican II* (Harvard University Press, 2008), 145. See also Peter Seewald, *Benedict XVI: A Life*, vol. 1: *Youth in Nazi Germany to the Second Vatican Council, 1927–1965*, trans. Dinah Livingstone (Bloomsbury

John XXIII ultimately called for Schema I to be redrafted more pastorally by a new commission.[43] Following this series of events, Schema III essentially became "buried" when it was sent "to be re-'organized'"; some of the topics and concerns of Schema III were brought under the umbrella of Schema XVII, later Schema XIII, which would become *Gaudium et Spes*.[44] The Second Vatican Council did not promulgate a document on morals or moral theology. *Gaudium et Spes* addresses key moral concepts like conscience, freedom, law, and human moral life by elucidating the relational and Christological character of the human person, marriage, and social life. It, however, has no explicit discussion of moral theology or moral method in itself. The most explicit statements from the Council on theological method and the discipline of moral theology are from the Decree on Priestly Training, *Optatam Totius*.

De Ordine Morali *and* Optatam Totius: *Unresolved Methodological Difficulties*

Whenever a moral theologian claims that Vatican II calls for a renewal in Catholic moral theology, the subsequent citation is typically *Optatam Totius*, no. 16: "Special care must be given to the perfecting of moral theology." How exactly moral theology ought to be perfected and what is wrong with moral theology such that it is in need of perfection are hinted at but not explicitly stated in the decree itself. *Optatam Totius* favors a more Scripture-based, personalist, and Christ-centered approach to moral theology, although it never explicitly rejects a legalist approach or criticizes *De Ordine Morali*. *Optatam Totius* emphasizes the fundamentally spiritual character of theology, asserting that the Bible, "as the soul of all theology," ought to be read and meditated on daily for the spiritual nourishment of students of theology (no. 16). Note that Sacred Scripture is not merely being appealed to here as a source of theological *content* but as an *activity*, an operation of theological method itself. The instruction is being given for students of theology to *meditate* on Scripture for nourishment and inspiration. The *activity* of meditating *on Scripture* is being identified as a foundational methodological activity for attuning oneself to God and entering into right relationship with

---

Continuum, 2020), 367; George Weigel, *Witness to Hope: The Biography of Pope John Paul II*, 1st ed. (Cliff Street, 1999), 161.

[43] O'Malley, *What Happened at Vatican II*, 150; Giuseppe Ruggieri, "The First Doctrinal Clash," in *History of Vatican II*, vol. 2: *The Formation of the Council's Identity First Period and Intersession (October 1962-September 1963)*, ed. Giuseppe Alberigo and Joseph A. Komonchak (Orbis Books, 1997), 265.

[44] Jan Grootaers, "The Drama Continues Between Acts," in *History of Vatican II*, vol. 2, 376, n. 36.

oneself and others. This activity of meditating on Scripture, however, does not exist in a vacuum. The decree instructs that "theological disciplines, in the light of faith and under the guidance of the magisterium of the Church, should be so taught that the students will correctly draw out Catholic doctrine from divine revelation" (no. 16).

The decree further underscores the turn to spirituality when it asserts that the "scientific exposition" of moral theology also ought to be "*more* nourished on the *teaching* of the Bible" in order that moral theology "be renewed through a more living contact with the mystery of Christ and the history of salvation" (no. 16). The activity of *meditating* on Scripture is connected to coming into *living contact* with the mystery of Christ and the history of salvation. This *living contact* appears to be epistemologically significant and morally efficacious insofar as it is *through* this living contact that the decree proposes that the theological disciplines be *renewed*. The vision of renewal and perfecting presented in *Optatam Totius* calls for moral theology to "shed light on the *loftiness* of the calling of the faithful *in Christ* and the *obligation* that is theirs of bearing fruit *in charity for* the life *of the world*" (no. 16).

Post-Conciliar Moral Theology as Ongoing Methodological Task

In direct contrast to the legalist framework of *De Ordine Morali, Optatam Totius* advocates a spiritual framework for morality. Although it is easy to harshly judge the Schema III writers and those who argued against this turn at the Council, their "rejection of the efforts to build moral theology on evangelical grounds and spiritual grounds and to give it a more positive and specifically Christian orientation," has a coherent, rational basis.[45] Those criticizing the spiritual turn in moral theology at the Council rightly grasped that if a field's foundational epistemology or formal criteria changes, then so too changes how its cumulative and progressive results are yielded. The fundamental critique of the personalist, Christ-centered, conciliar methodological turn is that it is not clear how one grasps truth in a universally accessible way, adjudicates moral disagreements, or morally evaluates particular cases. Critics say, "These positive orientations often confused moral theology with Christian asceticism."[46] They worried that it would result in confusion and a system of moral theology that "would not be helpful to confessors in dealing with concrete cases, and verged on the errors of situation ethics."[47] *Optatam Totius* does not provide solutions to these legitimate

---

[45] Komonchak, "The Struggle for the Council," 251.
[46] Komonchak, "The Struggle for the Council," 250.
[47] Komonchak, "The Struggle for the Council," 250.

questions about how truth and moral evaluation work in this new framework. Nor does it address the critique that such an approach inevitably devolves into moral subjectivism or a spiritualized relativism. Given what happens in Catholic moral theology in the wake of *Humanae Vitae*, this critique has teeth.

The Conciliar turn from a legalist to a spiritual moral framework is not a methodological turn per se. It is more precisely an epistemological turn (and arguably an ontological and anthropological turn) since knowing comes to be characterized as the involvement of the being of the knower in the known, evidenced by its use of *living contact* and *meditating* on Scripture as illuminative. I am *not* claiming that the Second Vatican Council shifts its conception of moral truth but its conception of how the knower comes to know that truth. It shifts from a more traditional epistemological framework to one that conceives knowledge as inherently relational or participatory. This framework is the epistemological inverse of the legalist framework, which requires the knower to know and obey moral law or precepts to be in right relationship with the known. The spiritual approach to moral theology needs further clarification and coherent development of its formal criteria, operations, and ordering as well as how it avoids devolving into moral subjectivism or relativism.

BEYOND TAKING SIDES: *VERITATIS SPLENDOR* IN NEW LIGHT

I propose a methodological narrative for post-conciliar moral theology that can make sense of "revisionists" and "traditionalists" both claiming to be in continuity with Vatican II and to have the same formal criteria, despite their radical methodological disagreements over the operations of law, conscience, and authority. Post-conciliar moral theology *is* the very task of developing a coherent moral theological method that is Christ-centered without devolving into moral relativism or returning to legalism. Both revisionist and traditionalist post-conciliar moral theology are better understood as attempts to take up this ongoing task. When situated within this narrative frame, as I will argue, *Veritatis Splendor* is a continuation of this methodological project and a response to how this methodological project has been taken up in post-conciliar moral theology.

Beyond a binary post-conciliar narrative, the methodological purpose and meaning of *Veritatis Splendor* more richly come into view. The story of *Veritatis Splendor* and its reception is, at its core, a story about what it means to do post-conciliar Catholic moral theology, a story that cannot be fully understood apart from the larger narrative of how Vatican II reorients Catholic moral theology away from a legalist framework to a spiritual framework. Two potential pitfalls of this approach to moral theology are a return to legalism or a turn to moral subjectivism. If viewed simply as taking sides in a contested debate, *Veritatis Splendor*'s key insights are defined out of view since those insights are beyond the binary and respond to difficulties that precede contemporary divisions over law and conscience.

Since an extensive exegesis of *Veritatis Splendor* is beyond the scope of the present article, in this final section, I draw out some of the key methodological insights previously occluded. First, I briefly draw out that *Veritatis Splendor*'s stated purpose is to address methodological division, and it intends to address this division on the level of formal criteria and their foundations. Turning to the first chapter, I argue that *Veritatis Splendor* affirms the Council and addresses the pitfall of legalism through its meditation on Matthew 19 and introduction of "encounter with Christ" as formal criterion for moral theological method. Turning to the second chapter, I argue that *Veritatis Splendor* addresses the pitfall of moral subjectivism as manifest in its treatment of certain post-conciliar methodological trends. Following this, I argue that the third chapter of *Veritatis Splendor* highlights the lives of the saints as sites for a path forward for post-conciliar moral theology beyond the methodological pitfalls a spiritual approach to morality faces.

Purpose of Veritatis Splendor

Veritatis Splendor states that it aims to treat "'more fully and more deeply the issues regarding the very foundations of moral theology'" (no. 5). To treat the foundation of any discipline is to treat its methodology. It is to treat the basis of its formal criteria, operations, and ordering of operations for achieving insights. The reason the encyclical gives for treating the very foundations of moral method is the emergence of "an overall and systematic calling into question of traditional moral doctrine, on the basis of certain anthropological and ethical presuppositions" (no. 4). As previously discussed, all methodological conflicts ultimately have their basis in ontological, epistemological, or anthropological disagreements or ambiguities and can only be fully adjudicated on that basis.

To clarify what the problem is with these "certain anthropological and ethical presuppositions," *Veritatis Splendor* explains that "at the root of these presuppositions is the more or less obvious influence of currents of thought which end by detaching human freedom from its essential and constitutive relationship to truth" (no. 4). It is identifying a problem with the way the relationship between truth and human subjectivity is being conceived. Again, intradisciplinary conflict over what it means for the human person to know truth, how the human person comes to know that truth, or how knowing truth, willing good, and acting virtuously relate to one another are methodological conflicts over formal criteria that ultimately have their basis in conflicts over ontology, epistemology, or anthropology. *Veritatis Splendor*, therefore, in aiming to treat the very foundations of moral theology, addresses moral theological method. It rightly recognizes the source of this methodological division and the proper ground upon which the conflict needs to be adjudicated.

Reaffirming the Council: Encounter with Christ as Basis for a Spiritual Framework

The first chapter of *Veritatis Splendor* begins with the activity of meditating on Matthew 19. The overall chapter is framed in terms of the question posed to Jesus by the rich young man: "Teacher, what good must I do to have eternal life?" (no. 6). *Veritatis Splendor* begins its meditation on this passage with the words that introduce the rich young man's question: "Someone came to him" (no. 6). Prior to the rich young man asking about the moral life or Jesus giving a reply, the rich young man *comes to* Jesus. It is here, in the meditation on the words "someone came to him," that the encyclical both addresses Vatican II's call for a renewal in moral theology and introduces the term "encounter" (no. 7). According to *Veritatis Splendor*, "In the young man . . . we can recognize every person who, consciously or not, *approaches Christ the Redeemer of man and questions him about morality*" (no. 7). The question of morality "is not so much about rules to be followed," but the full meaning of life and receiving in the Person of Christ "the only response capable of satisfying the human heart" (no. 7). *Veritatis Splendor* is affirming morality as being at its core about the human person and her relationship to God.

Further underscoring this, *Veritatis Splendor* explains that "precisely in this perspective, the Second Vatican Council called for a renewal of moral theology, so that its teaching would display the lofty vocation which the faithful have received in Christ" (no. 7). The encyclical thus both explicitly reaffirms the Council's turn from a legalist to a spiritual framework for moral theology and implicitly reaffirms this turn through its own consonant spiritual description of morality. Following these reaffirmations, *Veritatis Splendor* asserts that "in order to make this 'encounter' with Christ possible, God willed his Church" (no. 7). The term "encounter" is introduced here as a term of art set off by quotation marks used to describe the person's relationship to Christ in its disclosive and fulfilling character.[48]

---

[48] For philosophical and theological uses of "encounter" like this see Martin Buber, *I and Thou*, trans. Walter Kaufmann (Touchstone, 1996); Romano Guardini, "Europa und Christliche Weltanschauung," in *Stationen und Rack* (Echter, 1965).

Although *Veritatis Splendor* only uses the term "encounter" at a few key moments over the course of the encyclical, the term nicely distills the overall personalist, Christ-centered post-conciliar method the encyclical begins to articulate and for which it sets the groundwork.

In clarification of why and what is meant by "God willed his Church" to make this encounter with Christ possible, John Paul II quotes *Redemptor Hominis,* asserting that "the Church 'wishes to serve this single end: that each person may be able to find Christ, so that Christ may walk with each person the path of life'" (no. 7). The original context for the quotation is a discussion of union with Christ wherein the Church "sees its fundamental task in enabling that union [with Christ] to be brought about and renewed continually" (*Redemptor Hominis*, no. 13). This tells us that "encounter with Christ" signifies *involvement* in Christ, that is to say a kind of *union* and *relationship* with Christ as opposed to a mere physical meeting or thought. This also tells us that "encounter with Christ" signifies a personal relationship with Christ. It is an ongoing activity of human living, not a one-time thing. The reason why the church sees cultivating this encounter with Christ as its fundamental task is because "following Christ is . . . the essential and primordial foundation of Christian morality: just as the people of Israel followed God who led them through the desert towards the Promised Land (Exod 13:21), so every disciple must follow Jesus, towards whom he is drawn by the Father himself (John 6:44)" (no. 19).

Veritatis Splendor conceives of the interdependency of being, knowing, and willing in such a way that Christ "enlightens [the human person's] intelligence and shapes [her] freedom, leading [her] to know and love" by virtue of her being created and structured self-transcendently (no. 1). For the knower to encounter, follow, and be *involved in Christ* is qualitatively different from the knower being involved in any other known object or subject and as such transforms the knower toward her perfection. The reason for this is that Christ is the way, the truth, and the life (no. 2, see John 14:6). *He* is the Light who enlightens all human persons, not facts *about* him, but he himself (no. 1). Again, it is important to note here that *Veritatis Splendor*, like *Optatam Totius*, appears to be operating according to some kind of realist phenomenological or existential epistemology where the knower is involved in a way that impacts her living behavior or way of being in the world rather than sectioned off from the known.

By *"holding fast to the very person of Jesus,"* one becomes illumined (no. 19). *Veritatis Splendor*'s account of "encounter with Christ," understood as following and holding fast to Jesus, brings together the ontological, epistemological, and anthropological dimensions of moral discernment by asserting that the only true way to know the good to be done and to enact that good is to know and to be in Christ. Holding fast to the person of Christ in this way is simultaneously an illuminative spiritual practice and the disclosive ordering of formal criteria for moral theology in a spirituality-based framework. Connecting this personalist, Christ-centered method to law, *Veritatis Splendor* asserts that those who live or "walk by the Spirit . . . find in God's Law the fundamental and necessary way in which to practice love as something freely chosen and freely lived out" (no. 18). In contrast, those "who live 'by the flesh' experience God's law as a burden, and indeed as a denial or at least a restriction of their own freedom" (no. 18).

By setting forth obedience to law as a responsive activity of love, there is an attempt here by *Veritatis Splendor* to deal with the critique set out by those who favored a legalist framework. Law and obedience to law is born out of the spiritually and epistemologically transformative activity of being in an ever-deepening relationship with the person of Christ. True obedience to law in its richest and most complete sense is not the fulfillment of an imposed obligation or an action executed out of fear of punishment but a freely chosen corresponding response to the activity of loving and being loved. *Veritatis Splendor* is making the point that without the orientation and illumination of Christ, the *Logos*, how we experience and understand reality is defective (no. 18). Likewise, if our will does not coincide with Christ's, not only is it defective but our defective will then leaves us, like the rich young man, sorrowful, unfulfilled, and drawing away from love of God and love of neighbor.

Taking the Problem of Moral Evaluation Within a Spiritual Framework Seriously

After having dealt with the pitfall of returning to a pre-conciliar legalist approach in the first chapter by affirming the Conciliar turn to spirituality and posing "encounter with Christ" as the basis for a personalist, Christ-centered, and Scripture-based method for that approach, the second chapter of *Veritatis Splendor* turns to methodological tendencies in post-conciliar moral theology. Because of these post-conciliar developments, *Veritatis Splendor* asserts that "in order to 'reverently preserve and faithfully expound' the word of God, the Magisterium has the duty to state that some trends of theological thinking and certain philosophical affirmations are incompatible with revealed truth" (no. 29). What are these trends in theological thinking deemed incompatible with revealed truth?

Veritatis Splendor specifies that these "tendencies in contemporary moral theology, under the influence of the currents of *subjectivism and individualism* just mentioned, involve novel interpretations of the relationship of freedom to the moral law, human nature, and conscience, and propose *novel criteria* for the moral evaluation of acts" (no. 34, emphasis added). In my view, these tendencies are related to difficulties left unresolved by the Council and that, in the encyclical's view, have hit a critical point in need of discernment. What *Veritatis Splendor,* therefore, understands itself to be doing in the second chapter is correcting and intervening in post-conciliar methodological proposals that (whether by way of formal criteria, operation, or ordering of operations) fall prey to subjectivism and individualism or relativism.[49] Unlike the legalist moral theologians at Vatican II, *Veritatis Splendor* does not see the potential for or reality of moral method and its operations devolving into subjectivism as a reason to reject a spiritual framework for morality altogether.

Veritatis Splendor makes a point to say that "to undertake a critical discernment of these tendencies—a discernment capable of acknowledging what is legitimate, useful, and of value in them, while at the same time pointing out their ambiguities, dangers, and errors—we must examine them in the light of the fundamental dependence of freedom upon truth" (no. 34). This is why I say correcting and intervening in the theological conversation rather than rejecting altogether. *Veritatis Splendor* strives to discern what is legitimate in post-conciliar methodological developments given the warrants of Vatican II and what is illegitimate or insufficiently described in them, given the ontological, epistemological, and anthropological limits set out by divine revelation. This is why, in each of the four sections of chapter two, we see some recognition and complement of the good that a methodological theory or proposal about to be critiqued for some instantiation of subjectivism is attempting to protect or in which it has its basis.

For instance, in the second section, "Conscience and Truth," *Veritatis Splendor* affirms *Gaudium et Spes*'s description of conscience as "always summoning him to love good and avoid evil, the voice of conscience can, when necessary, speak to his heart more specifically" (no. 54, see *Gaudium et Spes,* no. 16). Earlier in the chapter, *Veritatis Splendor* recognizes that "this heightened sense of the dignity of the human person and of his or her uniqueness, and of the respect due to the journey of conscience, certainly represents one of the positive achievements of modern culture" (no. 31). That being said, the encyclical critiquing a subjectivist conception of conscience argues "it is the 'heart' converted to the Lord and to the love of what is good which is really the source of *true* judgments of conscience"

---

[49] To assess whether *Veritatis Splendor*'s critiques of specific tendencies in moral theology are accurate depictions of a specific theologian's exact argumentation is beyond the scope of this article. I am simply demonstrating that the target of the chapter is subjectivism.

such that "in order to 'prove what is the will of God, what is good and acceptable and perfect,' knowledge of God's law in general is certainly necessary, but it is not sufficient: what is essential is a sort of *'connaturality' between man and the true good*" (no. 64). *Veritatis Splendor* recognizes the radical significance and necessity of conscience and law to morality, but nonetheless asserts that although *necessary*, they are *insufficient* without a connaturality between the human person and the One who is Good, Jesus Christ.

Likewise, in the third section, "Fundamental Choice," *Veritatis Splendor* recognizes that "it has been rightly pointed out that freedom is not only the choice for one or another particular action.... Emphasis has rightly been placed on the importance of certain choices which 'shape' a person's entire moral life" (no. 65). The encyclical continues its affirmations, writing, "There is no doubt that Christian moral teaching, even in its Biblical roots, acknowledges the specific importance of a fundamental choice which qualifies the moral life and engages freedom on a radical level before God" (no. 66). *Veritatis Splendor* further explains that "this faith, which works through love, comes from the core of man, from his 'heart,' whence it is called to bear fruit in works" such that "in the Decalogue one finds, as an introduction to the various commandments, the basic clause: 'I am the Lord your God...'" (no. 66). Therefore, although *Veritatis Splendor* strongly critiques fundamental option theory for separating the transcendental and the categorial, it nevertheless emphasizes more so than any of the other theories being critiqued the profound insight that a fundamental choice is at the basis of the Christian moral life (no. 65). What, however, is of decisive significance for *Veritatis Splendor* is that this fundamental choice *is* the choice to follow Jesus, inseparable from temporal acts (no. 66).

More than Exemplars: The Martyrs, Saints, and Mary as Revelatory of the Path Forward

The third and final chapter of *Veritatis Splendor* sets out its purpose as being to "in a positive way . . . help all the faithful to form a moral conscience which will make judgments and lead to decisions in accordance with the truth" (no. 85). Like the first chapter, here *Veritatis Splendor* once again reaffirms and further emphasizes the need for Christian morality and, thereby, moral theology to be conceived of in a spiritual framework. Connecting faith to encounter with Christ, *Veritatis Splendor* asserts, "Faith is a decision involving one's whole existence. It is an *encounter*, a dialogue, a communion of love and of life between the believer and Jesus Christ, the Way, and the Truth, and the Life" (no. 88, emphasis added). This faith, this encounter with Christ, "possesses a moral content" (no. 89). *Veritatis*

Splendor insists that "it is urgent" for Christians to "rediscover the newness of the faith and its power to judge" since without this "faith is weakened and loses its character as a new and original criterion for thinking and acting in personal, family, and social life" (no. 88). Faith is "not simply a set of propositions to be accepted with intellectual assent" but an encounter with the living God that directly impacts the way one lives everyday life (no. 88).

The substantive addition to this final chapter is the incorporation of the meaning of those disciples who hold fast to the person of Jesus for the other people whom Jesus calls. It is ultimately *Veritatis Splendor*'s contention that "the proper place which *continuing theological reflection about the moral life* holds in the Church" is "in the living context of this new evangelization, aimed at generating and nourishing 'the faith which works through love' and in relation to the work of the Holy Spirit" (no. 108). This new evangelization "involves the proclamation and presentation of morality" such that it "will show its authenticity and unleash all its missionary force when carried out through the gift not only of the word proclaimed but also of the word lived" (no. 107). *Veritatis Splendor* culminates in a discussion of the martyrs and concludes with a prayer to Mary because "through the moral life, faith becomes 'confession,' not only before God but also before men: it becomes *witness*" (no. 89). This witness when encountered by other human persons parallel to the encounter with Christ is illuminative. As *Veritatis Splendor* notes, Christ does not only say, "I am the Light of the world" (John 8:12, see VS, no. 1) but also says to his disciples, "'You are the light of the world'" (no. 89, see Matt 5:14–16). The faith that becomes witness to other persons is not only a model or example of what a good life looks like but, more fundamentally, when encountered, an illuminative disclosure of truth and the meaning of reality that directs others to Christ and his loving encounter.

CONCLUSION: ENCOUNTER AS THE HEART OF METHOD AND LIGHT OF FAITH

The Second Vatican Council, while (re)turning to a more spiritual approach to moral theology, does not set out a clear *method* for the discipline within this new paradigm. It leaves methodological difficulties raised at the Council about this new approach unresolved. The Council ultimately leaves the question of how to do moral theology open and, thereby, leaves post-conciliar moral theology with the task of figuring out how to do moral theology according to this new paradigm. Post-conciliar moral theology on this reading *is* the methodological project of figuring out how to do moral theology in a way that fully incorporates Scripture, virtue, historicity, sociality, the human person, and a relationship with Christ into moral evaluation without devolving into moral subjectivism or relativism and without returning to a pre-conciliar legalist ethical method for moral evaluation. In my view, *Veritatis Splendor* is a response to this methodological task. When read in this light, *Veritatis Splendor* presents fruitful insights that reaffirm the vision of the Council against the pitfall of returning to legalism and deepen its vision against the pitfall of devolving into subjectivism or relativism.

Reading post-conciliar moral theology and *Veritatis Splendor* within a methodological law-conscience binary narrative leaves contemporary moral theology impoverished. It fails to acknowledge the unresolved methodological divisions at the Second Vatican Council, the underlying methodological agreement present in post-conciliar moral theology, and the potential resources *Veritatis Splendor* offers to those contemporary divisions. Reading *Veritatis Splendor* beyond a methodological binary narrative recognizes a larger horizon and deeper methodological narrative in which the contemporary methodological divisions themselves are embedded and according to which *Veritatis Splendor* is more fruitfully read. *Veritatis Splendor* returns to the original conciliar question of morality, spirituality, and law. *Veritatis Splendor*'s account of *encounter with Christ* understood as following and holding fast to the Person of Jesus, brings together the ontological, epistemological, and anthropological dimensions of moral discernment by asserting that the only true way to know the good to be done and enact that good is through encounter with Christ, the Incarnate Logos.

Through the concept of "encounter with Christ" and its emphasis on the illuminative power of the saints and martyrs, *Veritatis Splendor* plants seeds for the development of a method consistent with the methodological task set out by the Second Vatican Council, built from a foundational point of methodological continuity between "revisionists" and "traditionalists," and responds to unresolved methodological concerns from the Council. *Veritatis Splendor*'s insight that encounter with Christ is the hermeneutical key or formal criteria for the good life and human moral judgment is a decisive positive contribution to contemporary Catholic moral theology and post-conciliar moral theological method. *Veritatis Splendor* responds to the constructive methodological project the Second Vatican Council sets in motion. Its insight is that Catholic moral method and action theory must be grounded in the very being of the human person and the fact that God is a living God who dwells with us and in us, giving us new eyes and new hearts. This insight has already begun to flower in the work of John Paul II's successors, who affirm: "'Being a Christian is not the result of an ethical choice or a lofty idea, but the encounter with an event, a person, which gives life a new horizon and a decisive direction'" (*Evangelii Gaudium*, no. 7; see *Deus Caritas Est*, no. 1). These are not merely tender pious words but a roadmap for post-conciliar moral theology and the Christian moral life. They are a roadmap for a method grounded in a personalist and existential epistemology in which reality is only truly known when it is rightly felt and responded to according to the Sacred Heart of Jesus. M

Catherine Moon, PhD, is postdoctoral research fellow at the University of Virginia for the Institute for Advanced Studies in Culture. She specializes in fundamental moral theology, AI and technology ethics, and the thought of St. Edith Stein. She co-leads the AI & Education Research Group for the Centre for Digital Culture for the Dicastery for Culture and Education of the Holy See. She is also a member of the Institute for Advanced Catholic Studies' Generations in Dialogue Cohort on Medical Ethics: Trans-humanism and the Body. She has recently completed a monograph on Edith Stein's theory of human experience and its relevance to contemporary ethics and post-conciliar moral theology that is under contract with Lexington Books in the Edith Stein Studies series. She holds a PhD in moral theology and ethics from The Catholic University of America, an MTS from Boston College, and a BA from St. John's College Annapolis.

Veritatis Splendor and the Persistence of the Law-Conscience Binary in Catholic Moral Theology

Nicholas Ogle

Abstract: This essay considers why the conflict between law and conscience in modern Catholic moral theology that *Veritatis Splendor* sought to overcome has nevertheless persisted in the three decades since its publication. Without the further development of a theory of prudential judgment, *Veritatis Splendor* cannot adequately address the problem of moral uncertainty that has directly contributed to the law-conscience binary's enduring influence on contemporary moral theology. After examining the encyclical's discussion of conscience and the application of moral precepts, the essay explores what a theory of prudential judgment consistent with the teaching of *Veritatis Splendor* might look like, and how it would differ from the prevailing understanding of moral discernment among contemporary moral theologians. Rather than minimizing the significance of absolute moral norms in response to the problem of moral uncertainty, such an account would instead emphasize the essential role such norms play in any satisfactory solution to this problem.

I N 1985, SERVAIS PINCKAERS WROTE IN A CRUCIAL YET OFTEN neglected passage of his now-classic work, *The Sources of Christian Ethics*: "It is all too easy to say that today the era of the manuals is over and to take an opposite stand, pronouncing ourselves systematically in favor of freedom and conscience as opposed to law and authority. In so doing, we would be caught in the very spiral of the specific categories of moral theology that we wish to critique, notably the opposition between law and freedom."[1] Among those who gave heed to this warning was John Paul II, who eight years later in *Veritatis Splendor* set out to combat certain "currents of thought which end by detaching human freedom from its essential and constitutive relationship to truth" (no. 4). Although the extent of Pinckaers's influence on the 1993 encyclical remains a matter of speculation, there is little doubt that his critical perspective on dominant trends in post-

---

[1] Servais Pinckaers, OP, *The Sources of Christian Ethics*, trans. Mary Thomas Noble (The Catholic University of America Press, 1995), 279.

conciliar moral theology lies in the proximate background of its composition.² Like Pinckaers, John Paul II was deeply concerned with overcoming the conflict between law and conscience that has plagued Catholic moral theology throughout much of the modern period.³ While *Veritatis Splendor* is most well-known for its trenchant critique of proportionalist ethical theories and resolute defense of absolute moral prohibitions, its overarching aim is to present a vision of the Christian life that views the moral law not as a burden or threat to the dignity of conscience but a gift that invites us to "share in the divine Goodness revealed and communicated in Jesus" (no. 11). Thirty years after its publication, the encyclical's account of the inseparable connection between truth and freedom remains perhaps the single most significant attempt to liberate modern moral theology from the constraints of the law-conscience binary.

Yet, despite the significance of *Veritatis Splendor*, the field of Catholic moral theology arguably remains just as trapped in this binary today as it was three decades ago. In recent years, moral theologians have continued to champion revisionist theories of conscience that aim to safeguard human freedom by restricting the binding force of the moral law.⁴ This raises an important question: How can we explain the persistence of the law-conscience binary despite the best efforts of John Paul II to overcome it? If *Veritatis Splendor* helps illumine a path forward beyond the modern opposition between freedom and truth, why do revisionist accounts of the Christian moral life that pit the dignity of the individual conscience against the binding force of the moral law continue to thrive? Those sympathetic to the thought of John Paul II might be tempted to think that the law-conscience binary's enduring influence on moral theology can be adequately explained by the fact that *Veritatis Splendor* has still not been fully received. Thus, it is sometimes suggested that to move beyond the current impasse, we need only present anew the encyclical's sweeping

---

² For further discussion of Pinckaers's involvement in the drafting of *Veritatis Splendor*, see Craig S. Titus, "Servais Pinckaers and the Renewal of Catholic Moral Theology," *Journal of Moral Theology* 1, no. 1 (2012): 43–68, esp. 57–58; see also Romanus Cessario, OP, "On the Place of Servais Pinckaers († 7 April 2008) in the Renewal of Catholic Theology," *The Thomist* 73, no. 1 (2009): 1–27.

³ For an insightful analysis of the history of this conflict, see David Cloutier and Robert Koerpel, "Beyond the Law-Conscience Binary in Catholic Moral Thought," *Journal of Moral Theology* 10, no. 2 (2021): 160–93.

⁴ See, for example, many of the essays published in three recent edited volumes: *The Concept of Intrinsic Evil and Catholic Theological Ethics*, ed. Nenad Polgar and Joseph A. Selling (Lexington, 2019); *A Point of No Return? Amoris Laetitia on Marriage, Divorce, and Remarriage*, ed. Thomas Kneips-Port le Roi (Lit, 2017); and *Amoris Laetitia: Wendepunkt in der Moraltheologie?*, ed. Stephan Goertz and Caroline Witting (Herder, 2016).

vision of freedom and truth, albeit with certain minor revisions that target the latest manifestations of the law-conscience binary.[5]

While there is undoubtedly some truth to this suggestion, such a limited response to the current impasse in moral theology is ultimately bound to fail. Although we continue to have much to learn from *Veritatis Splendor*, it must be acknowledged that the encyclical fails to address certain crucial problems in Catholic moral theology that have directly contributed to the persistence of the law-conscience binary in the decades since its publication. Recent scholarship, for instance, has shown the need for further development of the encyclical's teaching on Christian obedience in accordance with a more nuanced account of moral growth and magisterial authority.[6] Setting these issues aside, this essay focuses specifically on the problem of moral uncertainty. It argues that while *Veritatis Splendor* presents a cogent defense of the absolute moral law, which ought to be unreservedly affirmed, it fails to adequately account for the difficulties that can arise when applying this law to specific cases. Without further developing a theory of prudential judgment that acknowledges the uncertainty which often characterizes the interpretation and application of moral precepts, *Veritatis Splendor* will be unable to adequately address one of the most pressing concerns motivating the development of contemporary revisionist theories of conscience.

The argument of the essay proceeds in two parts. In the first section, I critically examine *Veritatis Splendor*'s discussion of conscience and the application of moral precepts to lay bare its overall approach to the problem of moral uncertainty. This approach, I argue, is characterized by a failure to appreciate the indispensable role of prudence in bridging the gap between the generality of the moral law and the particularity of concrete situations, which sometimes allow for multiple legitimate moral interpretations. Consequently, in the second section, I consider what a theory of prudential judgment consistent with the teaching of *Veritatis Splendor* might look like and how it would differ from the prevailing understanding of moral discernment among contemporary moral theologians. I contend that, rather than minimizing the significance of absolute moral norms in response to the problem of moral uncertainty, such an account would instead

---

[5] For a recent argument along these lines, see Ryan Connors, "*Veritatis Splendor* at Thirty: Three Decades of Moral Teaching Founded on the Splendor of Truth," *National Catholic Bioethics Quarterly* 23, no. 4 (2023): 655–68.

[6] See, for example, David Elliot, "Irregular Unions and Moral Growth in *Amoris Laetitia*," *Journal of Moral Theology* 8, no. 2 (2019): 31–59, as well as Matthew Levering, "The Church as Temple of the Spirit: Is There Room for Magisterial Error?," *Communio* 50 (Spring 2023): 7–36.

emphasize the essential role such norms play in any satisfactory solution to it. Thus, in contrast with those who argue that a system of exceptionless moral precepts stands opposed to the development of a genuine culture of moral discernment, I conclude that such a system, when rightly understood, should instead be regarded as an indispensable element of it.

MORAL UNCERTAINTY AND PRUDENTIAL JUDGMENT IN *VERITATIS SPLENDOR*

To gain insight into *Veritatis Splendor*'s overall approach to the problem of moral uncertainty, it will be helpful to begin by examining its discussion of conscience and moral judgment. As is well known, this discussion is organized around John Paul II's criticism of so-called "creative" conceptions of conscience (nos. 54–64).[7] According to this family of views, the specific norms of the moral law ought to be regarded not as a "binding objective criterion," but as indications of a "general perspective" that must be interpreted by each of us individually in the concrete circumstances of our lives (no. 55). Obedience to the dictates of conscience therefore ought to lead "not so much to a meticulous observance of universal norms as to a creative and responsible acceptance of the personal tasks entrusted to him by God" (no. 55). For John Paul II, the essential problem with this view is that it proposes "a kind of double status of moral truth" (no. 56). While the validity of objective moral norms is affirmed on a "doctrinal and abstract level," a certain priority is nevertheless given to an "existential consideration" of the concrete reality to which such norms refer, making it possible for "one to do in practice and in good conscience what is qualified as intrinsically evil by the moral law" (no. 56). Accordingly, a separation is established "between the teaching of the precept, which is valid in general, and the norm of the individual conscience, which would in fact make the final decision about what is good and what is evil" (no. 56). If taken to an extreme, the Pope argues, such a separation would result in the eclipse of a shared moral standard by which we can hold each other accountable, leaving us with a merely subjective "criterion of sincerity, authenticity, and 'being at peace with oneself'" (no. 32).

---

[7] Although it is beyond the scope of this essay to demonstrate the accuracy of this criticism of revisionist moral theology, the influence of a "creative" conception of conscience is arguably reflected in Bernard Häring's *Free and Faithful in Christ: Moral Theology for Clergy and Laity*, vol. 1: *General Moral Theology* (Seabury, 1978), esp. 223–301, as well as Karl Rahner's late essay on "Conscience: Freedom and the Dignity of Human Decision," in *Theological Investigations*, vol. 22: *Humane Society and the Church of Tomorrow*, trans. Joseph Donceel, SJ (Crossroad, 1991), 3–13.

In contrast with this view, *Veritatis Splendor* defends the traditional teaching that "conscience expresses itself in acts of 'judgment' which reflect the truth about the good, and not in arbitrary 'decisions'" (no. 61). One could perhaps summarize John Paul II's account of conscience by saying that it is characterized not so much by *creativity* as by *receptivity*: "The dignity of this rational forum and the authority of its voice and judgments derive from the truth about moral good and evil, which it is called to listen to and to express" (no. 60). Thus, against those who appeal to a subjective criterion of sincerity or authenticity in defending the judgments of an erroneous conscience, the Pope maintains that "it is always from the truth that the dignity of conscience derives" (no. 63). Of course, this is not to deny the moral legitimacy of a conscience that errs because of invincible ignorance. Following *Gaudium et Spes*, no. 16, John Paul II acknowledges that such a conscience "does not lose its dignity, because even when it directs us to act in a way not in conformity with the objective moral order, it continues to speak in the name of that truth about the good which the subject is called to seek sincerely" (no. 62). Nevertheless, he insists that there can be no possibility of conflict between the objective requirements of the moral law and the judgments of a well-formed conscience. It is therefore mistaken to view the moral law as "only an 'ideal' which must then be adapted, proportioned, graduated to the so-called concrete possibilities of man" (no. 103), for to do so would be tantamount to denying that "before the demands of morality we are all absolutely equal" (no. 96).

In speaking here of the "demands of morality," John Paul II especially has in mind the Church's teaching regarding the existence of intrinsically evil actions prohibited "always and *per se*," regardless of the circumstances or further intentions of the acting person (no. 80). These are actions such as murder, theft, and adultery, which are "in no case compatible with the goodness of the will of the acting person, with his vocation to life with God and to communion with his neighbor" (no. 52). In other words, they are bad simply by virtue of their object, on which the morality of the human act "primarily and fundamentally" depends (no. 78).[8] Accordingly, John Paul II maintains that the negative precepts of the moral law that prohibit such actions do not admit of any legitimate exception: "They do not leave room, in any morally acceptable way, for the 'creativity' of any contrary determination whatsoever" (no. 67). Of course, the Pope is keenly aware that this teaching is "not infrequently seen as the sign of an intolerable intransigence, particularly with regard to the enormously

---

[8] For a helpful discussion of *Veritatis Splendor*'s teaching on the object of human action, see Stephen L. Brock, "*Veritatis Splendor* §78, St. Thomas, and (Not Merely) Physical Objects of Moral Acts," *Nova et Vetera* 6, no. 1 (2008): 1–62.

complex and conflict-filled situations present in the moral life of individuals and of society today" (no. 95). Nevertheless, he insists that it is "only by obedience to universal moral norms" that the human person finds "full confirmation of his personal uniqueness and the possibility of authentic moral growth" (no. 96). Consequently, he considers any attempt to safeguard human dignity by qualifying the binding force of moral prohibitions to be profoundly misguided, as this would ultimately undermine the very foundation upon which that dignity is established.

What are we to make of this account? On the one hand, I suspect that most moral theologians today would strongly sympathize with John Paul II's rejection of conscience-centered theories that deny the existence of an objective moral standard to which we are all equally accountable. Although the notion of intrinsic evil is certainly not uncontroversial, it nevertheless resonates with the widespread belief that certain kinds of behavior—say, rape or torture—are so morally abhorrent that they can never be justified under any circumstances. While some moral theologians might disagree with the Pope about exactly which actions should be included in this category, few would deny that at least some such actions exist. On the other hand, *Veritatis Splendor*'s strict dichotomy between creative and receptive theories of conscience is likely to strike many moral theologians as overly simplistic. Without further qualification, it would seem to suggest that any diversity of opinion regarding how the moral law ought to be applied in a particular case must stem from the corrupting influence of a creative conception of conscience. Granted, John Paul II does acknowledge the role of human reason in applying the moral law, observing that "the moral life calls for that creativity and originality typical of the person, the source and cause of his own deliberate acts" (no. 40). Thus, the opposition he posits between creativity and receptivity in moral judgment is by no means absolute. Nevertheless, his discussion of conscience largely overlooks the complexities and challenges that can arise when applying moral precepts to specific situations—even for those who view these moral precepts as universally binding. In other words, *Veritatis Splendor*'s account of conscience and moral judgment seems to suffer from a certain neglect of the problem of moral uncertainty.

This problem arises in cases where the object of an action is not immediately evident, making it difficult to determine how the moral law should be applied to the specific situation. While there will often be little doubt about whether a proposed course of action is morally permissible, complex situations nevertheless arise that generate what Oliver O'Donovan calls "a deliberative or reflective crisis," precisely because they seem open to various legitimate moral interpretations.[9] As a number of moral theologians and philosophers have recognized, there is a certain "complexity involved in act descriptions" that can make the straightforward application of moral precepts difficult.[10] For example, the question of whether a particular instance of killing should be classified as an act of murder or legitimate self-defense will not always be easy to discern, just as it will sometimes be unclear whether a particular business practice should be considered a valid market strategy or a form of worker exploitation. While it is both possible and necessary for us to identify what Elizabeth Anscombe calls the "hard core" of moral concepts such as murder and theft, we must also recognize that this core is "surrounded by a relatively fuzzy penumbra" where significant uncertainty can arise regarding whether a particular moral concept accurately describes a given action.[11]

Unfortunately, *Veritatis Splendor*'s neglect of the problem of moral uncertainty is not confined to its discussion of conscience but also extends to other sections of the encyclical. It is particularly evident in John Paul II's explanation of the difference in how positive and negative moral precepts apply to particular actions:

> In the case of the positive moral precepts, prudence always has the task of verifying that they apply in a specific situation, for example, in view of other duties which may be more important or urgent. But the negative moral precepts, those prohibiting certain concrete actions or kinds of behavior as intrinsically evil, do not allow for any legitimate exception. They do not leave room, in any morally acceptable way, for the "creativity" of any contrary determination whatsoever. Once the moral species of an action prohibited by a universal rule is concretely recognized, the only morally good act is that of obeying the moral law and of refraining from the action which it forbids. (no. 67)

According to this passage, the crucial difference between positive and negative precepts has to do precisely with the need for prudence in determining their application to concrete cases. Whereas positive precepts, which bind only under certain circumstances, require

---

[9] Oliver O'Donovan, *Resurrection and Moral Order: An Outline for Evangelical Ethics* (Eerdmans, 1994), 198.

[10] Cloutier and Koerpel, "Beyond the Law-Conscience Binary," 192. For further discussion of action description as a moral task that cannot be separated from reflection on the practices of a community, see Charles Pinches, *Theology and Action: After Theory in Christian Ethics* (Eerdmans, 2001) and Jean Porter, *Moral Action and Christian Ethics* (Cambridge University Press, 1995).

[11] Elizabeth Anscombe, "Murder and the Morality of Euthanasia," in *Human Life, Action, and Ethics: Essays by G. E. M. Anscombe*, ed. Mary Geach and Luke Gormally (Imprint, 2005), 262.

prudential judgment to verify their application to particular situations, negative precepts do not. Instead, they "forbid a given action *semper et pro semper* [literally, in every instance and at all times]" (no. 52; see also no. 82). Thus, once a behavior has been identified as belonging to a prohibited action type, there can be no question about whether the circumstances are such that the prohibition applies. Rather, that determination is, as it were, already built into the formulation of the precept.

Such an explanation seems straightforward. After all, the distinction between negative precepts that bind *semper et pro semper* and affirmative precepts that bind *semper et non pro semper* can be traced at least as far back as Aquinas, and has often been discussed by modern thinkers in terms of the difference between perfect and imperfect duties.[12] Perfect duties obligate everyone at all times to refrain from certain actions, while imperfect ones can require us to act in a variety of ways depending on the situation. There may be certain times and circumstances, for example, when an act of generosity or almsgiving that would normally be considered praiseworthy is rendered not only inappropriate but perhaps even blameworthy—such as when it would deprive those for whom one is responsible of the material resources they are owed. In contrast, there is never an occasion when an act of, say, extortion or slander is to be deemed morally permissible, let alone required. As John Paul II explains, whereas in the former kind of case "what must be done in any given situation depends on the circumstances, not all of which can be foreseen," the latter pertains to "behavior which can never, in any situation, be . . . a response which is in conformity with the dignity of the person" (no. 52).

Yet, upon further examination, such a distinction between perfect and imperfect duties, however valid in itself, nevertheless obscures from view the ineliminable aspect of judgment that informs moral deliberation at the level of action description. That is, it fails to capture how the determination of whether a precept binds *semper et pro semper* or merely *semper et non pro semper* depends not simply on whether it positively enjoins or negatively forbids certain kinds of action but, more fundamentally, on how such enjoined or forbidden actions are specified. Recall how, in the passage quoted above, the exceptionless binding force of a negative moral precept is premised

---

[12] For Aquinas, the difference between these two kinds of precept has to do with a certain asymmetry between action and omission. Whereas there can be no question whether an action that falls under the scope of a negative precept is sinful, an omission that falls under the scope of a positive precept is sinful only at the time during which the precept imposes an obligation. See *Summa Theologiae*, I-II, q. 71, a. 5, ad 3; II-II, q. 33, a. 2 (hereafter ST).

upon the fact that the "moral species of an action" prohibited by it has been "concretely recognized." By this, John Paul II seems to mean that negative moral precepts only apply to actions already identified as belonging to a prohibited action type. For example, it is only when behavior that results in the death of another human being is recognized not simply as an act of killing but as an instance of murder that there can be no doubt about its moral wrongness. Therefore, the relevant question is not whether murder can be justified under certain circumstances but how to determine when a particular act of killing should be deemed murderous.

On the other hand, the encyclical adopts a markedly different perspective when it comes to the positive moral precepts. In contrast to the negative precepts, where it was assumed that any action to which they refer is necessarily prohibited, there is no corresponding assumption that those actions that fall under the scope of a positive precept are always morally required. Rather, this will depend on the situation. As John Paul II notes, there may be competing duties "more important or urgent" that require one to refrain from such actions, at least for a time. For example, although there is an imperfect duty to feed the hungry, whether *I* am obligated to feed *this* hungry person *now* can only be determined after a careful consideration of the circumstances. What the encyclical fails to consider, however, is how the conditionality of the positive precepts is related to their lack of specificity. It is customary for positive precepts to be formulated in a highly general way, which means that prudence is normally required to determine their application to actions that fall under their scope. However, if the acts enjoined by such precepts are described more precisely, so as to take this prudential judgment into account (e.g., feed the hungry *at the right time, in the appropriate place, with suitable means, in the proper manner*, etc.), then there will no longer be any doubt about whether they impose an obligation in those situations to which they refer. A parallel observation applies to negative precepts: just as the positive precept to feed the hungry can be further specified in a way that expresses a perfect duty binding *semper et pro semper*, so can the absolute prohibition against murder be reformulated to express an imperfect duty to avoid killing that admits of certain exceptions. This symmetry underscores the role of specification and prudential judgment in applying both positive and negative precepts.

It is, therefore, mistaken to assume that the difference between positive and negative moral precepts can be explained simply in terms of the need for prudence in determining their application to particular situations of moral choice. On the contrary, it is evident that prudence is required in applying any moral precept whatsoever, regardless of whether it is positive or negative. The need for prudence is admittedly most evident when a precept is formulated to express an imperfect duty that imposes a moral requirement only under certain circumstances. However, even when a precept is further specified to express a perfect duty that binds without exception, prudential judgment is still needed to determine whether any particular action falls under its scope. The interpretive judgment required to accurately describe or correctly identify the object of an action is not limited to those that fall under general precepts, which admit certain exceptions, but applies universally to *all* actions. Thus, regardless of whether the precept in question expresses a perfect or imperfect duty, we cannot determine whether the acts that it enjoins or forbids ought to be performed or avoided here and now without some exercise of prudential judgment that interprets the precept and applies it to the situation at hand.

It is crucial to realize that the need for such prudential judgment does not result from any deficiency in the formulation of the law, as if the problem of moral uncertainty could be addressed simply by developing a more comprehensive specification of moral precepts. While an organized system of precepts can certainly assist deliberation by providing guidance on how to act in a wide variety of situations, it can never fully account for all the possible contingencies that may arise. Indeed, as Josef Pieper notes, "Any moral theology becomes truer and more genuine, and above all more capable of dealing with life, the more it expressly renounces such a claim."[13] Moreover, such a system cannot itself determine how we ought to classify any particular situation of moral choice we face. There is, as it were, an ineliminable gap between the generality of the moral law and the particularity of those concrete situations to which it refers, which prudential judgment alone can bridge. It may be tempting to think that once we have gathered all the morally relevant facts of a situation and properly consulted the moral law, the application of precepts will occur more or less automatically.[14] In reality, however, no system of moral precepts can interpret itself, no matter how specific or comprehensive. Rather, it is only what John Henry Newman calls the "living intellect"—whether our own or another's whose counsel we heed—that can apply the law to the situation we face here and now.[15]

---

[13] Josef Pieper, *The Four Cardinal Virtues: Prudence, Justice, Fortitude, Temperance* (University of Notre Dame Press, 1966), 28.

[14] Such a view is rightly rejected in the International Theological Commission's 2009 document *In Search of a Universal Ethic: A New Look at the Natural Law*, which states that "moral science cannot furnish an acting subject with a norm to be applied adequately and almost automatically to concrete situations" (no. 59).

[15] John Henry Newman, *An Essay in Aid of a Grammar of Assent* (University of Notre Dame Press, 2001), 277.

Put otherwise, a concrete action cannot ultimately be an object of theoretical demonstration but only of practical advice.[16]

Although *Veritatis Splendor* does not explicitly contradict these claims, it nevertheless reflects a general failure to appreciate their significance. This is particularly evident toward the end of the encyclical, where John Paul II asserts that the universal precepts of the moral law represent not only the "unshakable foundation" but also the "solid guarantee" of a just and peaceful society: "By protecting the inviolable personal dignity of every human being they help to preserve the human social fabric and its proper and fruitful development" (nos. 96–97). While such claims may seem unobjectionable at first, they nevertheless overlook the crucial fact that human dignity is protected not only by moral norms but, more importantly, by individual persons who properly conform their actions to them. That is to say, for such norms to provide the "solid guarantee" of peace and justice John Paul II ascribes to them, they not only need to be acknowledged and respected but understood and intelligently applied. Thus, while rejecting the absolute validity of the moral law in the name of freedom of conscience is certainly one way human dignity can be undermined and the social fabric unraveled, it is by no means the only one. If the moral law does not find prudent application in the judgments of individual moral agents, then the recognition of absolute moral prohibitions will be powerless to promote a more just and humane society. As Jean Porter puts it, "Respect for the moral law is a necessary, but not a sufficient condition for the attainment of genuine respect for other persons, both for individuals and for society as a whole."[17]

Setting these passages aside, perhaps no section of *Veritatis Splendor* has faced more criticism for neglecting the problem of moral uncertainty than its discussion of the Old Testament story of Susanna. In this discussion, John Paul II recounts how Susanna heroically resists the sexual advances of two unjust judges who threaten to condemn her to death if she refuses to comply with their wishes (no. 91). He then praises her as a "prime example" of "fidelity to the holy law of God even to the point of a voluntary acceptance of death," who ought to be extolled as a "perfectly clear witness" to the absoluteness of the moral order (no. 91). However, a number of moral theologians have challenged his interpretation of Susanna's decision, or at least

---

[16] See Livio Melina, *Sharing in Christ's Virtues: For a Renewal of Moral Theology in Light of* Veritatis Splendor, trans. William E. May (The Catholic University of America Press, 2001), 87.

[17] Jean Porter, "Moral Reasoning, Authority, and Community in *Veritatis Splendor*," *The Annual of the Society of Christian Ethics* 15 (1995): 214.

questioned whether it is as clear-cut a case as he suggests.[18] The problem, they argue, is that the encyclical simply assumes that Susanna is correct in her assessment that to submit to the judges would constitute a mortal sin of adultery without properly considering the duress under which such a decision would have been made. As Katherine TePas remarks, "From the context, it looks as if she was choosing not to be raped more so than choosing not to commit adultery."[19] Although it is true that Susanna does not face an immediate and certain threat to her life, the fact that she believes (on reasonable grounds) that she will be condemned to death if she resists clearly indicates that she was under significant coercion, which should at least complicate any straightforward application of the prohibition against adultery. Thus, TePas concludes that while the story of Susanna may serve as an inspiring example of devotion to God's law, it is "less convincing as an image of knowing what sin is in a given situation."[20]

Of course, one need not agree with this alternative interpretation of Susanna's predicament to appreciate the broader significance of the criticism. Even if John Paul II is ultimately right to affirm Susanna's own assessment of her situation, he does not elaborate as fully as one might hope on why he believes this assessment to be correct. This lack of elaboration is perhaps the result of his assumption that circumstances of coercion are not relevant to violations of negative precepts in the way they are for violations of positive ones. As he explains earlier on in the encyclical, "It is always possible that man, as the result of coercion or other circumstances, can be hindered from doing certain good actions; but he can never be hindered from not doing certain actions, especially if he is prepared to die rather than to do evil" (no. 52). While this is undoubtedly true, without further qualification it could be taken to mean that the threat of death never makes a significant difference in the moral assessment of whether a particular action violates a negative moral precept. Yet we sometimes do make precisely this sort of assessment. Consider, for example, the case of a cashier held at gunpoint who hands his employer's money over to a robber.[21] Such an act is not normally considered an instance of theft, because we consider it unreasonable to expect someone to

---

[18] See, for example, Katherine M. TePas, "'If You Wish to Be Perfect...': Images of Perfection in *Veritatis Splendor*," in Veritatis Splendor: *American Responses*, ed. Michael E. Allsopp and John J. O'Keefe (Sheed & Ward, 1995), 48–59; Cristina L. H. Traina, "Oh, Susanna: The New Absolutism and Natural Law," *Journal of the American Academy of Religion* 65, no. 2 (1997): 371–401; and Porter, "Moral Reasoning, Authority, and Community in *Veritatis Splendor*."

[19] TePas, "'If You Wish to Be Perfect," 56.

[20] TePas, "'If You Wish to Be Perfect," 56.

[21] The following examples are drawn from Porter, "Moral Reasoning, Authority, and Community in *Veritatis Splendor*," 211.

sacrifice his life for the sake of protecting another's property.[22] On the other hand, if the cashier were to fatally shoot an innocent bystander at the robber's command, we would likely judge him guilty of murder (albeit with mitigated culpability), precisely because we do expect each other to value and respect the lives of others as much as our own. As Jean Porter remarks, the difference between these two cases demonstrates how "moral concepts have built into them, so to speak, a set of judgments about the kinds of sacrifices that it is reasonable to expect of persons, and the kinds of coercion which we expect ourselves and others to withstand, in defense of given aims."[23] Thus, even if Susanna's decision to preserve her sexual integrity at the cost of her own life is deserving of praise and admiration, some justification must nevertheless be given for this judgment, given the complexity of her situation.

At this point, however, one might object that to admit this degree of uncertainty in the application of moral precepts would open the door to rampant abuse in the name of the generality of the moral law. After all, is not the purpose of specifying exceptionless moral rules precisely to eliminate such ambiguity?[24] If it is not unreasonable to question whether Susanna would have committed adultery had she submitted to the judges, who is to say that someone facing a far less serious threat should not also be excused for engaging in similar behavior?[25] To allow for such discretion in our moral judgments would seem to foster precisely the kind of moral laxity *Veritatis Splendor* was written to combat.

In response to this objection, we must first acknowledge that moral theologians have not always demonstrated sound judgment in applying the moral law to concrete situations. The casuistic tradition is replete with examples of moralists who subtly undermined the absolute validity of the moral law by casting doubt on what ought to have been straightforward moral judgments.[26] Nevertheless, it would

---

[22] See Aquinas, ST II-II, q. 62, a. 7 ad 3 and q. 78, a. 4.

[23] Porter, "Moral Reasoning, Authority, and Community in *Veritatis Splendor*," 211.

[24] For an influential account of absolute moral norms profoundly shaped by this concern, see John Finnis, *Moral Absolutes: Tradition, Revision, and Truth* (The Catholic University of America Press, 1991).

[25] There continues to be much debate about what degree of coercion is necessary for an unwanted sexual encounter to be considered an instance of rape. For a recent examination of this contentious issue, especially as it pertains to criminal law, see Kimberly Kessler Ferzan, "Consent, Culpability, and the Law of Rape," *Ohio State Journal of Criminal Law* 13 (2016): 397–439. For broader discussions, see Alan Wertheimer, *Coercion* (Princeton University Press, 1987) and *Consent to Sexual Relations* (Cambridge University Press, 2003).

[26] For an insightful overview of the casuistic tradition, with a helpful discussion of various "laxist" authors, see Stefania Tutino, *Uncertainty in Post-Reformation Catholicism: A History of Probabilism* (Oxford University Press, 2017), esp. 148–88.

be a mistake to think that the threat of laxism could be eliminated by adopting an absolutist stance that attempts to render moral judgment unnecessary. As we have already observed, the problem with this approach is that, no matter how strictly one wishes to enforce the moral law, such enforcement will inevitably require the exercise of prudence. As Porter puts it, "The difficulty with the project of living by the norms of morality without exercising any sort of interpretative judgment at all is not that it is unattractive or too stringent," but that it is "logically impossible."[27] Therefore, the proper response to the threat of laxism is not to attempt to eliminate the need for moral judgment altogether but to deepen our understanding of what its prudential exercise requires. We now turn to this task in the second part of this essay, where we will consider what a theory of prudential judgment consistent with the teaching of *Veritatis Splendor* might look like and how it would differ from the prevailing understanding of moral discernment among contemporary moral theologians.

EXCEPTIONLESS MORAL PROHIBITIONS AND THE TASK OF MORAL DISCERNMENT

Needless to say, it is far beyond the scope of this essay to develop a full-blown theory of prudential judgment. It ought to be observed, however, that such a theory would undoubtedly require a more sophisticated account of moral prohibitions, which takes into consideration their relative priority with respect to one another. When *Veritatis Splendor* discusses negative moral precepts, it tends to abstract from their specific characteristics to emphasize their systematic unity as elements of an absolutely valid moral law. Yet prohibitions posssess a complexity that must be considered when determining how they apply to particular cases.[28] We observed in the previous section how the prohibition against theft regulates human action in a more flexible manner than the prohibition against murder. In addition to the example discussed above, moral theologians have traditionally recognized a number of other exceptional situations in which an act that involves taking what belongs to another is morally justified.[29] In contrast, the prohibition against murder admits far less

---

[27] Porter, "Moral Reasoning, Authority, and Community in *Veritatis Splendor*," 210.
[28] This point is helpfully made by Alasdair MacIntyre in "How Can We Learn What *Veritatis Splendor* Has to Teach?," *The Thomist* 58, no. 2 (1994): 180.
[29] See Aquinas, ST II-II, q. 66, a. 7 and q. 120, a. 1. It is important to clarify that these cases are not, properly speaking, exceptions to the prohibition against theft but situations that fall outside the scope of the prohibition. For an insightful discussion of this point as it applies to exceptionless moral rules more generally, see Paul Ramsey, "The Case of the Curious Exception," in *Norm and Context in Christian Ethics*, ed. Gene Outka and Paul Ramsey (Charles Scribner's Sons, 1968), 67–138.

variability in its application. While it may not always be clear when a particular action should be considered an instance of the direct and voluntary killing of an innocent human being, it has traditionally been held that any such act of killing is *de facto* an instance of murder (see *Evangelium Vitae*, no. 57). Thus, while both precepts are exceptionless in the sense with which *Veritatis Splendor* is concerned, we nevertheless recognize an important difference in how they inform our judgment in particular situations of moral choice, with the latter applying in a more stringent way than the former due to the preeminent value of human life and the conditionality of the right to private property.

It should also be observed that such a theory would reject any strict division between moral discernment in concrete situations and rule-based forms of practical reasoning. It has sometimes been suggested that prudential judgment involves grasping a situation's unique character in a manner that cannot ultimately be subsumed under a general rule.[30] Karl Rahner, for example, argues in his existential ethics for the possibility of a "moral demand which is not identical with the validity of general principles, but is a concrete, particular, individual obligation."[31] The problem with this view, however, is that by insisting so emphatically on the absolute uniqueness of the particular situation, it risks making prudential judgment unintelligible as a form of practical wisdom that can be communicated to others.[32] Taken to an extreme, it would entail not only that concrete actions cannot be objects of demonstration but also that they cannot be objects of advice, since a norm that is valid in one situation would not necessarily apply to any other. While Rahner and other advocates of this view are rightly critical of a purely deductive model of practical reasoning that reduces the task of prudential judgment to the simple and straightforward application of moral rules, they are mistaken to conclude that it is not rule-governed at all. Although it may not always be clear how a moral precept applies to a particular case, there is no situation in which prudence might dictate acting in a manner that is not an intelligible expression of the universal requirements of the moral law.

---

[30] For an influential statement of this view, see Karl Rahner, SJ, *The Dynamic Element in the Church*, trans. W. J. O'Hara (Herder and Herder, 1964). Although there appears to be no direct influence between the two, this view shares a certain affinity with the "moral particularism" advocated by some contemporary analytic philosophers. See, for example, Jonathan Dancy, *Ethics Without Principles* (Clarendon, 2004).
[31] Rahner, *The Dynamic Element in the Church*, 16.
[32] Here I am indebted to the insights of Oliver O'Donovan in *Resurrection and Moral Order*, 181–203, as well as his more recent *Finding and Seeking: Ethics as Theology*, vol. 2 (Eerdmans, 2014), 225–30.

All of this may seem relatively uncontroversial, at least for those who adopt a broadly Thomistic or neo-Aristotelian approach to practical reasoning. On such a view, it is generally assumed that moral judgment characteristically involves the prudential application of moral precepts to particular cases in accordance with a nuanced understanding of the goods and values to which these precepts are ordered.[33] Nevertheless, this approach has faced significant criticism in recent years from moral theologians who contend that appeals to exceptionless moral norms are ill-equipped to address the problem of moral uncertainty.[34] This critique has been powerfully expressed in a recent article by Conor Kelly, who joins other prominent voices in Catholic moral theology calling for a shift from a preoccupation with exceptionless norms to a greater emphasis on conscience and moral discernment.[35] Kelly's contribution merits special attention because of its lucid and nuanced analysis of the problem of moral uncertainty, which presents an opportunity for constructive dialogue between revisionist moral theologians and those more sympathetic to the teaching of *Veritatis Splendor*.

While Kelly does not deny the existence of absolute moral norms, he nevertheless maintains that "the majority of moral decisions are not going to be made with reference to [them]; instead, these decisions will take place in an area where moral absolutes do not directly apply."[36] Accordingly, he suggests that moral theologians should "tread carefully when proposing moral rules" and "regard the pronouncement of absolute norms more as a last resort than as the default position."[37] Insofar as moral theologians are "committed to the task of improving moral discernment in the face of uncertainty," he argues that they should focus less on issuing definitive statements about intrinsically evil actions and direct more attention to prudential matters "that do admit variety and doubt."[38] At the very least, "the definition of absolute prohibitions should not be the primary focus of moral theology."[39] Rather, the task of the moral theologian today

---

[33] For further reflections along these lines, see Jean Porter, *Nature as Reason: A Thomistic Theory of the Natural Law* (Eerdmans, 2005), 309–321.

[34] See, for example, Nicholas Austin, "Moral Theology as Servant of Discernment: Reflecting on the Call of *Amoris Laetitia*," *Gregorianum* 99, no. 4 (2018): 739–758; James T. Bretzke, "Moral Theology and the Paradigm Shift of Vatican II," in *The Oxford Handbook of Vatican II*, ed. Catherine E. Clifford and Massimo Faggioli (Oxford University Press, 2023), 418–431; and James F. Keenan, SJ, "Receiving *Amoris Laetitia*," *Theological Studies* 78, no. 1 (2017): 193–212.

[35] Conor M. Kelly, "The Role of the Moral Theologian in the Church: A Proposal in Light of *Amoris Laetitia*," *Theological Studies* 77, no. 4 (2016): 931.

[36] Kelly, "The Role of the Moral Theologian in the Church," 931.

[37] Kelly, "The Role of the Moral Theologian in the Church," 932–933.

[38] Kelly, "The Role of the Moral Theologian in the Church," 931–932.

[39] Kelly, "The Role of the Moral Theologian in the Church," 931.

should be to promote the development of an ecclesial "culture of moral discernment" that can form the consciences of the faithful and empower them to act responsibly in areas of human life mostly unregulated by exceptionless moral norms.[40]

Kelly's article has much to commend it, and he is undoubtedly correct that the role of the moral theologian cannot simply be reduced to defining exceptionless moral prohibitions. After all, the task of moral discernment is not simply to identify sins to be avoided but ultimately to determine what singular course of action here and now would be most conducive to beatitude. Nevertheless, Kelly's framing of this task remains shaped by the law-conscience binary to an extent that obscures the crucial role exceptionless moral prohibitions play in the process of discernment. The problem with this framing is that no strict division can ultimately be sustained between intrinsically evil actions that are always and everywhere prohibited and so-called prudential matters, the moral permissibility of which can vary according to circumstances. Kelly seems to view these as two separate spheres of human activity, with moral prohibitions providing a sort of boundary that marks off the limits of permissible action while leaving the majority of moral decisions open to the prudential or conscientious judgment of individuals.[41] However, as we observed in the previous section, the difference between actions that fall under exceptionless moral prohibitions and those that fall under more general positive precepts is merely a superficial one, resulting from how the behaviors in question are described. What may initially appear as a moral failure related to some prudential matter will often, upon further reflection, be recognizable as an instance of an intrinsically evil type of action, and vice versa.[42]

For example, just as the murder of a trespasser can be more generally understood as a morally irresponsible attempt to protect one's property, a seemingly prudential matter such as the act of selling a car (when one knows it to be a lemon) can be recognized as an instance of the intrinsically evil act of fraud. In both cases, the difference between the two act descriptions results from how certain morally relevant details are incorporated into our explanation of what the agent is doing. From one perspective, these details can be viewed as mere circumstances that undermine the goodness of an otherwise

---

[40] Kelly, "The Role of the Moral Theologian in the Church," 944.
[41] See Kelly, "The Role of the Moral Theologian in the Church," 933.
[42] Often, but not always, since in many cases we lack the moral vocabulary necessary to describe such failures as intrinsically evil actions. However, this linguistic deficiency should not prevent us from recognizing them as such. On the contrary, I will argue below that it is an essential task of the moral theologian today to promote the development of such a vocabulary of prohibited action types.

morally acceptable act of protecting property or selling a car. From the other perspective, however, they are seen as essential features of the acts themselves, revealing the agent's behavior to be an instance of murder or fraud. Kelly's mistake—one frequently made not only by revisionist moral theologians but also many outspoken defenders of *Veritatis Splendor*—lies in assuming that these two kinds of description correspond to distinct categories of moral wrongdoing, when in fact *both* descriptions are true of *every* evil act.[43] That is to say, there is no failure of prudential judgment that does not result in the performance of an intrinsically evil act, and there is no intrinsically evil act that does not involve some sort of failure of prudential judgment.

This important truth has tended to be obscured by two mistaken assumptions that have profoundly shaped contemporary debates about intrinsically evil actions. The first is that prudential matters can be distinguished from such actions by the fact that judgments of their moral permissibility are uncertain and therefore susceptible to legitimate moral disagreement, whereas those regarding intrinsically evil actions are not. Consider, for example, John Finnis's claim in a recent essay that, unlike the application of negative precepts, the application of positive precepts is relative to assessments of circumstances about which "reasonable people often reasonably disagree."[44] Here Finnis specifically has in mind the moral directives of Catholic social teaching which, to his mind, raise questions of application "the Church is not equipped to answer authoritatively except in hypothetical form."[45] He writes: "Because the diagnosing of causalities, effects and side-effects, risks and probabilities is an inherently difficult and often uncertain matter, it is entirely possible for informed and well-catechized Catholics in good faith to hold diametrically opposed views on, say, climate change, migration policy, sentencing policy, healthcare policy, the organization of employment, laws of inheritance and taxation, and so on, while respecting all relevant moral principles and norms."[46]

Of course, Finnis is correct that the moral teachings of social encyclicals are often intertwined with historical, political, and scientific

---

[43] For an insightful elaboration of this point, to which the following discussion is indebted, see Therese Scarpelli Cory, "The Collapse of the Intrinsic/Prudential Judgment Distinction," *Church Life Journal: A Journal of the McGrath Institute for Church Life*, December 3, 2020, churchlifejournal.nd.edu/articles/the-collapse-of-the-intrinsic-prudential-wall/.

[44] John Finnis, "A Radical Critique of Catholic Social Teaching," in *Catholic Social Teaching: A Volume of Scholarly Essays*, ed. Gerard V. Bradley and E. Christian Brugger (Cambridge University Press, 2019), 557.

[45] Finnis, "A Radical Critique of Catholic Social Teaching," 566.

[46] Finnis, "A Radical Critique of Catholic Social Teaching," 573.

judgments in a manner that magisterial statements about intrinsically evil actions are not. This difference is recognized in *Donum Veritatis*'s teaching that the Church's "interventions in the prudential order" are subject to a degree of variability and uncertainty absent from its irreformable moral teachings (no. 24). However, while a juridical distinction between those moral teachings binding on all Catholics and those left up to the well-formed consciences of individual believers is certainly legitimate, it provides no basis whatsoever for the *moral* distinction Finnis posits between matters that allow for reasonable disagreement and others that do not.

This would follow only if (1) there could be no certainty about the intrinsic wrongness of an action apart from the determination of the Magisterium, and (2) those intrinsically evil actions about which a definitive pronouncement has been made were to admit of no uncertainty in their application. The falsity of this second claim has already been demonstrated in the above discussion.[47] The fact that we can say with absolute certainty that an act such as murder or theft is never morally justified does not mean there can be no legitimate disagreement about whether some concrete behavior constitutes such an act. On the contrary, it is evident that virtuous persons can hold opposing views on the application of both positive and negative precepts while still respecting all relevant moral principles and norms. As for the first claim, it need only be recalled that actions are not intrinsically evil because the Church prohibits them; rather, it prohibits them because it recognizes them as intrinsically evil. Just because the Magisterium has not (yet) pronounced definitively on the intrinsic wrongness of certain acts pertaining to, say, migration or sentencing policy does not mean that no such acts (e.g., the forced separation of migrant children from their parents or sentencing decisions based on opaque algorithmic judgments) could possibly be identified. Indeed, such a view—taken to an extreme—would seem to entail a kind of practical moral relativism, which assumes that even

---

[47] Admittedly, it is not logically inconsistent to acknowledge the need for prudential judgment in applying negative precepts to particular cases and yet to deny that these judgments are ever uncertain. Nevertheless, it would be incumbent upon anyone who holds such a view to demonstrate that cases of legitimate moral uncertainty (as opposed to culpable moral confusion) never actually arise, despite the appearance that they do. The success of such a demonstration, however, seems highly dubious. While the scope of legitimate moral disagreement can certainly be exaggerated, it is implausible to claim that no such disagreement is possible at all. A traditional example from the medieval period is the difference of opinion between St. Thomas and St. Bonaventure regarding whether a judge who orders the execution of a man he privately knows to be innocent, but who has judicially been proven guilty, is culpable of murder. For an insightful analysis of this case and the issue of moral uncertainty more generally, see G. E. M. Anscombe, "The Two Kinds of Error in Action," *The Journal of Philosophy* 60, no. 14 (1963): 398.

though there may be a moral truth about such matters, it is simply inaccessible to human reason.

The second mistaken assumption that informs the contemporary debate is that intrinsically evil actions can be distinguished from prudential matters by the fact that they involve especially serious violations of the moral law.[48] Indeed, it is commonly supposed that the category of intrinsically evil action is more or less equivalent to that of mortal sin. However, these are fundamentally distinct notions. To say that an action is evil by virtue of its object, regardless of the circumstances or further intention of the agent, is not at all to claim that it will necessarily turn one away from God as one's ultimate end. Although the standard list of intrinsically evil actions (murder, adultery, theft, etc.) certainly includes some mortally sinful behaviors, this is not due to any necessary connection between the two concepts. Their differentiation can be seen, for example, in Aquinas's discussion of beneficent lies. While he believes that lying of any kind is intrinsically evil and therefore never morally permissible, he nonetheless argues that when a lie is told to prevent an injustice, it should be considered a merely venial sin (ST II-II, q. 110, a. 3 and 4). Numerous other examples from the *Secunda Secundae* could be adduced of intrinsically evil actions that can be venial in kind, including negligence (q. 54), derision (q. 75), ingratitude (q. 107), hypocrisy (q. 111), boasting (q. 112), and flattery (q. 115). While Aquinas maintains that such actions are never justified under any circumstances, he nevertheless views them as relatively minor violations of the moral law.

The moral equivalence of intrinsically evil actions and failures regarding prudential matters can also be demonstrated by considering the interchangeability of the moral precepts that apply to them. We noted in the previous section how positive and negative precepts do not differ in their need for prudence in determining their application to particular situations; the assumption that they do is simply a result of how they are formulated. One implication of this view, which we have yet to consider, is that positive and negative precepts pertaining to the same sphere of human activity should not ultimately be considered distinct from one another but the same precept formulated in different ways. That is to say, just as a moral precept can be more or less specific in its formulation, it can also be reformulated into the opposite kind of precept without fundamentally altering how it

---

[48] This assumption finds expression, for example, in the USCCB document on *Forming Consciences for Faithful Citizenship*: "It is essential for Catholics to be guided by a well-formed conscience that recognizes that all issues do not carry the same moral weight and that the moral obligation to oppose policies promoting intrinsically evil acts has a special claim on our consciences and our actions" (no. 37).

regulates actions falling under its scope. Aquinas helpfully explains this point with reference to the precepts of the Decalogue:

> The affirmative precepts are distinct from the negative precepts when one is not included in the other. For instance, the precept that no man should be killed is not included in the precept about honoring one's parents, or vice versa. By contrast, when the affirmative precept is included in the negative one, or vice versa, then it is not the case that there are different precepts about the matter in question. For instance, the precept "You shall not steal" is not a different precept from "Take care of another's property" or "Return another's property to him" (ST I-II, q. 100, a. 4, ad 2).

Unfortunately, Aquinas does not elaborate any further on this point, leaving unexplored the question of what exactly it means for affirmative and negative precepts to be "included" [*comprehenditur*] in one another. Nevertheless, the immediate implications of his perspective are clear: any failure to properly observe a positive precept can, at the same time, be understood as a violation of a negative precept pertaining to the same sphere of action, since these two precepts are not fundamentally distinct. Similarly, any infringement of a negative precept can be interpreted as a failure to fulfill a corresponding positive precept. In short, there can be no violation of a positive precept which is not also a violation of a negative precept, and vice versa.

If this account is correct, then the task of improving moral discernment in the face of uncertainty will likely look quite different from what Kelly envisions. Instead of relegating absolute moral prohibitions to a narrow sphere of human action removed from most of our everyday concerns, effective discernment would instead result in their extension to virtually every area of human activity. Indeed, one of the surest signs of the ecclesial culture of moral discernment Kelly seeks to promote would be the development of a sophisticated moral vocabulary of prohibited action types that gives expression to the manifold ways in which human behavior can deviate from right reason. Kelly comes close to recognizing the importance of such a vocabulary when he argues that the Church needs a "common language that will allow people to explain the processes behind their decisions so that their moral choices do not have to be made alone, but can instead occur in a spirit of communal discernment."[49] Yet, out of an understandable—though ultimately misplaced—concern to avoid "a rigid dogmatism that attempts to answer every possible question with sweeping pronouncements," he overlooks the fact that this

---

[49] Kelly, "The Role of the Moral Theologian in the Church," 944.

language is precisely what moral prohibitions provide.[50] Kelly is certainly right to emphasize the need for moral theologians to embrace "the possibility of doubt and uncertainty, of a process of discernment that leads to a conclusion that does not fit in the standard box."[51] However, as we have observed in this essay, such discernment is in no way impeded by the applicability of an exceptionless moral prohibition to a particular domain of human action. On the contrary, the determination of whether a certain prohibition applies in a particular situation is precisely what, in many cases, moral discernment in the face of uncertainty will entail. Thus, contrary to Kelly's suggestion that moral theologians should regard the formulation of absolute moral norms as something of a last resort, what is actually needed to aid our discernment in situations of moral uncertainty is—perhaps surprisingly—not fewer prohibitions but more of them.

Of course, a complex system of moral prohibitions will only be effective in guiding discernment as long as it is paired with a nuanced understanding of the goods and values to which these prohibitions are ordered.[52] After all, the purpose of such a system is not ultimately to replace prudential judgment but to support it by providing what Oliver O'Donovan calls a "categorical structure" within which moral discernment can be successfully carried out.[53] To treat a set of moral prohibitions as if they provided a clear blueprint for human action that obviates the need for such discernment would only end up reinforcing the law-conscience binary we are striving to overcome. Thus, in advocating for the development of a more sophisticated vocabulary of moral prohibitions, I am not suggesting that moral theologians should embark on a misguided quest for a comprehensive specification of moral precepts that would eliminate the need for moral judgment altogether. On the contrary, the aim of the preceding discussion has been precisely to articulate a theory of prudential judgment that resists this false dichotomy. According to the view I have outlined, the application of exceptionless moral prohibitions is regarded not as any sort of alternative to or substitute for moral discernment but an essential feature of its responsible exercise.

---

[50] Kelly, "The Role of the Moral Theologian in the Church," 930.
[51] Kelly, "The Role of the Moral Theologian in the Church," 931.
[52] Although I lack the space to develop the point here, this nuanced understanding of moral prohibitions is always specific to the social practices of particular communities, apart from which the vocabulary of prohibited action types will not be fully intelligible. For further discussion of the inseparability of moral norms from the practices that give them meaning, see Pinches, *Theology and Action*, esp. 137–166.
[53] Oliver O'Donovan, *The Disappearance of Ethics: The Gifford Lectures* (Eerdmans, 2024), 108.

CONCLUSION

By now it should be evident how an account of prudential judgment consistent with the teaching of *Veritatis Splendor* would diverge from the prevailing understanding of moral discernment among contemporary moral theologians, to which Kelly's article gives lucid and nuanced expression. While acknowledging that the task of moral discernment is not simply to identify sins, it nevertheless recognizes that the formulation and application of exceptionless precepts constitutes an essential part of this task, without which it risks becoming unmoored from the moral law on which it is based. Accordingly, it regards the formulation of exceptionless moral precepts not as a threat to a genuine culture of moral discernment but as a necessary condition of its cultivation and enrichment. Although a system of prohibitions can certainly become rigid and unresponsive to the challenges of moral decision-making, this outcome is far from inevitable and provides little justification for the shift away from moral absolutes Kelly and other revisionist moral theologians have proposed. On the contrary, when integrated with practices of act description sensitive to the complexities of moral judgment, a sophisticated vocabulary of prohibited action types can serve as an invaluable resource for forming consciences and empowering the faithful to act responsibly in situations of moral uncertainty.[54] Ⓜ

Nicholas Ogle, PhD, is John and Daria Barry Fellow in the Program for Research on Religion and Urban Civil Society (PRRUCS) at the University of Pennsylvania. His research explores the nature of human action, practical reason, and moral responsibility, with a focus on the moral theology of Thomas Aquinas and its modern reception. He has published articles in the *Journal of the Society of Christian Ethics* and the *Scottish Journal of Theology* and is currently preparing a book manuscript entitled *The Problem of Moral Mistakes: A Thomistic Analysis*.

---

[54] I would like to thank Therese Cory, Ty Monroe, Veronica Ogle, and two anonymous reviewers for their helpful feedback on earlier versions of this essay.

The Pastoral Conversion of Moral Theology and "The Perspective of the Acting Person" in *Veritatis Splendor*

Matthew Kuhner

Abstract: This article considers the Second Vatican Council's trajectory of pastoral renewal in the church, specifically in its application to moral theology. In particular, Part I summarizes Pope Francis's reflections on moral theology throughout the first 11 years of his pontificate, attempting to articulate the contours of his vision of an "evangelical morality." This analysis reveals how Francis's vision represents a response to the Council's call for renewal in moral theology, inasmuch as it engages the integration of theology and pastoral action by foregrounding mercy "as the most radiant manifestation of God's truth." After this work of serene analysis, Part II considers how *Veritatis Splendor*—especially its second chapter— relates to the Council's pastoral trajectory. It is argued that John Paul II's encyclical does not stand outside the aforementioned trajectory of pastoral renewal, but rather makes an essential contribution to it, not only (as is usually suggested) because it made great strides in recovering a Christological and biblical context for moral reflection, but also because its contributions to moral action theory reflect, with scientific accuracy, the foundation required for a pastoral conversion of moral theology to take root and bear fruit. *Veritatis Splendor* provides what might be called a *pastoral action theory*, driven by the trajectory of pastoral renewal and evangelization called for by the Second Vatican Council and constituting the account of moral action necessary for Francis's vision of an "evangelical morality."

IN ONE OF THE MOST REMARKABLE MOMENTS OF RECENT ECCLESIAL history, John XXIII set forth an epoch-making charter for the Second Vatican Council:[1]

---

[1] This article is indebted to the attendees of the conference, "Human Action and the Drama of Accompaniment: The 30th Anniversary of *Veritatis Splendor*," hosted by St. Bernard's School of Theology and Ministry in Rochester, NY, many of whom offered insightful comments and critiques concerning an early version of this argument. Likewise, the article was significantly improved because of the excellent feedback offered by the anonymous reviewers and guest editors of the *Journal of Moral Theology*.

> What is needed, and what everyone imbued with a truly Christian, Catholic, and apostolic spirit craves today, is that [the church's] doctrine shall be more widely known, more deeply understood, and more penetrating in its effects on men's moral lives. What is needed is that this certain and immutable doctrine, to which the faithful owe obedience, be studied afresh and reformulated in contemporary terms. For this deposit of faith, or truths which are contained in our time-honored teaching is one thing; the manner in which these truths are set forth (with their meaning preserved intact) is something else. This, then, is what will require our careful, and perhaps too our patient, consideration. We must work out ways and means of expounding these truths in a manner more consistent with a predominantly pastoral view of the Church's teaching office.[2]

While this section of the Pope's opening address is frequently discussed in academic writing on the Council, its emphasis on morality is less observed. John XXIII is clear that a key concern within a "predominantly pastoral view of the Church's teaching office" is that doctrine will be "more penetrating in its effects on men's *moral* lives."[3] It is from these remarks that the conciliar and postconciliar emphasis on evangelization is born,[4] which does not concern the proclamation of the Gospel only but, as Paul VI writes, always elicits in the hearer "a genuine adherence . . . an adherence to a program of life—a life henceforth transformed—which [the Lord] proposes."[5]

---

[2] John XXIII, "Solemn Opening of the Second Vatican Council," Thursday, October 11, 1962, no. 6.5.

[3] Emphasis added. It is worth noting that the "*Pastoral* Constitution on the Church in the Modern World" (emphasis added), *Gaudium et Spes*, speaks frequently about moral action: "moral/morality" is used over two dozen times throughout the document.

[4] See Paul VI's great Apostolic Exhortation *Evangelii Nuntiandi*, an extended reflection on the nature and the demands of evangelization, intentionally promulgated on the tenth anniversary of the close of the Second Vatican Council. In observing this anniversary, Paul VI suggests that "the objectives [of the Second Vatican Council] are definitively summed up in this single one: to make the Church of the twentieth century ever better fitted for proclaiming the Gospel to the people of the twentieth century" (no. 2).

[5] *Evangelii Nuntiandi*, no. 23. See also *Evangelii Nuntiandi*, no. 23: "In a word, adherence to the kingdom, that is to say, to the 'new world,' to the new state of things, to the new manner of being, of living, of living in community, which the Gospel inaugurates. Such an adherence, which cannot remain abstract and unincarnated, reveals itself concretely by a visible entry into a community of believers. Thus those whose life has been transformed enter a community which is itself a sign of transformation, a sign of newness of life: it is the Church, the visible sacrament of salvation." John Paul II picks up this trajectory likewise in *Veritatis Splendor*, suggesting that "the new evangelization will show its authenticity and unleash all its missionary force when it is carried out through the gift not only of the word proclaimed but also of the word lived" (no. 107).

During the Council, *Optatam Totius*, the Decree on Priestly Training, provided an initial statement concerning how the pastoral vision of the church's teaching office should unfold within moral theology per se:

> Special care must be given to the perfecting of moral theology. Its scientific exposition, nourished more on the teaching of the Bible, should shed light on the loftiness of the calling of the faithful in Christ and the obligation that is theirs of bearing fruit in charity for the life of the world. (no. 6)

This lapidary statement demarcates the challenge of renewal: even the "scientific exposition" of moral theology must be for the sake of "bearing fruit in charity for the life of the world."

Francis's pontificate has offered a unique synthesis of reflection on evangelization, pastoral action, and moral theology, allowing these conciliar and post-conciliar themes to converge in new ways. In *Evangelii Gaudium*, Francis quite famously called for ecclesial renewal in language that echoes the conciliar address of John XXIII:

> I dream of a "missionary option," that is, a missionary impulse capable of transforming everything, so that the Church's customs, ways of doing things, times and schedules, language and structures can be suitably channeled for the evangelization of today's world rather than for her self-preservation. The renewal of structures demanded by *pastoral conversion* can only be understood in this light: as part of an effort to make them more mission-oriented, to make ordinary pastoral activity on every level more inclusive and open, to inspire in pastoral workers a constant desire to go forth and in this way to elicit a positive response from all those whom Jesus summons to friendship with himself. (no. 27, emphasis added)

This "pastoral conversion" of the church appears to arise from the same fundamental impulse as John XXIII's call for a "predominantly pastoral view of the Church's teaching office." Likewise, just as *Optatam Totius* sought to challenge moral theology in light of that pastoral view, so also Francis has called for the continued renewal of moral theology, precisely by way of a "pastoral conversion" of moral theology, or as he puts it, "evangelical morality."[6]

This article will reflect upon the Second Vatican Council's emphasis on evangelization and pastoral action, specifically in application to moral theology. Part One considers Francis's reflections

---

[6] Pope Francis, "Discorso ai Partecipanti al Convegno Internazionale di Teologia Morale, Promosso dalla Pontificia Università Gregoriana e dal Pontificio Istituto Teologico Giovanni Paolo II per le Scienze del Matrimonio e della Famiglia," May 13, 2022.

on moral theology throughout the first eleven years of his pontificate, attempting to articulate the contours of his vision of an "evangelical morality." Such an analysis will reveal how Francis's vision represents a response to the Council's call for renewal in moral theology, inasmuch as it engages the integration of theology and pastoral action by foregrounding mercy as "the most radiant manifestation of God's truth."[7] After this work of more serene analysis, Part II considers how *Veritatis Splendor*—especially its second chapter—relates to the Council's pastoral trajectory. Here I will suggest that John Paul II's encyclical does not stand outside the aforementioned trajectory of pastoral renewal, but rather makes an essential contribution to it, not only (as is usually suggested) because it made great strides in recovering a Christological and biblical context for moral reflection, but also because its contributions to moral action theory reflect, with scientific accuracy, the foundation required for a pastoral conversion of moral theology to take root and bear fruit. I will suggest, then, that *Veritatis Splendor* provides what might be called a pastoral action theory, driven by the trajectory of pastoral renewal and evangelization called for by the Second Vatican Council and constituting the account of moral action necessary for Francis's vision of an "evangelical morality."

FRANCIS: "EVANGELICAL MORALITY" AND MERCY AS THE "RADIANT MANIFESTATION OF TRUTH"

Taking into account the major documents of his pontificate, as well as several key addresses and audiences, I will articulate Francis's vision of "evangelical morality" in summary form. In order to do so, I highlight two observable features of "evangelical morality" ultimately and inseparably united by the theological principle standing at the center of his vision, namely, *mercy*.[8]

The first observable feature of Francis's vision of "evangelical morality" is the persistent description of the church's moral teaching as a *response* to the love of God. In *Evangelii Gaudium*, Francis writes:

> Before all else, the Gospel invites us to respond to the God of love who saves us, to see God in others and to go forth from ourselves to

---

[7] *Amoris Laetitia*, no. 311.
[8] In what follows, I greatly benefited from two excellent articles that provide distinct but complementary summaries of Francis's vision of moral theology: Cathleen Kaveny, "Francis and Healthcare Ethics," *Theological Studies* 80, no. 1 (2019): 186–201, esp. 187–193; Alessandro Rovati, "Mercy is a Person: Francis and the Christological Turn in Moral Theology," *Journal of Moral Theology* 6, no. 2 (2017): 48–69.

seek the good of others. Under no circumstance can this invitation be obscured! All of the virtues are at the service of this response of love. If this invitation does not radiate forcefully and attractively, the edifice of the Church's moral teaching risks becoming a house of cards, and this is our greatest risk. It would mean that it is not the Gospel which is being preached, but certain doctrinal or moral points based on specific ideological options. The message will run the risk of losing its freshness and will cease to have "the fragrance of the Gospel." (no. 11)

These words come at the conclusion of a section titled, "From the Heart of the Gospel," wherein Francis observes the demands of communicating the Gospel message. Perhaps the most pressing demand for authentic proclamation today, according to the Apostolic Exhortation, is the consideration of the "integrity of the Gospel message" (no. 39), which presupposes "a fitting sense of proportion" in the art of proclamation (no. 38), while nevertheless permitting all the truths of the faith and the virtues to illuminate one another. Only in this way can the Gospel message avoid deformation (no. 39). To this extent, it would be a mistake to be concerned with the integrity of the church's moral teachings apart from the integrity of the Gospel as such; moral teaching is *always* a response of love to God's loving invitation, and moral discourse should "radiate" this fact. For Francis, this is why moral teaching cannot be something distinct from the Gospel as a whole and its proclamation; but it also accounts for why moral teaching is so important: the church's moral teachings are indeed invitations to love, invitations to respond to the unexpected and overwhelming love of God.[9] The following sentence from *Amoris Laetitia* summarizes this line of reflection:

> The teaching of moral theology should not fail to incorporate these considerations [i.e., the necessity of mercy], for although it is quite true that concern must be shown for the integrity of the Church's moral teaching, special care should always be shown to emphasize and encourage the highest and most central values of the Gospel, particularly the primacy of charity as a response to the completely gratuitous offer of God's love. (no. 311)

---

[9] The vision relayed here is one of the most remarkable and central threads of *Veritatis Splendor*. See Part II for further discussion of this point. An echo of this can also be heard in the likewise famous sentence of Benedict XVI's encyclical, *Deus Caritas Est*: "Being Christian is not the result of an *ethical choice* or a lofty idea, but the encounter with an event, a person, which gives life a new horizon and a decisive direction" (no. 1, emphasis added). Christian identity does not result from an ethical choice; the ethical choice arises as a response to the encounter with Christ.

The understanding of morality as a response to God's love appears to be the most significant context for Francis's consistent and tenacious opposition to a casuistic morality, which he says characterized his own early studies. In his own account, a casuistic morality represents a "cold morality, a theoretical morality,"[10] which takes up the study of cases and determines "up to this point it is possible, up to this point it is not possible, from here yes, from here no,"[11] and thereby loses the integrity of the Gospel message. Cathleen Kaveny has shown, quite convincingly, that casuistry in its most basic meaning ("the practice of discernment about what to do in particular situations") can be done in a manner consistent with Francis's vision of discernment and pastoral conversion.[12] Kaveny helps highlight that the essential drive of Francis's statements criticizing a "casuistic morality" indicates a relationship of opposition with his understanding of an "evangelical morality": the love of God, and our loving response, must always constitute the basis of moral teaching in the church, as is required by a total dedication to evangelization. Should casuistical sophistry become the overarching frame for moral discourse—the manipulation of law in favor of freedom, or freedom in favor of law—then the role of moral teaching in the context of the Gospel is lost. Joseph Cardinal Ratzinger echoes the same point, which highlights well the crux of Francis's opposition to casuistry: "The older type of moral theology no longer allowed people to see the great message of liberation and freedom given to us in the encounter with Christ. Rather, it stressed above all the negative aspect of so many prohibitions, so many 'no's. These are no doubt present in Catholic ethics, but they were no longer presented for what they really are: the concretization of a great 'yes.'"[13]

If the first observable feature of Francis's vision of "evangelical morality" is its character as a *response to* God's love, the second observable feature is the necessity of proclaiming the church's moral teaching *in* love. If others are to be invited to take up a response to the love of God through charity and virtue, it is necessary for those mediating this invitation to accompany others precisely *in* love, espousing "a pastoral discernment filled with merciful love, aimed at understanding, forgiving, accompanying, and above all, integrating"

---

[10] Pope Francis, "Address to Participants in the Conference Promoted by the Alphonsian Academy," March 23, 2023.
[11] Pope Francis, "Discorso ai Partecipanti al Convegno Internazionale di Teologia Morale," May 13, 2022.
[12] "A Defense of Casuistry," *Commonweal* 150, no. 1 (January 2023), www.commonwealmagazine.org/casuistry-pope-francis-morality-theology-thomism-kaveny.
[13] Joseph Cardinal Ratzinger, "The Renewal of Moral Theology: Perspectives of Vatican II and *Veritatis Splendor*," in *Joseph Ratzinger in* Communio, vol. 1: *The Unity of the Church* (Eerdmans, 2010), 184.

(*Amoris Laetitia*, no. 312). The practical demands of this model of proclamation—thoroughly imbued with the "pastoral conversion" called for above—were articulated well in an address Francis made ten years after *Evangelii Gaudium*:

> Every moral-theological proposal has, in the final analysis, this foundation: the love of God is our guide, the guide of our personal choices and our existential journey. As a consequence, moral theologians, missionaries, and confessors are required to enter into a living relationship with the People of God, engaging in particular with the cry of the least, to understand their real difficulties, to look at existence from their perspective, and to offer them answers that reflect the light of the eternal love of the Father.[14]

Notice that, in this description, the identification of the church's moral teaching as a response to God's love is presupposed; the primary emphasis here is upon the one mediating the proposal of the church's moral teaching. If the one receiving the proposal is to understand that moral action is a response to the love of God, then the one proposing that teaching should "reflect the light of the eternal love of the Father" precisely *in* the proposal itself.

For Francis, St. Alphonsus is the greatest model of this feature of "evangelical morality." Francis has consistently highlighted this Doctor of the Church and patron saint of moral theologians throughout his papacy, following in the steps of John Paul II's Apostolic Letter *Spiritus Domini* ("On the Bicentenary of the Death of St. Alphonsus de Liguori"). In particular, Francis notes that Alphonsus made the decision "to place himself at the service of consciences that sought, even amid a thousand difficulties, the right thing to do, faithful to God's call to holiness."[15] Because he was a man for others, who saw the need to invite people to encounter the love of God precisely in his own witness of love for them, Alphonsus "was neither lax nor strict. He was a realist in the true Christian sense, because he understood clearly that 'at the very heart of the Gospel is life in community and

---

[14] Pope Francis, "Address to Participants in the Conference Promoted by the Alphonsian Academy," March 23, 2023. See also *Amoris Laetitia*, nos. 307–312, and *Misericordiae Vultus*, especially no. 12: "The Church's first truth is the love of Christ. The Church makes herself a servant of this love and mediates it to all people: a love that forgives and expresses itself in the gift of oneself. Consequently, wherever the Church is present, the mercy of the Father must be evident. In our parishes, communities, associations, and movements, in a word, wherever there are Christians, everyone should find an oasis of mercy."

[15] Pope Francis, "Message to Mark the 150th Anniversary of the Proclamation of St. Alphonsus Maria de Liguori *Doctor Ecclesiae*," March 23, 2021.

engagement with others.'"[16] In this sense, we must follow Alphonsus, who "offered constructive answers to the challenges of the society of his time, through popular evangelization, indicating a style of moral theology capable of holding together the need for the Gospel and human fragility."[17] Ultimately, such "true fraternity" with others—who stand in such need of the Gospel of God's love, including its encouragement to virtuous living as a response of love to God—is only possible because God exhibits such fraternity first. As Francis writes,

> I invite moral theologians, missionaries, and confessors to enter into a living relationship with the people of God, and to look at existence from their angle, to understand the real difficulties they encounter and to help heal wounds, because only true fraternity is "capable of seeing the sacred grandeur of our neighbor, of finding God in every human being, of tolerating the nuisances of life in common by clinging to the love of God, of opening the heart to divine love and seeking the happiness of others just as their heavenly Father does."[18]

In an Alphonsian key, Francis recalls this point in discussing the proclamation of the church's teaching on the family: "The radiation of this divine plan [for the family], in the complexity of today's condition, requires a special intelligence of love, as well as a strong evangelical dedication, animated by great compassion and mercy for the vulnerability and fallibility of love between human beings."[19] Such an "intelligence of love" strives to intelligently put forward the

---

[16] Pope Francis, "Message to Mark the 150th Anniversary of the Proclamation of St. Alphonsus Maria de Liguori *Doctor Ecclesiae*," March 23, 2021. See also John Paul II, *Spiritus Domini*: "Alphonsus was responsible for the renewal of moral theology; through contact with the people he encountered in the confessional, especially during his missionary preaching, he gradually and with much hard work brought about a change in his mentality, progressively achieving a correct balance between rigorism and liberty."

[17] Pope Francis, "Message to Mark the 150th Anniversary of the Proclamation of St. Alphonsus Maria de Liguori *Doctor Ecclesiae*," March 23, 2021. See also Francis, "Letter to the Grand Chancellor of the 'Pontificia Universidad Católica Argentina' for the 100th Anniversary of the Founding of the Faculty of Theology," March 3, 2015: "Even good theologians, like good shepherds, have the odor of the people and of the street and, by their reflection, pour oil and wine onto the wounds of mankind."

[18] Pope Francis, "Message to Mark the 150th Anniversary of the Proclamation of St. Alphonsus Maria de Liguori *Doctor Ecclesiae*," March 23, 2021, quoting *Evangelii Gaudium*, no. 92.

[19] Pope Francis, "Discorso alla Comunita Accademica del Pontificio Istituto 'Giovanni Paolo II' per Studi su Matrimonio e Famiglia," October 27, 2016, no. 3.

Gospel, led all the while by love of those persons receiving the proclamation.[20]

On this point, it is worth observing that these two features of Francis's vision of "evangelical morality"—as a response *to* love and a proclamation *in* love—do not necessarily reduce or blunt the intellectual rigor required by moral theology. Rather, as Francis notes in an address to an Alphonsian Academy conference, "The Church expects from the Pontifical Alphonsian Academy that it will be able to reconcile scientific rigor and closeness to the holy faithful People of God, that it will give concrete answers to real problems, that it will accompany and formulate humane moral proposals, attentive to the salvific Truth and the good of people."[21] For Francis, "evangelical morality" does not so much require the *extension* of scientific moral theology to something other than its primary object of study and reflection, as much as it requires the *recognition in fact* of a "virtuous circularity" between theology and pastoral action: "Pastoral practice cannot be deduced from abstract theological principles, just as theological reflection cannot limit itself to reiterating the practice."[22] Rather, "Theology and pastoral care go together. A theological doctrine that does not allow itself to be oriented and shaped by the evangelizing purpose and pastoral care of the Church is equally unthinkable as a pastoral care of the Church that does not know how to treasure revelation and its tradition with a view to better understanding and transmission of the faith."[23] Within Francis's vision, this "virtuous circularity" is related to that "special intelligence of love" noted above: "You learn so as to live: theology and holiness

---

[20] Francis's discussion of an "intelligence of love" was echoed in an address concerning theological method: "Benedict XVI rightly asked all sciences to widen the boundaries of scientific rationality in a sapiential sense. This widening also needs to take place in theology, so that it can be a discipline critical for the life of every human being and the entire People of God, uniting science and virtue, critical reasoning and love. Catholic faith is a faith that works through charity: otherwise it is a dead faith (cf. James 2:26). A sapiential theology is thus a theology of love, because 'whoever does not love does not know God, for God is love' (1 John 4:8)" ("Greeting to the Members of the International Network of Societies for Catholic Theology," May 10, 2024).

[21] Pope Francis, "Address to Participants in the Conference Promoted by the Alphonsian Academy," March 23, 2023. It is worth noting how similar this formulation is to one of the central assertions of Paul VI's Apostolic Exhortation *Evangelii Nuntiandi*: "Fidelity both to a message whose servants we are and to the people to whom we must transmit it living and intact is the central axis of evangelization" (no. 4).

[22] Pope Francis, "Discorso ai Partecipanti al Convegno Internazionale di Teologia Morale," May 13, 2022.

[23] Pope Francis, "Discorso alla Comunita Accademica del Pontificio Istituto 'Giovanni Paolo II' per Studi su Matrimonio e Famiglia," October 27, 2016, no. 5.

are inseparable."[24] Practically speaking, this suggests once again that "teaching and studying theology means living on a frontier, one in which the Gospel meets the needs of the people to whom it should be proclaimed in an understandable and meaningful way."[25]

For Francis, just as "evangelical morality" does not signal an abandonment of scientific rigor, it also does not suggest an adaptation or gradualness of the law in order to make the "frontier life" of moral theology possible in practice.[26] Rather, the "virtuous circularity" between theology and pastoral action is again, a recognition of fact; it is the observation of a *polar* relationship that cannot be understood according to an *antagonistic* or a *displacive* understanding, wherein theology and pastoral action stand in opposition to one another or ultimately displace each other.[27] This is why, as *Amoris Laetitia* relates, "A lukewarm attitude, any kind of relativism, or an undue reticence in proposing that ideal [God's plan for marriage in all its grandeur] would be a lack of fidelity to the Gospel *and also of love on*

---

[24] Pope Francis, "Letter to the Grand Chancellor of the 'Pontificia Universidad Católica Argentina,'" March 3, 2015.

[25] Pope Francis, "Letter to the Grand Chancellor of the 'Pontificia Universidad Católica Argentina,'" March 3, 2015. See also Francis, *Ad Theologiam Promovendam*, no. 7: "Wisdom holds Truth and Charity together internally in a 'solid circle,' so that it is impossible to know the truth without practicing charity."

[26] See *Amoris Laetitia*, no. 295: "Saint John Paul II proposed the so-called 'law of gradualness' in the knowledge that the human being knows, loves, and accomplishes moral good by different stages of growth.' This is not a 'gradualness of law' but rather a gradualness in the prudential exercise of free acts on the part of subjects who are not in a position to understand, appreciate, or fully carry out the objective demands of the law. For the law is itself a gift of God which points out the way, a gift for everyone without exception; it can be followed with the help of grace, even though each human being 'advances gradually with the progressive integration of the gifts of God and the demands of God's definitive and absolute love in his or her entire personal and social life.'"

[27] For a discussion concerning what might be considered an antagonistic or displacive understanding of theology and pastoral action, see William P. George, "Moral Statement and Pastoral Adaptation: A Problematic Distinction in McCormick's Theological Ethics," *The Annual of the Society of Christian Ethics* 12 (1992): 135–156. See especially the emblematic story relayed on 154–155: "James Gustafson, in conversation with his students, has occasionally told of lively discussions years ago with Paul Ramsey and Bernard Häring. Ramsey and Gustafson would be at odds over a particular case and Häring would offer a clarifying comment: 'well, Ramsey's right morally, but Gustafson's right pastorally.' To which Gustafson would reply, 'if I'm right pastorally, then why am I not right morally?'" Indeed, the unsatisfactory nature of Häring's comment is noted well by Gustafson, and George's article supports Gustafson's response with significant theological reflection that requires careful consideration (though I am not in agreement with his proposed vision of the relationship between ethics and pastoral action, which seems to me to displace ethics [teachings, principles, etc.] with pastoral action). Francis's polar vision seems to intentionally avoid such an approach, with a much more organic vision of the polar relationship between moral theology and the demands of pastoral action.

the part of the Church for young people themselves" (no. 306, emphasis added). This statement constitutes the foundation for the section themed "The Logic of Pastoral Mercy," paragraphs 307 to 312. The circularity of the "logic of pastoral mercy" means that a lack of fidelity to the Gospel *is* a lack of love for young people; likewise, a lack of love for young people *is* a lack of fidelity to the Gospel. Thus, when it comes to the pastoral discernment of particular cases, Francis suggests in *Amoris Laetitia* that "this [pastoral] discernment [of particular cases] can never prescind from the Gospel demands of truth and charity as proposed by the Church"; to the contrary, it is actually the case that, "for this discernment to happen, the following conditions must necessarily be present: humility, discretion, and love for the Church and her teaching, in a sincere search for God's will and a desire to make a more perfect response to it" (no. 300).[28] To give anything less than the grandeur of the Gospel is a failure to love; to fail to love human persons, especially in their failures and their fragility, is a failure to be faithful to the Gospel message.[29]

For Francis, all that has been said here erupts from and is held together by "the beating heart of the Gospel" (no. 309): mercy.[30] The

---

[28] Francis quotes *Misericordiae Vultus*, no. 12. See also *Amoris Laetitia*, no. 297: "Naturally, if someone flaunts an objective sin as if it were part of the Christian ideal, or wants to impose something other than what the Church teaches, he or she can in no way presume to teach or preach to others; this is a case of something which separates from the community (cf. Matt 18:17). Such a person needs to listen once more to the Gospel message and its call to conversion."

[29] See *Amoris Laetitia*, no. 311: "At times we find it hard to make room for God's unconditional love in our pastoral activity. We put so many conditions on mercy that we empty it of its concrete meaning and real significance. That is the worst way of watering down the Gospel." For further discussion of how Francis's vision of "evangelical morality" in no way promotes laxism, see David Cloutier, "Moral Theology in Service of the Work of the Spirit: Synthesizing Pinckaers and Francis Against Moralities of Obligation," *Journal of Moral Theology* 8, no. 2 (2019): 13–30, especially 21ff.

[30] Francis's emphasis on mercy reflects a broader development in the church over the past 150 years that has foregrounded divine mercy in a radical way. Benedict XVI discussed this trajectory in a rare interview given in 2015: "For me it is a 'sign of the times,' the fact that the idea of the mercy of God should become more and more central and dominant—starting from Sister Faustina, whose visions in various ways reflect deeply the image of God held by the men of today and their desire for the divine goodness. John Paul II was deeply impregnated by this impulse, even if this did not always emerge explicitly. But it is certainly not by chance that his last book, published just before his death, speaks of God's mercy. Starting from the experiences which, from the earliest years of life, exposed him to all of the cruel acts men can perform, he affirms that mercy is the only true and ultimate effective reaction against the power of evil. Only where there is mercy does cruelty end, only with mercy do evil and violence end. Francis is totally in agreement with this line. His pastoral practice is expressed in the fact that he continually speaks to us of God's mercy. It is mercy that moves us toward God, while justice frightens us before Him. In my view,

two observable features of "evangelical morality"—a response *to* God's love and the proclamation of moral teaching *in* love—as well as the "virtuous circle" of theology and pastoral action it presupposes, are held together by the fact that "mercy is not just a pastoral attitude but it is the very substance of the Gospel of Jesus."[31] Mercy is precisely the *substance* of the Gospel and the church's teaching, *and* the shape of all pastoral action, converging in the person of Jesus Christ. Elsewhere he writes: "Mercy has become living and visible in Jesus of Nazareth, reaching its culmination in him. . . . Jesus of Nazareth, by his words, his actions, and his entire person reveals the mercy of God. . . . The Church is called above all to be a credible witness to mercy, professing it and living it as the core of the revelation of Jesus Christ" (*Misericordiae Vultus*, nos. 1, 25). "Evangelical morality," then, is not simply a response to God's love generally, but a specific response to his mercy: "Christian morality is a response, it is the heartfelt response before the surprising, unforeseeable—even 'unfair' according to human criteria—mercy of One who knows me, knows my betrayals and loves me just the same, appreciates me, embraces me, calls me anew, hopes in me, has expectations of me."[32] Likewise, "evangelical morality" proposes the Church's teachings in love precisely because the experience of mercy in every proclamation of the Gospel message is precisely an experience of the very content of the message: (divine) mercy is believable because I have experienced mercy (in this missionary disciple). As Francis relates in *Misericordiae Vultus*, "Mercy is not

---

this makes clear that, under a veneer of self-assuredness and self-righteousness, the man of today hides a deep knowledge of his wounds and his unworthiness before God. He is waiting for mercy" (www.catholicnewsagency.com/news/33591/full-text-of-benedict-xvis-recent-rare-and-lengthy-interview). In addition to the developments mentioned by Benedict, it is worth noting the memorable words of John XXIII in his opening address of the Second Vatican Council: "The Church has always opposed . . . errors, and often condemned them with the utmost severity. Today, however, Christ's Bride prefers the balm of mercy to the arm of severity. She believes that present needs are best served by explaining more fully the purport of her doctrines, rather than by publishing condemnations." See also Kaveny, "Francis and Catholic Healthcare Ethics," 189–190. See also Rovati, "Mercy is a Person: Francis and the Christological Turn in Moral Theology," 58ff.

[31] Pope Francis, "Letter to the Grand Chancellor of the 'Pontificia Universidad Católica Argentina,'" March 3, 2015. See Rovati, "Mercy is a Person," 64: "For the Pope, pastoral care is nothing else than seeing things with the eyes of Christ, imitating him who 'goes out to everyone without exception.' This is why any attempt to pit doctrinal and pastoral considerations against each other ought to be rejected for, as Francis beautifully said, 'Christian doctrine is called Jesus Christ.'"

[32] Pope Francis, "Address to the Communion and Liberation Movement," March 7, 2015. See also *Amoris Laetitia*, no. 311: "We should always consider 'inadequate any theological conception which in the end puts in doubt the omnipotence of God and, especially, his mercy.'"

only the working of the Father; it becomes a criterion for knowing who his true children are. In a word, we are called to show mercy because mercy was first shown to us" (no. 9).[33]

A pitting of mercy against justice and justice against mercy (in God and the church) would certainly cause this vision of "evangelical morality" to break down into an irreconcilable tension between proclamation of church teaching and personal accompaniment. For Francis, however, "Mercy is the fullness of justice and the most radiant manifestation of God's truth" (no. 311). In *Misericordiae Vultus*, he notes: "God does not deny justice. He rather envelopes it and surpasses it with an even greater event in which we experience love as the foundation of true justice" (no. 21). God's mercy, his divine love that pursues us and stoops to pick us up and heal us, is thus that hidden center uniting those two observable features of "evangelical morality," and the centripetal force that makes possible the "virtuous circle" of theology and pastoral action it requires.

VERITATIS SPLENDOR, "THE PERSPECTIVE OF THE ACTING PERSON," AND PASTORAL ACTION THEORY

Part I of this paper attempted to unfold Francis's vision of "evangelical morality," suggesting that it proposes a vision of moral theology steeped in the Second Vatican Council's emphasis on evangelization and pastoral action. I now turn to John Paul II's landmark encyclical on moral teaching, *Veritatis Splendor*, to consider how it relates to the trajectory of pastoral renewal and evangelization called for by the Second Vatican Council. It is reasonable to ask whether chapter two of *Veritatis Splendor* in particular represents a move away from the conciliar trajectory of pastoral renewal and evangelization, inasmuch as it offers several negative pronouncements upon certain trends in moral theology. A closer look at the purpose of the encyclical, and then at chapter two itself, offers a modest (and in no way comprehensive) response to this question.

At the outset John Paul II situates *Veritatis Splendor* explicitly within the Conciliar trajectory of renewal indicated by John XXIII and *Optatam Totius*. John Paul II writes,

> For the [rich] young man [see Matt 19:16], the *question* is not so much about rules to be followed, but *about the full meaning of life*. This is in fact the aspiration at the heart of every human decision and action, the quiet searching and interior prompting which sets freedom in motion. This question is ultimately an appeal to the absolute Good

---

[33] See further Alessandro Rovati, "Mercy is a Person," 62: "We can be witnesses of mercy for the world because the Lord has looked upon us with mercy."

which attracts us and beckons us; it is the echo of a call from God who is the origin and goal of man's life. Precisely in this perspective the Second Vatican Council called for a renewal of moral theology, so that its teaching would display the lofty vocation which the faithful have received in Christ, the only response fully capable of satisfying the desire of the human heart. (no. 7)[34]

This emphasis on the "full meaning of life" and "the desire of the human heart" is a remarkable testimony to the encyclical's deeply pastoral interest in proposing the Gospel, not simply as discrete ethical decisions or limitations on actions, but rather as a proclamation "for the life of the world," recalling the words of *Optatam Totius*. John Paul II writes, quite famously: "*The moral life presents itself as the response* due to the many gratuitous initiatives taken by God out of love for man" (*Veritatis Splendor*, no. 10). Thus, the first observable feature of Francis's "evangelical morality" noted above—morality as a *response* to the love of God—is the very departure point for John Paul II's encyclical; the continuity on this point is difficult to overstate.

Furthermore, as is often recognized, *Veritatis Splendor* represents a remarkable development in the unfolding of a moral vision "nourished more on the teaching of the Bible" that the Council recommended.[35] The meditation on the "Rich Young Man" from Matthew's Gospel as the narratival *inclusio* grounds the discussion of morality in Scripture, while also providing a vivid illustration, biblically and Christologically, of what it means for the moral life to

---

[34] See also *Veritatis Splendor*, no. 29: "The Second Vatican Council invited scholars to take '*special care for the renewal of moral theology*,' in such a way that 'its scientific presentation, increasingly based on the teaching of Scripture, will cast light on the exalted vocation of the faithful in Christ and on their obligation to bear fruit in charity for the life of the world.' The Council also encouraged theologians, 'while respecting the methods and requirements of theological science, to look for *a more appropriate way of communicating* doctrine to the people of their time; since there is a difference between the deposit or the truths of faith and the manner in which they are expressed, keeping the same meaning and the same judgment.' This led to a further invitation, one extended to all the faithful, but addressed to theologians in particular: 'The faithful should live in the closest contact with others of their time, and should work for a perfect understanding of their modes of thought and feelings as expressed in their culture.'"

[35] See Servais Pinckaers, "The New Law in *Veritatis Splendor*," *Josephinum Journal of Theology* 17, no. 2 (2011): 209: "In keeping with the Second Vatican Council's recommendation to bring moral theology to fuller perfection by a presentation more deeply enriched by Scripture, John Paul II has wished to strengthen the bonds between Catholic moral teaching and the Gospel, bonds which have grown too slack." Francis takes up this bond between Catholic moral teaching and the Gospel likewise in *Amoris Laetitia*, no. 6: "I will begin with an opening chapter inspired by the Scriptures, to set a proper tone."

present itself as a response to God: if the questions asked of the young man are questions addressed to the heart of every human person (see no. 8 and no. 117 of the encyclical), then this Gospel dialogue shows that the moral life is always indeed a response to the "initiatives taken by God [in Jesus Christ] out of love for man."

When the encyclical transitions to its assessment of certain trends in moral theology, it does so in the firm self-understanding that this engagement is a requirement of evangelization:

> In addressing this Encyclical to you, my Brother Bishops, it is my intention to state *the principles necessary for discerning what is contrary to 'sound doctrine,'* drawing attention to those elements of the Church's moral teaching which today appear particularly exposed to error, ambiguity, or neglect.... Because the Church has been sent by Jesus to preach the Gospel and to "make disciples of all nations ... teaching them to observe all" that he has commanded (cf. Matt 28:19–20), *she today once more puts forward the Master's reply* [to the question, "Teacher, what good must I do to have eternal life?"], a reply that possesses a light and a power capable of answering even the most controversial and complex questions. (no. 30)

Thus, whatever negative pronouncements are included in chapter two, the document addresses these as an implicit requirement *with a view towards* the broader, positive proposal of the Gospel; they are driven by the need to proclaim the integral message of the Gospel, and the primary purpose is not to draw attention to the errors, but rather to "elements of the Church's moral teaching." It might be said, with Ratzinger, that according to this vision the "no's" in Catholic moral teaching are "the concretization of a great 'yes.'"[36]

Further, it is significant that the stated purposes of *Veritatis Splendor* are very specific: "To reflect on the whole of the Church's moral teaching, with the precise goal of recalling certain fundamental truths of Catholic doctrine which, in the present circumstances, risk being distorted or denied" (no. 4). The encyclical's purpose is not, therefore, to reflect on the Church's moral teaching in the life of the church as a whole, nor is it, like *Amoris Laetitia*, a consideration of a central mystery of the church's teaching ("On Love in the Family"); such broader purposes would necessitate a more universal and pastoral dimension. *Veritatis Splendor* sets out to recall "certain fundamental truths of Catholic doctrine" at risk in current circum-stances, thereby signaling both the encyclical's importance and its specificity. Along these lines, it is striking to consider the fact that John Paul II's Apostolic Exhortation *Familiaris Consortio*, "On the Role of the

---

[36] Joseph Cardinal Ratzinger, "The Renewal of Moral Theology," 184.

Family in the Modern World," represents a much more comprehensive approach, treating fundamental truths of doctrine while also spending considerable time on the total pastoral care of the family. Francis's caution against a "gradualness of the law" in Chapter Eight of *Amoris Laetitia*—as opposed to the "law of gradualness" in authentic pastoral care—is drawn from a central pastoral section of *Familiaris Consortio* ("The Moral Progress of Married People"). Such a pastoral principle does not appear in *Veritatis Splendor*.[37]

Nevertheless, if the "virtuous circle" of theology and pastoral action observed by Francis is correct, then the more narrow, doctrinal focus of *Veritatis Splendor* does not render it set apart from pastoral concern. Indeed, according to that virtuous circle, those "certain fundamental truths of Catholic doctrine" highlighted by *Veritatis Splendor* are necessary for authentic pastoral action; if those fundamental truths stressed by *Veritatis Splendor* "risk being distorted and denied," then so too does pastoral action. As quoted above, Francis suggests that "pastoral care of the Church is . . . unthinkable as a pastoral care . . . that does not know how to treasure revelation and its tradition with a view to better understanding and transmission of the faith."[38] In faithfulness to this polar vision of moral theology and pastoral action, I would argue that one of the most potent and explosive contributions of *Veritatis Splendor* to the conciliar trajectory of pastoral renewal occurs precisely in chapter two, within what are perhaps the most intellectually and doctrinally rigorous paragraphs of the document, namely, the discussion of the object of the moral act. These paragraphs contain a remarkable articulation of moral action as a dimension and demand of the Gospel, and they likewise have significant implications for the development of authentic pastoral action; in fact, they constitute what I would call a pastoral action theory. In particular, the well-known statement in no. 78 of *Veritatis Splendor*—that "in order to be able to grasp the object of an act which specifies that act morally, it is therefore necessary to

---

[37] See *Familiaris Consortio*, no. 34: "Married people too are called upon to progress unceasingly in their moral life, with the support of a sincere and active desire to gain ever better knowledge of the values enshrined in and fostered by the law of God. They must also be supported by an upright and generous willingness to embody these values in their concrete decisions. They cannot however look on the law as merely an ideal to be achieved in the future: they must consider it as a command of Christ the Lord to overcome difficulties with constancy. 'And so what is known as 'the law of gradualness' or step-by-step advance cannot be identified with 'gradualness of the law,' as if there were different degrees or forms of precept in God's law for different individuals and situations. In God's plan, all husbands and wives are called in marriage to holiness, and this lofty vocation is fulfilled to the extent that the human person is able to respond to God's command with serene confidence in God's grace and in his or her own will."
[38] Pope Francis, "Discorso alla Comunita Accademica del Pontificio Istituto 'Giovanni Paolo II' per Studi su Matrimonio e Famiglia," October 27, 2016, no. 5.

place oneself *in the perspective of the acting person*"—represents an essential theological presupposition for Francis's vision of "evangelical morality," particularly the proclamation of moral teaching *in love* through the art of accompanying and ultimately integrating. Given the voluminous discussion and debate concerning the interpretation of no. 78 and the adjacent paragraphs in chapter two, the following treatment will not be systematic, but rather extend a discussion of its basic content to the context of pastoral renewal.[39]

At the outset, it is crucial to observe that the first sentence of no. 78 cites Thomas Aquinas's *Summa Theologiae* I-II, q. 18, a. 6, in which the Angelic Doctor articulates a nuanced vision of human action: he suggests that the moral adjudication of a single, voluntary human act requires the consideration of a two-fold action (within that act, as it were), with two distinct objects: the "object of the interior act of the will," related to the intention (end), the "what for" of the actor— *as well as* the "object of the external action . . . that on which the action is brought to bear," the chosen behavior of the actor. Thus, for Thomas, and likewise for *Veritatis Splendor*, both the intention of the actor and the proximate, chosen behavior are essential in determining the moral species of the act, i.e., whether that act is *good* or *evil*. The encyclical is quite clear that *neither* of these dimensions, taken on their own merits, is "neutral" *vis-à-vis* good or evil: the interior *purpose* of the actor is always ordered or disordered with regard to the human person's *ultimate* end, God, and the external *behavior* of the actor is either capable or not capable of being ordered to that ultimate end. Concerning the interior purpose or intention of the actor, *Veritatis Splendor* writes in no. 72: "Acting is morally good when the choices of freedom are in conformity with man's true good and thus express the voluntary ordering of the person towards his ultimate end: God

---

[39] The following may be consulted for a more systematic consideration of *Veritatis Splendor*, no. 78: David Crawford, "Experience of Nature, Moral Experience: Interpreting *Veritatis Splendor*'s 'Perspective of the Acting Person,'" *Communio* 37 (2010): 266–282; Kevin L. Flannery, "Placing Oneself 'In the Perspective of the Acting Person': *Veritatis Splendor* and the Nature of the Moral Act," in *Live the Truth: The Moral Legacy of John Paul II in Catholic Health Care*, ed. Edward J. Furton (National Catholic Bioethics Center, 2006): 47–49; Steven A. Long, "*Veritatis Splendor* §78 and the Teleological Grammar of the Moral Act," *Nova et Vetera* 1 (2008): 139–156; William F. Murphy, "A Reading of Aquinas in Support of *Veritatis Splendor* on the Moral Object," *Logos: A Journal of Catholic Thought and Culture* 11 (2008): 100–126; Martin Rhonheimer, "The Perspective of the Acting Person and the Nature of Practical Reason: The 'Object of the Human Act' in Thomistic Anthropology of Action," *Nova et Vetera* 2 (2004): 461–516. For a more detailed explanation of what I attempt to articulate in the following paragraphs, see Matthew Kuhner, "'The Perspective of the Acting Person' and Moral Action: Reading *Veritatis Splendor* no. 78 with Servais Pinckaers, OP," *Journal of Moral Theology* 10, no. 1 (2021): 73–101.

himself, the supreme good in whom man finds his full and perfect happiness." Concerning the external, chosen behavior, *Veritatis Splendor* cites the *Catechism of the Catholic Church*, no. 1761: "There are certain specific kinds of behavior that are always wrong to choose, because choosing them involves a disorder of the will, that is, a moral evil." Note that the intrinsically evil character of such behaviors arises *precisely because* they are not capable of being ordered "teleologically" towards the person's authentic good; it is not enough to think of intrinsically evil acts as external, physical patterns of behavior apart from the acting person. As *Veritatis Splendor* notes, "Christian ethics, which pays particular attention to the moral object [i.e., a freely chosen kind of behavior], does not refuse to consider the inner 'teleology' of acting, inasmuch as it is directed to promoting the true good of the person" (no. 78). The vision of moral acts unfolded in no. 78, inspired by the action theory of Aquinas, is deeply significant: it is necessary "to place oneself in the perspective of the acting person" in order to understand the morality of the total, unified action, insofar as it is the result of an interior act of the will *and* an external act: an external behavior chosen for a *purpose*, under the deliberation of the *will*.

The crucial role played by no. 78 comes into greater view when considering the encyclical's criticisms of certain moral theories, such as consequentialism, proportionalism, and "fundamental option" theories. For *Veritatis Splendor*, each of these theories distorts or departs from the aforementioned vision of moral action. For example, *Veritatis Splendor* is concerned that "fundamental option" theories reduce the external, chosen behavior to a "premoral" or "physical good" emptied of moral significance, seeking the moral determination of the act in the "fundamental option" of the interior act of the will alone.[40] But John Paul II suggests that this evacuation of moral significance on the part of the external, chosen behavior occurs

---

[40] See, for example, *Veritatis Splendor*, no. 65: "A *distinction* thus comes to be introduced *between the fundamental option and deliberate choices of a concrete kind of behavior*. In some authors this division tends to become a *separation*, when they expressly limit moral 'good' and 'evil' to the transcendental dimension proper to the fundamental option, and describe as 'right' or 'wrong' the choices of particular 'innerworldly' kinds of behavior: those, in other words, concerning man's relationship with himself, with others, and with the material world. There thus appears to be established within human acting a clear disjunction between two levels of morality: on the one hand the order of good and evil, which is dependent on the will, and on the other hand specific kinds of behavior, which are judged to be morally right or wrong only on the basis of a technical calculation of the proportion between the 'premoral' or 'physical' goods and evils which actually result from the action. This is pushed to the point where a concrete kind of behavior, even one freely chosen, comes to be considered as a merely physical process, and not according to the criteria proper to a human act."

precisely because this vision of the "fundamental option" does "not do justice to the rational finality immanent in man's acting and in each of his deliberate decisions" (no. 67). In other words, such a "fundamental option" position does not only remove the moral significance of the external act *but also fails to properly attend to the interior act of the will*. The rational finality of the choice is itself eviscerated, since considering the external action as "premoral" or simply "physical" is actually to downplay the actor's choice of that action towards an end. Though such "fundamental option" theories strive to foreground the interior act of the will and the significance of intention in determining the morality of a given act, it does so by untethering the purpose of the actor from their external behaviors, a move which ultimately *devalues*—does "not do justice to"—the way in which the rational finality of the actor *permeates the entirety of their external actions*. Ultimately, as John Paul II suggests, "to separate the fundamental option from concrete kinds of behavior means to contradict the substantial integrity or personal unity of the moral agent in his body and in his soul" (no. 67). The "fundamental option" theories described in *Veritatis Splendor* thus fail to obtain the perspective of the acting person, inasmuch as the unity of the acting person is put in jeopardy; it is no longer possible to understand the actions of the person through their *purpose* and their *behavior* in the world, understood organically, holistically, and hylomorphically.

Placing oneself in the perspective of the acting person, then, requires one to see *both* the behavior *and* the "what for" of the actor, namely, how the acting person understands *this chosen behavior* as fitting for *the good of their person*. Only by taking seriously these dimensions of the act can one really take on the acting person's perspective; otherwise, the engagement of their perspective will remain partial or fragmentary. In this sense, *Veritatis Splendor* appears to argue that "fundamental option" theories, consequentialism, and proportionalism fail to place themselves in the perspective of the acting person, precisely because they variously fail to give full due to what every acting person *does* when they act: for that acting person thinks their chosen behavior really matters, and that this chosen behavior matters because it was deliberately chosen for a particular reason and a particular purpose.

Ultimately, *Veritatis Splendor*'s emphasis on the importance of "placing oneself in the perspective of the acting person" through a consideration of the integrated whole of human action *undergirds and makes possible* the vision of "evangelical morality" proposed by Francis, precisely at the level of action theory.[41] Indeed, I think it

---

[41] For further evidence of this point *vis-à-vis* the application of "the perspective of the acting person" to the question of Communion for the divorced and remarried in the

justified to call this a *pastoral action theory*. If "discernment must help to find possible ways of responding to God and growing in the midst of limits" (*Amoris Laetitia*, no. 305), if the "art of accompaniment" requires "a pedagogy which will introduce people step by step to the full appropriation of the mystery" (*Evangelii Gaudium*, no. 171), and if all of this begins by coming alongside them "in the moral state in which they find themselves,"⁴² it will be necessary to place oneself in the perspective of the acting person; only from such a perspective of *taking on the place of the other in respect and love*, by understanding the importance given by the other to their concrete behaviors and intentions, might one begin to aid them in seeing how the behaviors they choose might be more authentically ordered to their ultimate end, God, their greatest good and joy.⁴³

CONCLUSION

In a 1995 essay titled, "The New Law in *Veritatis Splendor*," Servais Pinckaers argues quite convincingly that John Paul II's encyclical represents a remarkable response to the Second Vatican Council's call for renewal in moral theology, a renewal borne from the pastoral heart of the Council. At the same time, he reflects soberly on the broader impact of this renewal:

---

context of *Amoris Laetitia*, see Anthony Hollowell, "Moral Impossibility and Communion to the Divorced and Remarried," *Journal of Moral Theology* 13, no. 2 (2024): 42–43: "Francis's call for discernment follows as a pastoral consequence of Pope John Paul II's Thomistic personalism, for although *Veritatis Splendor* teaches that the object is determined in the perspective of the acting person, the object can still be discerned by those outside the acting person, and some valuable elements (but not the only elements) of such discernment can be found in the conscience of the acting person."

⁴² Pope Francis, "Address to Participants in the Conference Promoted by the Alphonsian Academy," March 23, 2023.

⁴³ See *Amoris Laetitia*, no. 308, citing *Evangelii Gaudium*, no. 270: "Jesus 'expects us to stop looking for those personal or communal niches which shelter us from the maelstrom of human misfortune, and instead to enter into the reality of other people's lives and to know the power of tenderness. Whenever we do so, our lives become wonderfully complicated.'" See also David Cloutier and Robert Koerpel, "Beyond the Law-Conscience Binary in Catholic Moral Thought," *Journal of Moral Theology* 10, no. 2 (2021): 193: "Francis consistently preaches inclusion of any and all who might be struggling with living out the fullness of the Church's teachings—and we might add that this is true regardless of the area of teaching, sexual or social, life issue or economic justice issue. Yet that inclusion does not legitimate views contrary to the Church's teachings, when construed properly not simply as arbitrary ecclesial laws but as the 'principles' of the final end of human sexuality involved in the Church's moral vision."

> In one sense, all is yet to be done, for it is not so easy to pass from a too natural morality, focusing on obligations and prohibitions, to a morality open to the dynamism of the Gospel. . . . We perceive the dynamism of evangelical morality. In contrast to legalistic morality, which halts at the fulfillment of obligations, it spontaneously goes further, as life tends towards growth and maturity, as love aspires to its perfection. . . . This is the direction in which *Veritatis Splendor* leads us.[44]

The fact that "all is yet to be done" in the articulation of an "evangelical morality" undoubtedly highlights why Francis has taken up this trajectory anew, furthering it in significant ways that require further thought and development still, especially among moral theologians and pastors. At the same time, Pinckaers's words highlight the deep continuity among the Second Vatican Council, *Veritatis Splendor*, and Francis's vision of "evangelical morality." May this trajectory of renewal, permeated by a "predominantly pastoral view of the Church's teaching office," continue to unfold, in the light of the Gospel and under the guidance of the Holy Spirit, "an ethics conceived not as a series of precepts but as the event of an encounter, of a love that then also knows how to create corresponding actions."[45]

Matthew Kuhner, PhD, is vice president/academic dean and associate professor of systematic theology at St. Bernard's School of Theology and Ministry in Rochester, NY, and he serves on the editorial board of *Communio: International Catholic Review*.

---

[44] Servais Pinckaers, OP, "The New Law in *Veritatis Splendor*," *Josephinum Journal of Theology* 17, no. 2 (2010): 215–216.
[45] Ratzinger, "The Renewal of Moral Theology," 184.

Amoris Laetitia Develops the Subjective Conscience from *Veritatis Splendor*

Matthew P. Schneider

Abstract: The subjective and objective aspects of conscience often exist in tension in Catholic theology: there is a need to affirm that an objective law exists by which proper conscience formation is judged, while acknowledging a subjective aspect in each person, obliged to follow her, even erroneous, conscience. Although not the focus of either *Veritatis Splendor* or *Amoris Laetitia*, these two papal documents demonstrate these dual aspects of conscience well and allow a better understanding of conscience together than they could apart. Reading each in light of the other provides a fuller view and illuminates the tension between the two aspects of conscience. *Veritatis Splendor* provides a clear explanation of the objective aspect of conscience while briefly mentioning the subjective. *Amoris Laetitia* briefly reaffirms the objectivity of conscience and then dramatically expands on its subjectivity, spending significant time on mitigating factors and the formation of conscience as both a starting point and an end goal. This paper analyzes these documents in dialogue with Charles Curran as contrary view to the two popes.

IN CATHOLIC TEACHING, THERE IS A CONSTANT TENSION BETWEEN the objective and subjective elements of conscience, described both as the voice of God leading a person to moral truth and their personal judgment of a particular moral situation. *Veritatis Splendor* effectively specifies conscience's objective aspect, while *Amoris Laetitia* expands papal teachings on the subjective aspect but without denying the objectivity of conscience.

This essay seeks to read each papal document in light of the other to maintain the productive tension between the objective and subjective elements of conscience.[1] Several scholars have already read *Amoris Laetitia* in light of *Veritatis Splendor*,[2] but the opposite

---

[1] I presented an early version of these arguments during the conference "Human Action and the Drama of Accompaniment: The 30th Anniversary of *Veritatis Splendor*," St. Bernard's School of Theology and Ministry, Rochester, NY, September 29-October 1, 2023.

[2] Angel Perez-Lopez, "*Veritatis Splendor* and *Amoris Laetitia*: Neither Lamented nor Celebrated Discontinuity," *Nova et Vetera* 16, no. 4 (Fall 2018): 1173–1204; Jose

approach is less common and usually focused on applying the practical elements of *Amoris Laetitia* rather than reflecting on the issue of conscience. This essay does not present a radical new proposal but identifies a connection unexplored in existing literature. In doing so, it seeks to push back against those who argue that what *Amoris Laetitia* teaches is what *Veritatis Splendor* condemns as a form of "creative" conscience (*Veritatis Splendor*, no. 54).[3] At the same time, the article rejects the position of those who over-contextualize intrinsic evil as described in *Veritatis Splendor*, no. 79, to the point of turning it into a meaningless category that almost never exists in concrete moral choices. Both of these views put the two documents in opposition to each other,[4] while the essay seeks to show their harmony by claiming that objectivity and subjectivity both exist in each individual conscience and that the individual is always called to integrate the objective aspect of conscience into the subjective one.[5]

To provide the backdrop for examining *Veritatis Splendor*'s and *Amoris Laetitia*'s views on conscience, I will start by considering four preliminaries that give us the context necessary to understand these documents with greater precision. In particular, I will focus on the hermeneutic of continuity, conscience in the magisterium before *Veritatis Splendor*, conscience in Thomas Aquinas, and the objectivity-subjectivity of conscience in Charles Curran as a view contrary to the one held by the two popes. After these preliminaries,

---

Granados, Stephen Kampowski, and Juan Jose Perez-Soba, *Accompanying, Discerning, Integrating: A Handbook for the Pastoral Care of the Family According to* Amoris Laetitia (Emmaus Road, 2017); Matthew Schneider, "Does the Text of *Amoris Laetitia* Allow Communion for the Divorced and Remarried? Part 1," *Homiletic & Pastoral Review*, February 12, 2019, www.hprweb.com/2019/02/does-the-text-of-amoris-laetitia-allow-communion-for-the-divorced-and-remarried/; Matthew Schneider, "Does the Text of *Amoris Laetitia* Allow Communion for the Divorced and Remarried? Part 2," *Homiletic & Pastoral Review*, March 10, 2019, www.hprweb.com/2019/03/does-the-text-of-amoris-laetitia-allow-communion-for-the-divorced-and-remarried-2/; Robert Fastiggi, "Responding to the Five Dubia from *Amoris Laetitia* Itself," *La Stampa*, March 12, 2018, www.lastampa.it/vatican-insider/en/2018/03/12/news/responding-to-the-five-dubia-from-amoris-laetitia-itself-1.33989886/.

[3] For a description and response to this kind of critique, see Antonio Autiero, "Resistances to *Amoris Laetitia*: A Critical Approach," *Journal of Moral Theology* 11, no. 2 (2022): 9, doi.org/10.55476/001c.37339.

[4] For an example of scholars who place John Paul II and Francis in opposition to each other, see Todd A. Salzman and Michael G. Lawler, "*Amoris Laetitia*: Towards a Methodological and Anthropological Integration of Catholic Social and Sexual Ethics," *Theological Studies* 79, no. 3 (2018): 637, doi.org/10.1177/0040563918784772.

[5] Autiero seems to hold a similar view by explaining that we must keep together "the objective level of morality established on the basis of the acts carried out and the subjective level affirming the primacy of the person and his or her moral substance" ("Resistances to *Amoris Laetitia*," 10).

the essay examines each of the documents considered and their relationships.

PRELIMINARIES

Hermeneutic of Continuity

To be understood according to the mind of the church, papal documents should be read through a hermeneutic of continuity. While the school of thought to which I belong considers that this way of interpreting the relationship between magisterial documents is correct,[6] it must be recognized that its approach is not universal, which warrants a brief explanation. To provide the latter, let us turn to Benedict XVI's way of contrasting hermeneutic of discontinuity and continuity. Though he describes these in relation to Vatican II, the same logical framework can apply to other magisterial texts as well. Benedict XVI first describes the hermeneutic of discontinuity, rupture, or suspicion:

> It asserts that the texts of the Council as such do not yet express the true spirit of the Council. It claims that they are the result of compromises in which, to reach unanimity, it was found necessary to keep and reconfirm many old things that are now pointless. However, the true spirit of the Council is not to be found in these compromises but instead in the impulses toward the new that are contained in the texts.[7]

This approach ultimately derives from a secular hermeneutic of suspicion that stands contrary to a Christian or theological way of reading magisterial texts. In contrast, the hermeneutic of continuity or reform takes seriously what John XXIII established as the goals of Vatican II, namely, to "transmit the doctrine, pure and integral, without any attenuation or distortion, which throughout twenty centuries, notwithstanding difficulties and contrasts, has become the common patrimony of men."[8] Benedict XVI describes this process not

---

[6] For example, Perez-Lopez argues that any sound interpretation of a passage from a magisterial document must pay attention to its literal meaning, be compatible with other affirmations in the document, and be coherent with other magisterial documents ("*Veritatis Splendor* and *Amoris Laetitia*," 1188).

[7] Benedict XVI, "Christmas Greetings to the Members of the Roman Curia and Prelature," December 22, 2005, www.vatican.va/content/benedict-xvi/en/speeches/2005/december/documents/hf_ben_xvi_spe_20051222_roman-curia.html.

[8] John XXIII, "Opening Speech at Vatican II," October 11, 1962, vatican2voice.org/91docs/opening_speech.htm.

merely as a static repetition of existing dogmas but as presenting them anew for current and future generations.

In the speech closing Vatican II, Paul VI critiqued how the hermeneutic of suspicion was too influenced by culture at the expense of tradition: "Some have been inclined to suspect that an easy-going and excessive responsiveness to the outside world, passing events, cultural fashions, temporary needs, an alien way of thinking . . . may have swayed persons and acts of the ecumenical synod, at the expense of the fidelity which is due to tradition."[9] Following the council, the spirit of rupture manifested both in those who promoted a spirit contrary to the council's text and the traditionalists who viewed it as a moment of apostasy. This view of the council presented a greater obstacle than liturgy to the reunion of the Lefebvrists (Society of St. Pius X) under John Paul II.[10] Ratzinger would critique both extremes that interpret Vatican II as a moment of rupture or change of doctrine. Since at least 1985, he explicitly argued in favor of reading post-conciliar teachings in continuity rather than rupture with pre-conciliar ones.[11]

Using a hermeneutic of continuity works bidirectionally: one can read new magisterial teachings in light of old ones and vice versa. In fact, it functions much like how we read one passage of Scripture in light of the whole Bible and the analogy of faith or superstructure of various truths (*Catechism*, nos. 112 and 114). This method of reading will help us understand *Veritatis Splendor* and *Amoris Laetitia* as mutually interpretative.

Existing Magisterial Teaching

Let us now turn to providing an overview of what the magisterium taught regarding conscience before the publication of *Veritatis Splendor*. This analysis will help us establish a broader magisterial framework for reading John Paul II's and Francis's teachings on conscience together.

In 1690, the Holy Office condemned several Jansenist propositions. The third condemned proposition establishes a significant limit to conscience: "It is not licit to follow a [probable] opinion, even if the

---

[9] Paul VI, "Conclusion of the II Vatican Council: Speech at the Last Public Session," December 7, 1965, www.vatican.va/content/paul-vi/en/speeches/1965/documents/hf_p-vi_spe_19651207_epilogo-concilio.html.
[10] Gilles Routhier, "The Hermeneutic of Reform as a Task for Theology," *Irish Theological Quarterly* 77, no. 3 (2012): 220, 223 232, doi.org/10.1177/0021140012443635.
[11] Routhier, "The Hermeneutic of Reform," 233.

most probable among the probable ones."[12] This condemnation demonstrates that if a person's conscience is not absolutely certain about the right course of action but has an understanding of what is likely moral, they can and should act in accord with that understanding. This implicitly acknowledges that one cannot ignore the subjective aspect of conscience.

In 1956, the Holy Office issued an instruction on situation ethics. While erring in the opposite direction from the Jansenists, this moral system was condemned as well. As the instruction explains, situation ethics holds that "the decisive and ultimate norm of conduct is not the objective right order, determined by the law of nature and known with certainty from that law, but a certain intimate judgment and light of the mind of each individual."[13] The last phrase about an individual's mental judgment accurately describes one aspect of conscience, but the followers of situation ethics err when this judgment is no longer grounded in the principles of a higher law and relies solely on the individual's situation.

In 1963, John XXIII issued the encyclical *Pacem in Terris*, which characterizes conscience thus: "The world's Creator has stamped man's inmost being with an order revealed to man by his conscience; and his conscience insists on his preserving it. Men 'show the work of the law written in their hearts. Their conscience bears witness to them.' And how could it be otherwise? All created being reflects the infinite wisdom of God. It reflects it all the more clearly, the higher it stands in the scale of perfection" (no. 5, quoting Romans 2:15). This description reveals conscience as both objective and subjective. Objectively, it indicates that a divine order exists, stamped on each person, and reflecting God's wisdom. The subjective element appears in how this order is uniquely stamped on each person, but the emphasis here falls primarily on the objective aspect.

Gaudium et Spes addresses conscience meaningfully twice. The first relevant paragraph emphasizes the objective nature of conscience. It begins thus: "In the depths of his conscience, man detects a law which he does not impose upon himself, but which holds him to obedience" (no. 16), strongly affirming the objective aspect of an external law to which conscience must correspond. The same paragraph then shifts to the subjective element: "Conscience is the most secret core and sanctuary of a man. There he is alone with God, Whose voice echoes in his depths" (no. 16). Autiero summarizes this duality by explaining that we must always recognize "the objective

---

[12] Heinrich Denzinger and Peter Hünermann, eds., *Enchiridion Symbolorum: A Compendium of Creeds, Definitions, and Declarations of the Catholic Church*, trans. Robert Fastiggi and Anne Englund Nash, 43rd ed. (Ignatius, 2012), no. 2303.
[13] Denzinger and Hünermann, *Enchiridion Symbolorum*, no. 3918.

level of morality established on the basis of the acts carried out and the subjective level affirming the primacy of the person and his or her moral substance."[14] Such a description positions the eternal law given by God as the ultimate arbiter of conscience and source of its objectivity. In particular, this conciliar passage establishes that conscience represents both a judgment measured against objective law and also an intimate, subjective judgment through which we strive to hear God's voice more clearly. Later on, *Gaudium et Spes* focuses more on the formation of conscience: "In order for individual men to discharge with greater exactness the obligations of their conscience toward themselves and the various groups to which they belong, they must be carefully educated to a higher degree of culture through the use of the immense resources available today to the human race" (no. 31). The need for conscience formation acknowledges both the subjective nature and the possibility of malformation of conscience while also recognizing a more objective standard toward which we can strive to form conscience.

Vatican II also promulgated *Dignitatis Humanae*, a declaration focusing on religious liberty. It affirms that "every man has the duty, and therefore the right, to seek the truth in matters religious in order that he may with prudence form for himself right and true judgments of conscience, under use of all suitable means" (no. 3). While this document specifically addresses religious matters, its principles seem applicable to other areas, provided they do not contravene natural law or directly harm other human beings. For example, one can choose their country of residence based on conscience but cannot choose violent assault in liberty of conscience. A Catholic might avoid meat based on conscience, although not required, or submit a conscience exemption to a vaccine based on sincerely held beliefs, even if based on dubious science. This strongly emphasizes the subjective aspect of conscience and the fact that there is an inherent value in respecting this internal conscience even when erroneous.

Persona Humana from the Congregation for the Doctrine of the Faith addresses conscience in novel ways in two paragraphs. First, it establishes that a good conscience aligns with church teachings by indicating that "a spirit of docility to the Church's teaching" and "what an upright conscience dictates in concrete cases"[15] refer to the same reality. An upright conscience dictates in concrete cases what accords with church teaching. Later, the same document repeatedly notes the

---

[14] Autiero, "Resistances to *Amoris Laetitia*," 10.
[15] Congregation for the Doctrine of the Faith, *Persona Humana*: Declaration on Certain Questions Concerning Sexual Ethics, December 29, 1975, no. 11, www.vatican.va/roman_curia/congregations/cfaith/documents/rc_con_cfaith_doc_1 9751229_persona-humana_en.html.

need for enlightening consciences both in confronting new ethical questions and in the confessional.[16] This second citation parallels the second paragraph above from *Gaudium et Spes* as both emphasize the need for forming or enlightening consciences, demonstrating both the objective and subjective aspects of conscience.

Finally, John Paul II articulated important principles regarding conscience in *Dominum et Vivificantem*. He notes that conscience is a gift based on the *Imago Dei*: "To man, created to the image of God, the Holy Spirit gives the gift of conscience, so that in this conscience the image may faithfully reflect its model" (no. 36). We cannot overlook this divine origin of conscience, explaining why conscience serves as each person's divine interior voice. John Paul II further emphasizes the objectivity of conscience by explaining that "a result of an upright conscience is, first of all, to call good and evil by their proper name" (no. 43). At the same time, he also observes that "man's inmost being [is] . . . the sanctuary of human consciences" (no. 42), thus reaffirming the interiority and privacy of conscience *Gaudium et Spes* articulated.

In the magisterial teachings preceding *Veritatis Splendor*, we find both objective and subjective aspects of conscience clearly identified. However, these documents do not develop conscience as extensively as *Veritatis Splendor* and *Amoris Laetitia* would later do. Referring to them serves to establish that the church's official teachings recognize the presence of objective and subjective aspects of conscience. Furthermore, the documents just analyzed also refer to freedom of conscience, conscience formation, the secrecy of conscience, and its divine origin. These are all elements John Paul II and Francis further elaborate in their own magisterial teaching.

Aquinas

John Paul II seems set on presenting a Thomistic view, and Francis himself declares that "everything written in *Amoris Laetitia* is Thomistic, from beginning to end."[17] Thus, an overview of Thomas Aquinas's understanding of conscience provides important context to understand the writings of both popes and further supports a harmonious reading of their teaching. Surprisingly, given the emphasis on conscience in modern moral theology, Aquinas dedicates no specific question in the *Summa* to it. However, three articles in the *Summa* describe his thoughts on conscience.

---

[16] Congregation for the Doctrine of the Faith, *Persona Humana*, no. 13.
[17] Pope Francis, "Opening of the Pastoral Congress of the Diocese of Rome," June 16, 2016, www.vatican.va/content/francesco/en/speeches/2016/june/documents/papa-francesco_20160616_convegno-diocesi-roma.html.

First, Aquinas addresses whether conscience is an intellectual power and concludes that it is an act rather than a power as it can be set aside or ignored. He observes that the word conscience "implies the relation of knowledge to something: for conscience may be resolved into '*cum alio scientia*,' i.e., knowledge applied to an individual case" (ST I, q. 79, a. 13). This etymology reveals conscience's subjective nature as it represents the knowledge the person has regarding an individual case rather than some perfect external law. At the same time, Aquinas writes that conscience "is said to witness, to bind, or incite, and also to accuse, torment, or rebuke" (ST I, q. 79, a. 13), a characterization that suggests a more objective dimension, given that a witness testifies not merely to subjective knowledge but something external. Finally, Aquinas explains, "Sometimes the name conscience is given to the first natural habit—namely, 'synderesis'" (ST I, q. 79, a. 13). Accordingly, this article explains that conscience can be understood equivocally or analogically and is characterized by both subjective and objective elements.

Two subsequent articles examine erring conscience, thereby introducing an emphasis on the subjectivity of conscience, considering that a purely objective conscience could not err. The first article asks whether a will is evil if it contradicts erroneous reason and concludes that such a will would indeed be evil. Aquinas explains that "to inquire whether the will is evil when it is at variance with erring reason, is the same as to inquire 'whether an erring conscience binds'" (ST I-II, q. 19, a. 5). The goodness or evil of the will depends on the object as perceived by reason or conscience, not on its intrinsic goodness or vileness. Aquinas notes, "The will that is at variance with erring reason or conscience, is evil in some way on account of the object [as perceived], on which the goodness or malice of the will depends; not indeed on account of the object according as it is in its own nature; but according as it is accidentally apprehended by reason as something evil to do or to avoid" (ST I-II, q. 19, a. 5). He explains this because "the object of the will is that which is proposed by the reason" (ST I-II, q. 19, a. 5). Since conscience represents a judgment of reason, then, we can conclude that the goodness or evilness of an object corresponds to conscience's judgment of it. The next article continues this topic, addressing the opposite question of whether a will is good if following an erring reason and establishing Aquinas's position on whether an erring conscience excuses a person (ST I-II, q. 19, a. 6).

Overall, Aquinas presents a view aligned with the previously examined magisterial teachings by recognizing both objective and subjective aspects of conscience and emphasizing the need to form subjective conscience in accordance with objective moral law. Furthermore, he also acknowledges that one has a duty to follow an errant but invincibly ignorant conscience.

Charles Curran

Examining Catholic theologians who write about conscience but do not always align with papal teachings provides another valuable context for understanding the two documents considered. Charles Curran serves as an example of this perspective. Despite his disagreement with objective church teachings on significant matters,[18] part of his account of conscience identifies the objective-subjective tension highlighted so far in a way that appears compatible with John Paul II's and Francis's teachings on this topic. However, Curran ultimately overemphasizes the subjective aspect of conscience to a degree that extends well beyond what *Veritatis Splendor* and *Amoris Laetitia* teach. This section explains Curran's general view of conscience, while what he wrote about John Paul II's moral theology will be considered in later sections of the essay.

Curran's initial treatment of the tension between objective and subjective elements appears reasonably sound. In an early work, he clearly articulates both dimensions: "Conscience forms its judgment discursively from the objective principles of the moral order; but at the same time, there is also a direct connatural knowing process. The dictate of conscience is concrete, subjective, individual, and existential."[19] This presentation acknowledges both the objective aspects found in the principles of the moral order as the foundation of conscience's dictates and its subjective aspects manifested in connatural knowledge and particular judgments of specific acts. Overall, Curran seems to recognize "the primacy of the subjective" while acknowledging "the importance of the objective."[20]

Curran also correctly observes that moral theology can sometimes become too hyper-focused on training confessors at the expense of the broader theological context.[21] For example, he critiques the manuals by noting their overemphasis on the distinction between mortal and venial sin[22] and for the fact that, while expressing the objective law

---

[18] For example, Curran has expressed disagreements with what the church teaches regarding divorce, abortion, euthanasia, homosexual acts, sex outside marriage, contraception, sterilization, and masturbation. Curran's statements against church teaching on these matters are catalogued in Schubert M. Ogden, "Academic Freedom and Tenure: The Catholic University of America," *Academe* 75, no. 5 (1989): 29, doi.org/10.2307/40249738.

[19] Charles E. Curran, *Christian Morality Today: The Renewal of Moral Theology* (Fides, 1966), 17.

[20] Charles E. Curran, *The Catholic Moral Tradition Today: A Synthesis, Moral Traditions, and Moral Arguments* (Georgetown University Press, 1999), 189.

[21] Charles E. Curran, *Directions in Fundamental Moral Theology* (University of Notre Dame Press, 1985), 221–222.

[22] Curran, *The Catholic Moral Tradition Today*, 191.

effectively, they gave the impression that "the law spells out all of one's moral obligations and conscience passively conforms to the existing laws."²³ While conscience should ideally function this way, Curran correctly observes that subjective conscience does not always process moral law so directly. In fact, Curran goes further and seems to overemphasize the subjective dimension of conscience. He presents three models for understanding morality: deontological, teleological, and relational.²⁴ All three models have important insights, but he appears to diminish the deontological aspect to the point of irrelevance, creating what John Paul II would later criticize as an excessively teleological theory. Curran summarizes his view in four steps: (1) the importance of the relational model; (2) the subjectivity of the individual conscience; (3) conscience as cognitive, affective, and moral, not merely cognitive; and (4) specific metaphysical theories of conscience.²⁵ The notable absence from this summary of the deontological model—the most objective one—is noteworthy and points to Curran's over-emphasis on the subjective dimension of conscience. Thus, it is not surprising that, in a more recent publication, Curran offers a simplified definition of conscience that, while adequate, does not capture the subjective-objective tension he recognizes in parts of his work: "Conscience is generally understood as a judgment about the morality of an act to be done or omitted, or already done or omitted by the person."²⁶

Curran seems to elevate the subjective aspect of conscience to a degree that risks overshadowing objective morality completely. He states, "The external law is static and very incomplete. It does not and cannot express the totality of man's relationship with God."²⁷ While it is true that the external law God puts into creation and in which human beings participate through the natural law is unchanging, it is incomplete only in the sense that its principles are often general and may not immediately resolve every issue of conscience. This incompleteness does not indicate a lack of guidance for human action but simply indicates that the law's guidance functions more as a guardrail defining boundaries than as a command prescribing specific decisions made in conscience. For example, while eternal law establishes that human beings should spend daily time in prayer, it does not specify exactly what prayers a Catholic should recite each day; thus, one must exercise personal judgment of conscience to decide between *lectio divina*, the rosary, or other devotions. Still,

---

²³ Curran, *Directions in Fundamental Moral Theology*, 227.
²⁴ Curran, *Directions in Fundamental Moral Theology*, 228.
²⁵ Curran, *Directions in Fundamental Moral Theology*, 243–244.
²⁶ Curran, *The Catholic Moral Tradition Today*, 172.
²⁷ Curran, *Christian Morality Today*, 20.

Curran further emphasizes the subjective dimension of conscience by noting that "there are no infallible criteria to determine if the decision of conscience is true."[28] The best criteria we can use, he continues, are peace and joy. Now, while those elements hold value in deeper discernment where there is no obvious objective breaking of natural law, like determining a calling to a specific religious community, Curran's statement seems to ignore the cases in which objective rules of natural, eternal, or ecclesiastical law clearly indicate that one option represents an incorrect choice. In such cases, an infallible criterion for choice does exist. In the end, even Curran would likely argue that experiencing peace and joy about murdering someone to collect life insurance proceeds would not constitute a true judgment of conscience.

Curran's lack of focus on the objectivity of the moral order comes in part from his questioning of the authority of the magisterium. He accepts infallible teachings but sees no obligation to follow non-infallible magisterium, no matter how authoritative. For example, he accurately notes that in *Evangelium Vitae*, no. 62, John Paul II condemns direct abortion in the strongest terms short of an ex-cathedra statement. Yet, Curran argues that this teaching on abortion is "not definitive or infallible teaching"[29] and that, accordingly, direct abortion can be moral under certain circumstances. His judgment about the magisterium's lack of authority to teach infallibly or definitively on moral matters is not limited to the case of abortion. Instead, Curran claims that "the teaching of the papal magisterium on complex moral issues is not always a certain truth."[30] Judging by the context, he uses the word "complex" not just to refer to cases of prudence or cases where not all teachings are in accord. Instead, Curran considers complex even things that would not be considered such by many moral theologians, like abortion and sexual activity outside of marriage, and thus ends up directly opposing multiple church teachings. It must be recognized that the comment quoted above does have a degree of truth, given that there are statements on moral matters made by the magisterium at different times discordant with each other and that, accordingly, cannot all be certainly true.[31] However, Curran takes this principle to such an extreme point as to entail that almost no moral precepts remain certainly true unless they

---

[28] Curran, *The Catholic Moral Tradition Today*, 189.
[29] Charles E. Curran, *The Moral Theology of Pope John Paul II* (Georgetown University Press, 2005), 132.
[30] Curran, *The Moral Theology of Pope John Paul II*, 133.
[31] For a recent example, see the changes to the *Catechism* regarding the death penalty. Linda Bordoni, "Pope Francis: 'Death Penalty Inadmissible,'" *Vatican News*, August 2, 2018, www.vaticannews.va/en/pope/news/2018-08/pope-francis-cdf-ccc-death-penalty-revision-ladaria.html.

are infallibly defined, a position that functionally eliminates the objective aspect of conscience.

In conclusion, while Curran's views on conscience initially appear orthodox with a slight emphasis on the subjective that would be in line with the teachings of *Amoris Laetitia*, on further examination, they seem to go significantly further than Francis's proposal. Curran loses sight of the objective law articulated by the magisterium, something that both John Paul II and Francis consider essential for forming conscience. Thus, his analysis of conscience ends up emphasizing its subjective character to an extreme degree and rejecting some of the church's settled moral teachings.

VERITATIS SPLENDOR ON CONSCIENCE

In the previous section, we considered four preliminaries that ground the essay's interpretation of *Veritatis Splendor* and *Amoris Laetitia*. The magisterial teaching on conscience before the publication of *Veritatis Splendor* and Aquinas's framework show that conscience has two aspects: objective and subjective. The hermeneutic of continuity guides us to read John Paul II's and Francis's teachings on conscience as complementary rather than contradictory while simultaneously acknowledging that each pope emphasizes one of the dimensions of conscience more than the other. Finally, Curran's perspective on conscience provides an alternative account that can be compared with *Veritatis Splendor* and *Amoris Laetitia* to highlight how, contrary to Curran, these papal texts maintain the productive tension between the objective and subjective sides of conscience.

Veritatis Splendor emphasizes the objectivity of conscience and how it accords with natural and eternal law. It addresses subjectivity briefly and primarily in connection to the possibility of error. This section examines six key aspects of John Paul II's teachings on conscience: the reasons for writing the encyclical, the emphasis on objectivity and the object of the act, the possibility of error, the notion of invincible error, the importance of discerning whether an error is vincible or invincible, and the formation of conscience.

When examining *Veritatis Splendor*, one must consider its primary purpose, namely, to refute proportionalism, consequentialism, fundamental option theory, and other excessively teleological theories. While extensive debate exists about how to understand these theories with precision,[32] the encyclical's fundamental concern with

---

[32] Louis Janssens, "Teleology and Proportionality," *Bijdragen*, January 1, 1994, doi.org/10.2143/BIJ.55.2.2015240; Richard A. McCormick, "Some Early Reactions to *Veritatis Splendor*," *Theological Studies* 55, no. 3 (1994), doi.org/10.1177/004056399405500303.

them is that they grant excessive autonomy to the subjective conscience and simplify the objective eternal law such that final ends take priority over the object of the act. Curran claims that "John Paul II's approach to conscience is totally consistent with his overall perspective,"[33] which he describes as being fearful of the subjectivism and individualism present in today's world. How fearful John Paul II is can be debated, but it is clear Curran sees such views as the interlocutor to whom John Paul II is responding in *Veritatis Splendor*. Countering these theories requires reinforcing the objective aspect of conscience, which thus becomes the element *Veritatis Splendor* decides to emphasize.

Veritatis Splendor states unequivocally, "*The morality of the human act depends primarily and fundamentally on the 'object' rationally chosen by the deliberate will*" (no. 78, emphasis original). Although this object is chosen based on conscience's judgment, what is emphasized is its objective morality. The subsequent paragraph further elaborates, "*One must therefore reject the thesis . . . which holds that it is impossible to qualify as morally evil according to its species—its 'object'—the deliberate choice of certain kinds of behavior or specific acts, apart from a consideration of the intention for which the choice is made or the totality of the foreseeable consequences of that act for all persons concerned*" (no. 79, emphasis original). Certain objects are specified in a manner and to a degree that, in an objective sense, no moral justification exists for them, regardless of potential good outcomes. These are often referred to as intrinsically evil acts based on an extrinsic and objective morality. This objectivity is further expressed in the specific discussion of conscience:

> The dignity of this rational forum [conscience] and the authority of its voice and judgments derive from the truth about moral good and evil, which it is called to listen to and to express. This truth is indicated by the "divine law," *the universal and objective norm of morality.* The judgment of conscience does not establish the law; rather, it bears witness to the authority of the natural law and of the practical reason with reference to the supreme good (no. 60, emphasis original).

Conscience should reflect the divine law, which serves as the ultimate source for objectivity in conscience.

Moving on to the subjectivity of conscience, *Veritatis Splendor* notes the possibility of error:

---

[33] Curran, *The Moral Theology of Pope John Paul II*, 126.

Conscience, as the judgment of an act, is not exempt from the possibility of error. As the Council puts it, "not infrequently conscience can be mistaken as a result of invincible ignorance, although it does not on that account forfeit its dignity; but this cannot be said when a man shows little concern for seeking what is true and good, and conscience gradually becomes almost blind from being accustomed to sin." In these brief words the Council sums up the doctrine which the Church down the centuries has developed with regard to the erroneous conscience. (no. 62, quoting *Gaudium et Spes*, no. 16)

This acknowledgment of the possibility of ignorance explicitly refers to the subjective nature of conscience, as the objective law is free from error. When discussing the possibility of error, it is worth noting what *Veritatis Splendor* states elsewhere about conscience: "The individual conscience is accorded the status of a supreme tribunal of moral judgment which hands down categorical and infallible decisions about good and evil" (no. 32). If conscience is individual, it is inherently subjective and thus may or may not align with objective truth. This creates the fundamental tension between conscience's dual—objective and subjective—aspects.

In recognizing that conscience can err, *Veritatis Splendor* also explores the possibility of invincible error, that is, an error for which the person erring is not morally culpable. As John Paul II explains, an "error of conscience can be the result of an invincible ignorance, an ignorance of which the subject is not aware and which he is unable to overcome by himself" (no. 62).[34] At the same time, though, John Paul II emphasizes the objectivity of evil even in cases of invincible ignorance: "It is possible that the evil done as the result of invincible ignorance or a non-culpable error of judgment may not be imputable to the agent; but even in this case it does not cease to be an evil, a disorder in relation to the truth about the good" (no. 63). Interestingly, while invincible appears four times in the two consecutive paragraphs of *Veritatis Splendor* cited above, the encyclical does not offer any guidance on discerning or distinguishing between vincibly and invincibly ignorant consciences. As we will see, *Amoris Laetitia* offers criteria that help distinguish between the various forms of ignorance.

In summary, *Veritatis Splendor* recognizes the goodness of following an errant conscience while noting its errant nature, as it is only subjectively rather than objectively right. Curran opposes John Paul II's teachings about the issue of invincibly ignorant consciences

---

[34] The existence of invincible ignorance is relevant not only to questions regarding moral theology but also when it comes to Catholic teaching regarding the possibility of salvation for those who are formally members of other religions through no fault of their own but follow their conscience fully. See *Lumen Gentium*, no. 16.

by claiming that St. Alphonsus Liguori "says it is the common opinion of theologians . . . that an act done in invincible ignorance is not only not imputable to the agent but also can be a good and meritorious act. John Paul II, with his emphasis on the primacy of objective truth, does not want to accept the position of St. Alphonsus and the common position of theologians today."[35] Yet, Curran does not cite any specific text of John Paul II to justify such a critique and seems to misunderstand what the pope teaches about this matter. In fact, John Paul II states that an invincibly ignorant conscience "continues to speak in the name of that truth about the good which the subject is called to seek sincerely" (no. 62). Although this quote does not directly state that following an invincibly ignorant conscience is meritorious, it implies it. If even such an invincibly erroneous conscience keeps speaking the name of truth and the subject is called to follow it sincerely, it is hard to argue that John Paul II considers this unmeritorious, as Curran suggests.

When it comes to the distinction between the objective and subjective elements of conscience, *Veritatis Splendor* aims to address a particularly problematic view of conscience that would "permit one to do in practice and in good conscience what is qualified as intrinsically evil by the moral law" (no. 56). However, the case of an invincibly ignorant conscience differs fundamentally from the view opposed by John Paul II. The invincibly ignorant conscience does not consider the action intrinsically evil but considers it good because, through no fault of the ignorant person, it does not know its objective morality. Instead, John Paul II is concerned about moral theories that, without being ignorant of the objective or external evaluation of an action as intrinsically evil, still decide to characterize it as good.

On this point, John Paul II emphasizes the reality that the church's teachings constitute the objective law. He states, "It would be a very serious error to conclude . . . that the Church's teaching is essentially only an 'ideal' which must then be adapted, proportioned, graduated to the so-called concrete possibilities of man" (no. 103).[36] This establishes a distinct and objective rule beyond the merely subjective law adapted to man. John Paul II seeks to clarify that one cannot intentionally pursue such adaptation or propose a theory of conscience formation that would circumvent error. Yet, simultaneously, he points to the need to follow a sure judgment of conscience even if erroneous: "The judgment of conscience also has an imperative character: man must act in accordance with it. If man acts against this judgment or, in a case where he lacks certainty about the rightness and goodness of a

---

[35] Curran, *The Moral Theology of Pope John Paul II*, 128–129.
[36] The encyclical is quoting from John Paul II, "Address to Those Taking Part in a Course on 'Responsible Parenthood,'" March 1, 1984, no. 4.

determined act, still performs that act, he stands condemned by his own conscience" (no. 60). This represents consistent church teaching and leads us to the final point from *Veritatis Splendor*, namely, the essential role of conscience formation in the moral life.

John Paul II stresses the importance of forming consciences. Referring to Matthew 6:22–23, "The eye is the lamp of the body," he states: "The words of Jesus just quoted also represent a call to form our conscience, to make it the object of a continuous conversion to what is true and to what is good" (no. 64). This indicates the need to form conscience in accord with objective truth. Furthermore, John Paul II identifies the magisterium as a source for this formation: "Christians have a great help for the formation of conscience in the Church and her Magisterium. As the Council affirms: 'In forming their consciences the Christian faithful must give careful attention to the sacred and certain teaching of the Church'" (no. 64, quoting *Dignitatis Humanae*, no. 14). This stands in contrast to views like Curran's which elevate the subjective conscience at the expense of the objective standard and remove the foundation on which John Paul II bases conscience formation.

In summary, in response to various moral theories, *Veritatis Splendor* emphasizes the objective nature of conscience through the primacy of the moral object of the act in judging morality. While it briefly mentions the subjective nature of conscience, this discussion appears primarily in relation to the possibility of invincible ignorance and the importance of following a sure conscience even if invincibly ignorant.

AMORIS LAETITIA ON CONSCIENCE

Amoris Laetitia does not approach conscience from the point of view of fundamental moral theology as *Veritatis Splendor* does but from the point of view of the pastoral care of those who, without being validly married from the point of view of the church, cohabitate and are in a romantic relationship. Accordingly, its teachings emphasize the subjective aspect of conscience to respond to the pastoral concerns such situations raise. While Francis reaffirms the objective nature of the moral law and thus of conscience, he expands significantly on John Paul II's treatment in three ways through which we can read *Veritatis Splendor* anew: the presence of mitigating factors, the necessity of conscience formation, and judging whether a conscience errs due to vincible or invincible ignorance.

The Objectivity of Conscience Repeated

Francis reaffirms John Paul II's view on the objectivity of conscience without significant development, except for a slight difference in emphasis that implicitly responds to one of Curran's critiques of John Paul II. Francis declares, "If someone flaunts an objective sin as if it were part of the Christian ideal, or wants to impose something other than what the Church teaches, he or she can in no way presume to teach or preach to others" (no. 297). Francis's use of "objective sin" seems to refer to actions whose object is morally illicit when viewed externally, thus affirming the principle of intrinsic evil. His reference to the "Christian ideal" seems to echo John Paul II's assertion that church law constitutes an objective standard for man, not merely an abstract ideal.

Regarding conscience's objectivity, Francis offers a modest development: "Given that gradualness is not in the law itself, this discernment can never prescind from the Gospel demands of truth and charity, as proposed by the Church" (no. 300).[37] John Paul II does not talk about graduality in this manner in *Veritatis Splendor* and, when he does, he focuses on the fact that we cannot have "different degrees or forms of precept in God's law for different individuals and situations" (*Familiaris Consortio*, no. 34). Rather than focusing on the external forum, Francis emphasizes how the law of gradualness must be part of moral discernment, which we could consider a slight development when compared to John Paul II's analysis. *Amoris Laetitia*'s treatment of gradualness bridges the objective and subjective dimensions, while the concern for not departing from truth, charity, or church teaching reinforces the objective aspect of conscience: a well-formed conscience judges in accord with "the Gospel demands of truth and charity, as proposed by the Church" (no. 300). This affirmation of conscience's objective dimension stands in contrast to Curran's denial of the deontological aspect.

Regarding the objectivity of conscience, Curran argues that "John Paul II develops his understanding of conscience in terms of a legal model. Even references to the role of God and to the Holy Spirit . . . put the emphasis on law and obedience."[38] He then critiques this view as inadequate by noting that "the vast majority of our moral decisions are not made by reference to a law. The most important decisions in life—marriage partner, vocation, friends, coping with limitations, short-comings, and sufferings of human existence—are not made in

---

[37] Francis is here quoting from XIV Ordinary General Assembly of the Synod of Bishops, *Relatio Finalis*, no. 86.
[38] Curran, *The Moral Theology of Pope John Paul II*, 127.

response to a law."³⁹ Curran's change of terms from "by reference to" to "in response to" is subtle but very significant. A young person does not choose a marriage partner in response to a law, but a good discernment of a marriage partner would be made with reference to various laws. For example, considering the sixth commandment, a person should ask whether the possible marriage partner would be faithful. It is true that we do not discern between ethical choices such as whether to join this or that religious community *in response to* a law. However, even in these cases, we must discern *by reference to* the law to be sure whether the options we are considering are moral: if the law were to describe one option as immoral, that would exclude it from good discernment. Nonetheless, there is a reasonable argument that John Paul II's language is legalistic in his objectivity, which is why Francis's use of the terminology of "Christian ideal" and "gradualness" is a welcome shift that helps us move away from excessive legalism in ethics while maintaining the objectivity of conscience. Thus, we can say that Francis indirectly responds to Curran's critique of John Paul II.

Mitigating Factors on Conscience

Francis's emphasis on the subjective dimension of conscience emerges clearly in his discussion of mitigating factors that can produce objectively erroneous yet subjectively certain consciences. This section will center on paragraph 305, its famous footnote 351, and paragraph 303 of *Amoris Laetitia*.

In paragraph 305, Francis articulates how mitigating factors can create an erroneous conscience: "Because of forms of conditioning and mitigating factors, it is possible that in an objective situation of sin—which may not be subjectively culpable, or fully such—a person can be living in God's grace, can love, and can also grow in the life of grace and charity, while receiving the Church's help to this end" (no. 305). This observation illustrates the distinction between sin as an objective versus subjective act: sin is a violation of one's conscience rather than merely an objectively incorrect action. Here, Francis organically develops John Paul II's treatment of invincibly ignorant consciences, explaining both the distinction between objective and subjective culpability and identifying various factors that can cause this disparity.

Footnote 351 immediately follows the passage quoted in the prior paragraph. It states: "'I want to remind priests that the confessional must not be a torture chamber, but rather an encounter with the Lord's

---

³⁹ Curran, *The Moral Theology of Pope John Paul II*, 128.

mercy' (*Evangelii Gaudium*, no. 44). I would also point out that the Eucharist 'is not a prize for the perfect, but a powerful medicine and nourishment for the weak' (*Evangelii Gaudium*, no. 47)" (no. 305, n351). While the main text indicates the potential presence of mitigating circumstances suggesting an invincibly ignorant conscience, the quoted passage from *Evangelii Gaudium* provides more specificity. Just before the "torture chamber" reference cited in this footnote, Francis enumerates several mitigating factors: "Imputability and responsibility for an action can be diminished or even nullified by ignorance, inadvertence, duress, fear, habit, inordinate attachments, and other psychological or social factors" (*Evangelii Gaudium*, no. 44, quoting *Catechism*, no. 1735). As we can see, Francis's teachings provide a more detailed framework for understanding the subjective aspect of conscience, since whereas *Amoris Laetitia* describes what might constitute an invincibly ignorant conscience, *Veritatis Splendor* limits itself to affirming its possibility.

Paragraph 303 of *Amoris Laetitia* further develops this treatment of factors potentially causing invincible ignorance by acknowledging the validity of striving to follow conscience even when it is not in perfect alignment with objective reality. It states,

> Conscience can do more than recognize that a given situation does not correspond objectively to the overall demands of the Gospel. It can also recognize with sincerity and honesty what for now is the most generous response which can be given to God, and come to see with a certain moral security that it is what God himself is asking amid the concrete complexity of one's limits, while yet not fully the objective ideal (no. 303).

While an imperfectly formed, and thus partially ignorant, conscience remains less than ideal, an effort to improve and follow one's conscience represents a positive moral development. This seems to extend the principles of *Dignitatis Humanae* regarding religious matters to broader moral matters. While this sentence can be interpreted as sanctioning the non-formation of conscience contrary to *Veritatis Splendor*, the context and additional statements in *Amoris Laetitia* indicate an ongoing call to pursue conscience formation. In fact, the paragraph simply addresses how mitigating circumstances affect culpability for objectively wrong actions by affirming that ignorant or erroneous consciences may render an individual inculpable for an objectively immoral action. Thus, we see how Francis elaborates on the subjective factors that can produce a fully or partially invincibly ignorant conscience. This development enables a more nuanced understanding of the possibility of invincible ignorance mentioned in *Veritatis Splendor*.

Forming Consciences

Amoris Laetitia establishes conscience formation as a foundational focus early on: "We have been called to form consciences, not to replace them" (no. 37). This represents a significant pastoral development. Historically, pastoral practice often positioned the parish priest as the arbiter of all moral decisions down to judgments about reading popular literature. *Amoris Laetitia* suggests a more efficacious approach, namely, to form consciences so that people may make most moral decisions through their well-formed conscience rather than defaulting to pastoral consultation over routine moral questions. This demonstrates a subjective dimension in the gradual development of well-formed consciences, as opposed to a false objectivity where all moral decisions are predetermined.

Later, *Amoris Laetitia* quotes paragraph 1735 of the *Catechism* to explain how conscience can be malformed and uses it to list a second time the mitigating factors that appear in the passage from *Evangelii Gaudium* quoted in footnote 351. Francis employs this list of possible malformations to address the need for conscience formation: "Pastoral discernment, while taking into account a person's properly formed conscience, must take responsibility for these situations. Even the consequences of actions taken are not necessarily the same in all cases" (no. 302).[40] While this paragraph addresses a specific point about marriage and family, it also establishes a broader principle: consciences must be formed within people's concrete situations. Historical precedents demonstrate this point. For example, conscience formation of recently converted warriors in the Middle Ages started where they were with their existing ideal of heroic raiding parties. Furthermore, to use another historical example, St. Thorlak of Iceland in the twelfth century had to criticize the chieftain of the island for maintaining a formal marriage for the purpose of forging a political alliance while keeping a concubine (Thorlak's sister) whom he genuinely loved.[41] Although the island had converted to Christianity in recent generations, they still needed conscience formation. From this point of view, we could say that Francis describes the starting point of conscience formation while John Paul II limits his discussion to the endpoint. Both are needed, given that any formation process requires knowledge of both the start and endpoint. University classes present a good analogy where course goals give us a clear endpoint, and prerequisites give us a clear starting point. Although conscience

---

[40] Francis is here quoting XIV Ordinary General Assembly of the Synod of Bishops, *Relatio Finalis*, no. 85.
[41] Aimee O'Connell and John C. Wilhelmsson, *Thorlak of Iceland: Who Rose Above Autism to Become Patron Saint of His People* (Chaos To Order, 2018), 210.

formation is not as information-heavy as academic coursework, the same principle applies: understanding the current subjective state of the person as the starting point and the objectively well-formed conscience as the endpoint is essential for determining the appropriate formative path.

The subsequent paragraph begins by acknowledging "certain situations which do not objectively embody our understanding of marriage" (no. 303). This serves as a starting point for discussing conscience formation: "Naturally, every effort should be made to encourage the development of an enlightened conscience, formed and guided by the responsible and serious discernment of one's pastor, and to encourage an ever greater trust in God's grace" (no. 303). The conscience of the one forming can recognize that a certain situation, while objectively disordered, may represent the current limit of what can be asked of this individual. This principle manifests in confession where guiding someone towards objective morality, or the "ideal," as Francis likes to say, may require incremental steps. Francis continues,

> Yet conscience can do more than recognize that a given situation does not correspond objectively to the overall demands of the Gospel. It can also recognize with sincerity and honesty what for now is the most generous response which can be given to God, and come to see with a certain moral security that it is what God himself is asking amid the concrete complexity of one's limits, while yet not fully the objective ideal (no. 303).

The paragraph concludes, "In any event, let us recall that this discernment is dynamic; it must remain ever open to new stages of growth and to new decisions which can enable the ideal to be more fully realized" (no. 303). Ongoing discernment remains essential for moving persons toward the truth. Here, discernment appears linked to conscience formation, thus suggesting that continuous discernment functions as a synonym for conscience formation. Francis's use of the word "ideal" differs from John Paul II's. For both of them, in fact, the objective standard of the church's law remains not merely as a lofty ideal expected only of canonized saints but an ideal towards which each person is guided.

The last relevant paragraph on conscience formation states, "A good ethical education includes showing a person that it is in his own interest to do what is right" (no. 265). This insight proves valuable because people are naturally inclined toward perceived good. Thus, people become more disposed to embrace conscience formation when they come to view it as beneficial, that is, as something connected to the larger goods of flourishing and beatitude.

To summarize, *Amoris Laetitia* significantly expands upon *Veritatis Splendor*'s treatment of conscience formation. While John Paul II simply notes Jesus's call to formation and the church's role in providing it, Francis addresses what this ongoing formation entails extensively. In particular, Francis emphasizes that conscience formation involves guiding rather than replacing consciences, that it must begin from where people are, and that conscience formation needs particular attention in complicated relationships. Overall, Francis demonstrates the importance of conscience's subjective dimension in formation, while reaffirming John Paul II's emphasis on the objective dimension rather than developing it further.

Judging Consciences

Amoris Laetitia illustrates the complexity of judging consciences via a specific example. Addressing the situation of romantic partners divorced and civilly "remarried," that is, cohabitating, it explains: "There are also the cases of . . . 'those who have entered into a second union for the sake of the children's upbringing, and are sometimes subjectively certain in conscience that their previous and irreparably broken marriage had never been valid'" (no. 298, quoting *Familiaris Consortio*, no. 84). This presents a case where subjective conscience judges a marriage invalid due to some defect. Whether this judgment proves correct or not, the annulment cannot be granted since marriage vows maintain the presumption of validity and cannot be nullified by information that cannot be proven publicly or to the proper officers in a canonical court. However, this example importantly demonstrates how conscience's judgments can diverge from externally visible realities. Although the person in the example cannot get remarried, the mere fact of their moral certainty in conscience may be either accurate or erroneous. Furthermore, if erroneous, whether it is the fruit of vincible or invincible ignorance remains unclear. Only through self-disclosure of conscience can we begin to understand the subjective culpability, and even then, certainty may continue to be elusive. For example, while it may appear that full knowledge of the moral law would preclude the possibility of an individual possessing invincible ignorance, one could maintain invincible ignorance regarding matters of fact—for example, their spouse's will against children on the wedding day—rather than matters of law. The inherent inaccessibility of internal subjective conscience to external observers exemplified here speaks to a broader principle about conscience's fundamentally private nature.

Francis also addresses the challenge faced by those with relatively well-formed and nevertheless still weak consciences. *Amoris Laetitia* observes: "Often we prove inconsistent in our own convictions, however firm they may be; even when our conscience dictates a clear moral decision, other factors sometimes prove more attractive and powerful" (no. 265). The process does not end with conscience formation; rather, conscience's judgments must become actualized in concrete decisions leading to specific actions. This observation cautions against judging other people's consciences harshly based solely on external factors by acknowledging the universal weakness caused by concupiscence. Concupiscence often clouds conscience's clarity, and even the greatest saints experience it. St. Therese of Lisieux, for example, noted how her concupiscence manifested in excessive fear of abandonment or rejection in childhood, requiring grace to eventually overcome this tendency.[42] Nevertheless, human beings generally maintain an awareness of the guidance of conscience and its judgment. While they can perceive their own conscience's subjectivity, they remain unable to perceive or access the conscience of another. This constitutes a return to the teaching of *Gaudium et Spes*: "Conscience is the most secret core and sanctuary of a man. There he is alone with God, Whose voice echoes in his depths" (no. 16). Conscience remains our most intimate and inaccessible dimension, even if a judgment is sometimes possible based on what persons ought to know in conscience. For instance, in cases of theft or rape, it is reasonable to conclude that the perpetrator is culpable, as they ought to know those acts are immoral, and their conscience ought to have judged them accordingly. Still, there remains an essential challenge in judging consciences that highlights the fundamentally private interior nature of each conscience, which constitutes an essential aspect of its subjectivity. Individual consciences may be misinformed on moral law and relevant facts or clouded by concupiscence. Such realities require that we exercise charity in our judgments.

Objections

Several objections or points of disagreement have been noted in the preliminaries and are better addressed in literature specifically focused on those preliminary topics. For example, not all scholars agree with such a strong hermeneutic of continuity in reading these documents, but that question precedes the central argument of this essay and is thus presumed. However, one objection specific to this analysis of *Veritatis Splendor* and *Amoris Laetitia* warrants consideration.

---

[42] Paul C. Vitz and Christina P. Lynch, "Thérèse of Lisieux from the Perspective of Attachment Theory and Separation Anxiety," *International Journal for the Psychology of Religion* 17, no. 1 (2007), doi.org/10.1080/10508610709336854.

It is important to address the quasi-magisterial status Francis gave to the Argentinian bishops' guidelines on *Amoris Laetitia*. Francis approved this interpretation in a letter and published both that letter and the guidelines in *Acta Apostolicae Sedis*.[43] These guidelines largely directed priests to discern subjective consciences with individuals. While this significantly affects some aspects of interpreting *Amoris Laetitia*, it seems to have little effect on the argument presented herein. Conscience appears only twice in these guidelines. First, when the Argentinian bishops write that "it is always important to guide people to stand before God with their conscience,"[44] a statement that affirms and largely promotes the objective understanding of conscience John Paul II emphasizes and Francis reaffirms. Second, conscience is used in reference to doing an "examination of conscience" after divorce, which does not really affect the arguments presented in the essay.

There is debate about whether some of the claims in the guidelines' sixth paragraph may negate the objective aspect of conscience. There, the Argentinian bishops offer "the possibility of having access to the sacraments of Reconciliation and Eucharist" for couples where one party is divorced and civilly remarried if "there are limitations that mitigate responsibility and culpability."[45] Three responses to this possible objection are appropriate. First, the sacramental discipline recommended by the guidelines does not seem to directly affect the argument in this article, as the Argentinian bishops maintain Francis's emphasis on subjective conscience in a productive tension with John Paul II's treatment of objective conscience. At no point, in fact, do the guidelines deny objective conscience. Second, reading one paragraph of a magisterial document in opposition to another rather than finding a way to harmonize them contradicts the very hermeneutic of continuity that, this essay argues, is the only correct way of thinking about the relationship between different papal teachings. Third, considering that the guidelines state that the scenario in paragraph six refers to situations in which complete continence is not possible, it seems likely that this paragraph describes a situation where only one

---

[43] Cindy Wooden, "Pope's Letter to Argentine Bishops on *Amoris Laetitia* Part of Official Record," *National Catholic Reporter / Catholic News Service*, December 5, 2017, www.ncronline.org/vatican/popes-letter-argentine-bishops-amoris-laetitia-part-official-record.

[44] Bishops of the Buenos Aires Pastoral Region, "Basic Criteria for the Implementation of Chapter VIII of *Amoris Laetitia*," no. 8. Translation: Crux staff, "Guidelines of Buenos Aires Bishops on Divorced/Remarried," September 16, 2016, cruxnow.com/global-church/2016/09/guidelines-buenos-aires-bishops-divorcedremarried. Original in *Acta Apostolicae Sedis* 108, no. 10 (October 2016): 1074.

[45] Bishops of the Buenos Aires Pastoral Region, "Basic Criteria," no. 6, AAS 108, no. 10, 1073.

of the two romantic partners wants to conform to church teaching. For instance, a divorced and remarried individual might face a dilemma where their partner threatens to leave the family if sexual relations cease. In such a case, the individual seeking continence must confront the challenge of having to choose between their desire to follow what the church teaches and the potential financial and emotional hardship that would fall on their children if the partnership were to end.

The later part of the paragraph provides further indication that this suggested interpretation and, accordingly, the document is opening the possibility of accessing the sacraments to an individual member of the couple rather than both parties. In fact, the document states that access to the sacraments is a possibility "when a *person* believes he/she would incur a subsequent fault by harming the children of the new union."[46] Such a situation raises difficult questions about whether, from the standpoint of objective Christian morality, a person can morally accept sexual advances of their legal but not real or sacramental spouse for the sake of protecting their children. However, considering and responding to this question is beyond the scope of this article and does not directly affect its central claims.

CONCLUSION

Veritatis Splendor has served its purpose well by arguing against proportionalism and other subjectivist moral theories that started in the 1960s and continue even today. While it still remains relevant, the twenty-first century has seen a return of an earlier error wherein morality is overly objectified, failing to consider the subjective experience of the one committing an immoral act, which actually constitutes a sin. Accordingly, *Amoris Laetitia* responds more to this latter tendency, but the combination of these two documents provides the balance necessary to maintain the center of Catholic theology. *Amoris Laetitia* provides a more subjective lens through which the objective truths *Veritatis Splendor* emphasizes can be viewed.

Contrary to views that would consider the moral theology of John Paul II surpassed, the approaches of the two documents to conscience are in tension but not contradictory. Everything *Amoris Laetitia* says regarding conscience demonstrates that it intends to clarify against over-objectification rather than eliminate the objectivity of conscience. In fact, although Francis expands on the subjective aspect of conscience in *Amoris Laetitia*, he also reaffirms the objective one. Reading *Amoris Laetitia* as denying the objective conscience expressed in *Veritatis Splendor* it explicitly confirms contradicts both

---

[46] Bishops of the Buenos Aires Pastoral Region, "Basic Criteria," no. 6, AAS 108, no. 10, 1073 (emphasis added).

a hermeneutic of continuity and a reasonable and coherent reading of the exhortation's text.

The goal of *Amoris Laetitia* is to be concrete and specific and thus avoid abstractions: when discussing malformed consciences, for example, it cites more than once a list of possible causes for the distortion of conscience rather than merely mentioning the possibility that malformation may exist. Emphasizing the starting point in conscience formation helps illuminate the path better than knowing only the endpoint. Together, *Veritatis Splendor* and *Amoris Laetitia* demonstrate the constant tension between the objective and subjective aspects of conscience and provide a fuller understanding of conscience than either document alone could offer. 🅼

Matthew P. Schneider, SThD, is a priest with the Legionaries of Christ and will be joining the faculty and formation team at Holy Apostles College and Seminary in Connecticut. He holds a Sacred Theology Doctorate in Moral Theology from the Pontifical Atheneum Regina Apostolorum in Rome. He has written widely, including *God Loves the Autistic Mind: Prayer Guide for Those on the Spectrum and Those Who Love Us* (Pauline, 2022), which won an award from the Association of Catholic Publishers.

Moral Law and Pastoral Praxis from *Veritatis Splendor* to the Magisterium of Francis

Gustavo Irrazábal

Abstract: Thirty years ago, Pope John Paul II's *Veritatis Splendor* confronted what it considered a moral crisis in which freedom, understood as autonomy without limits, led to the denial of the objective truth, especially the truth of revelation and natural law. Therefore, it strongly reaffirmed the relationship of faith to moral law and the doctrine of intrinsically evil acts, unlawful in all circumstances. The text rejected so-called "pastoral solutions," which postulated exceptions to moral absolutes by exaggerating the singularity of concrete situations. Pope Francis's magisterium addresses a different problem: the inherent complexity and fragility of the human condition in this world. For this reason, he is primarily concerned with the dangers of rigorism and legalism, as can be seen in the exhortation *Gaudete et Exsultate*. The declaration *Dignitas Infinita*, with its unconditional condemnation of acts that violate human dignity, may open a way for overcoming the tension between the teachings of the two pontiffs and contributing to a renewal of moral theology and pastoral praxis which avoids the danger of both rigorism and overburdening personal consciences for lack of clear normative references.

THIRTY YEARS AGO, THROUGH HIS ENCYCLICAL *VERITATIS Splendor*, John Paul II attempted to establish the limits of theological discussion and redirect the process of moral renewal promoted by the Second Vatican Council, especially by confirming the traditional doctrine on the existence of intrinsically evil acts, that is, acts considered illicit whatever the intention or circumstances.

This encyclical was passionately questioned by some and defended by others, deepening divisions among moral theologians. Only exhaustion and the multiplication of disciplinary measures succeeded in calming tensions, albeit in a more apparent than real way. Following the pontificates of John Paul II and Benedict XVI, moral revisionism emerged with bolder proposals, which reflected the ever growing cultural and moral pluralism of western societies. In this context, the direction given to the moral magisterium by Pope Francis, characterized by a more pastoral than doctrinal approach to moral issues, and his silence on *Veritatis Splendor* and the *intrinsece malum*, may give the impression that the latter are already part of the past.

In the present article, I argue that there is a profound tension between the two pontiffs in the moral field, evidenced in the fact that John Paul II rejects "pastoral solutions" while Francis resorts to them. This contrast shows that the question of how to reconcile doctrinal objectivity and pastoral prudence in the face of concrete situations has not yet been satisfactorily resolved. Consequently, confrontations have arisen between those who consider that the emphasis on the former entails a danger of rigorism and those who believe that insistence on the latter leads to disorder.

In the first two parts of my paper, I will compare some teachings of *Veritatis Splendor* with Francis's exhortation *Gaudete et Exsultate* to illustrate the main aspects of this conflict. In the last part, I intend to show that the declaration *Dignitas Infinita* constitutes an effort of the present pontificate to show continuity with the preceding official teaching regarding moral absolutes while seeking a new synthesis, more context-sensitive, based on the unique dignity of all human beings and their fundamental rights.

VERITATIS SPLENDOR: RESPONSE TO A MORAL CRISIS

Veritatis Splendor arose from a controversial diagnosis.[1] According to this encyclical, Catholic morality is threatened by "a genuine crisis" (no. 5), described as "a new situation . . . within the Christian community itself, which has experienced the spread of numerous doubts and objections of a human and psychological, social and cultural, religious and even properly theological nature, with regard to the Church's moral teachings" (no. 4). At its root, this is "a crisis of truth" (no. 32), which has resulted in a confusion between good and evil, caused by the influence of certain "currents of thought which end by detaching human freedom from its essential and constitutive relationship to truth" (no. 4).

---

[1] Questioning this diagnosis, Maura Anne Ryan observes: "I grant that there is a worrisome moral subjectivity in the air. . . . It is difficult, however, to find his description of the cultural crisis facing the church today persuasive. . . . For one thing, 'culture' is a far more complex phenomenon than this encyclical grants" ("'Then Who Can be Saved?' Ethics and Ecclesiology in Veritatis Splendor," in Veritatis Splendor: American Responses, ed. M. E. Allsopp and J. J. O'Keefe [Sheed & Ward, 1995], 11). For Servais Pinckaers, on the other hand, "c'est incontestablement la crise de la morale qui s'est développée dans l'Église et dans la société depuis un quart de siècle" ("It is unquestionably the crisis of morality that has developed in the Church and in society over the last quarter century"), *Pour une lecture de* Veritatis Splendor (Mame, 1995), 9.

In view of this increasingly relativistic mentality, the encyclical confirms the doctrine of intrinsically evil acts, that is, acts illicit *semper et pro semper*, whatever the intention that inspires them or the circumstances in which they are performed. In this regard, the correlation between eternal life, commandments and the beatitudes (chapter one), and Christian moral anthropology (chapter two) are seen respectively as the biblical and philosophical foundations of the existence of those negative precepts and constitute the rationale for the rejection of so-called "pastoral solutions" (chapter three).

The Commandments as "the Beginning of Freedom" (no. 13)

In his double response to the Rich Young Man's question about eternal life, Jesus connects the obedience to the commandments to the call to follow him (Matthew 19:16–21; *Veritatis Splendor*, nos. 19–21). *Veritatis Splendor* relies on this biblical text to formulate the delicate relationship between the natural order reflected in the commandments and the order of grace contained in the Sermon on the Mount.

According to St. Augustine, the commandments are "the *first necessary step on the journey towards freedom*, its starting point, the beginning of freedom" (no. 13). It is, nevertheless, in the Sermon on the Mount, the "*magna carta*" of Gospel morality, where Jesus shows that the commandments should not be understood just as a minimum limit not to be exceeded, but rather as a moral and spiritual journey towards perfection, at the heart of which is love (no. 15).

Considering the intimate and reciprocal link between the commandments and the Beatitudes, the document intends to go beyond the dialectics between law and freedom. Jesus's invitation to the young man ("come, follow me") reveals "the particular dynamic of freedom's growth towards maturity, and at the same time *they bear witness to the fundamental relationship between freedom and divine law.* Human freedom and God's law are not in opposition; on the contrary, they appeal one to the other" (no. 17).

Moral Law and Intrinsically Evil Acts

The second chapter lays out the anthropological and moral foundations of the commandments as negative precepts valid *semper et pro semper* (nos. 52, 82). Christian ethics is "teleological" in the sense that it conceives the moral goodness of an action as its conformity with the perfection of the person. This conformity is grasped by reason in the very being of each person, considered in their integral truth, and therefore in their natural inclinations, which always have a spiritual dimension as well. The ordered structure of "personal goods" apprehended by reason in light of the "good of the person" constitutes the universal and immutable contents of natural law (no. 79).

Prudence always has the task of verifying whether positive precepts are to be applied or not in a specific situation; however, negative precepts, which prohibit certain concrete actions as intrinsically evil, do not allow for any legitimate exception, because choosing them involves a disorder of the will, that is, a moral evil (*Catechism of the Catholic Church*, no. 1761). These acts, which contradict the good of the person made in God's image, are by their very nature "incapable of being ordered" to God on account of their very object, quite apart from the ulterior intentions and the circumstances (no. 79).

The So-Called "Pastoral Solutions"

John Paul II is aware that the uncompromising affirmation of absolute prohibitions can be objected to for its supposed rigidity, that is, for its inability to adapt to the complexity of human life. On the other hand, he recognizes that, as martyrdom attests, "maintaining a harmony between freedom and truth occasionally demands uncommon sacrifices and must be won at a high price" (no. 102).

However, the overcoming of temptation and sin and the fulfillment of the law of God are always possible with the help of divine grace and the collaboration of human freedom. It would be a grave error to think that the Gospel is nothing but an "ideal" to be adapted to "the so-called concrete possibilities" of the individual, because these possibilities are not those of persons dominated by concupiscence but of persons redeemed by Christ (no. 103). True mercy is the understanding for human weakness, but not the pretension of making this weakness the criterion of the truth about the good. The latter is precisely an expression of Pharisaism which seeks to eliminate awareness of one's own limits and sin. "In our own day this attitude is expressed particularly in the attempt to adapt the moral norm to one's own capacities and personal interests, and even in the rejection of the very idea of a norm" (no. 105).

The most direct practical consequence of this vision, although formulated earlier in the encyclical, can now be understood in all its significance, namely, the rejection of so-called "pastoral solutions:"

> In order to justify these positions (i.e., the "creative" understanding of conscience), some authors have proposed a kind of double status of moral truth. Beyond the doctrinal and abstract level, one would have to acknowledge the priority of a certain more concrete existential consideration. The latter, by taking account of circumstances and the

situation, could legitimately be the basis of certain *exceptions to the general rule* and thus permit one to do in practice and in good conscience what is qualified as intrinsically evil by the moral law. A separation, or even an opposition, is thus established in some cases between the teaching of the precept, which is valid in general, and the norm of the individual conscience, which would in fact make the final decision about what is good and what is evil. On this basis, an attempt is made to legitimize so-called "pastoral" solutions contrary to the teaching of the Magisterium, and to justify a "creative" hermeneutic according to which the moral conscience is in no way obliged, in every case, by a particular negative precept. (no. 56)

According to the encyclical, consistency between moral doctrine and pastoral praxis demands a rejection of "exceptions to the general rule," understood as attempts to justify the performance of intrinsically evil acts. The objective moral requirement in the concrete case is an application of universal norms, and pastoral action must be limited to accompanying people in their efforts to respond to this requirement. *Veritatis Splendor* does not consider the possibility that the interpretation of the general norm might need some revision in the light of the particular situation.

FRANCIS'S NEW APPROACH: *GAUDETE ET EXSULTATE*

Having briefly presented the contents of *Veritatis Splendor* relevant to our scope, the second part of this paper addresses the novelties Pope Francis brings to the process of moral renewal. To this end, the exhortation *Gaudete et Exsultate* constitutes a good starting point.[2] In fact, this document refers directly and indirectly to numerous fundamental themes of *Veritatis Splendor* (although, surprisingly, without quoting it even once), and does so with clearly different accents, reflecting a shift in the Catholic magisterium.

In addition, the second chapter, entitled "The Enemies of Holiness," which differs in its tone from the rest, is a remarkably harsh condemnation of "contemporary Gnosticism and Pelagianism" that reflect "a narcissistic and authoritarian elitism," distinctive of those who, instead of evangelizing, exhaust their energies in inspecting and verifying (no. 35). Considering these polemical labels (which should not be interpreted in a technical sense),[3] it is difficult to avoid the

---

[2] Pope Francis, *Gaudete et Exsultate* (2018), www.vatican.va/content/francesco/en/apost_exhortations/documents/papa-francesco_esortazione-ap_20180319_gaudete-et-exsultate.html.

[3] Congregation for the Doctrine of the Faith, Letter *Placuit Deo*, March 1, 2018, www.vatican.va/roman_curia/congregations/cfaith/documents/rc_con_cfaith_doc_2 0180222_placuit-deo_en.html. With reference to the deviations "to which the Holy

impression that they are mainly addressed to those who consider Francis's moral magisterium as conflicting with *Veritatis Splendor* and, especially, its teaching about intrinsically evil acts.[4]

Beatitudes and Commandments

Chapter three of *Gaudete et Exsultate* is mostly dedicated to the Beatitudes, the fundamental dispositions that characterize the believer's lifestyle and concretize his or her configuration with the Lord (no. 63). Compared to *Veritatis Splendor* (no. 16), much more attention is devoted in this exhortation to the Beatitudes, including a meditation on each of them (nos. 66–94). It is true that the former insists on the call to perfection, interpreted in the spirit of the Sermon on the Mount; but, at the same time, it stresses the importance of the commandments as "the first and indispensable condition for having eternal life" (no. 17). Perfection entails the dynamic of freedom's growth towards maturity in self-giving, which requires a fundamental relationship between freedom and divine law (no. 17), even though the Beatitudes, as basic attitudes, do not coincide exactly with the commandments (no. 16).

On the other hand, the concern for obedience to the commandments, central to *Veritatis Splendor,* is not explicitly present in *Gaudete et Exsultate*. While "obedience" is mentioned twenty-seven times in *Veritatis Splendor*, it appears just once in *Gaudete et Exsultate*, as "obedience to the Gospel" (no. 173), not specifically to God's law. This may be explained by considering that the problem faced by *Gaudete et Exsultate* is not a crisis of moral life caused by the relativization of the commandments, but their absolutization by rigorist sectors, who seek to apply them without considering the peculiarity of different situations, as well as the limits and difficulties of many believers.

In *Gaudete et Exsultate*, the centrality of the commandment of love is frequently pointed out (nos. 55; 92; 154) to warn about the dangers of legalism: the "obsession with the law" (no. 57), "the thicket of

---

Father Francis has often referred," that is, neo-Pelagianism and neo-Gnosticism, this letter points out that "the comparison with the Pelagian and Gnostic heresies refers only to general common features, without entering into judgments on the exact nature of the ancient errors," bearing in mind that the difference between the secularized historical context of today and that of the first Christian centuries, in which these heresies were born, is great, for which reason the text limits itself to pointing out "a certain familiarity" with some contemporary movements (no. 3).

[4] As one example among many: W. Brandmüller, R. Burke, C. Caffarra, and J. Meisner, "Seeking Clarity: A Plea to Untie the Knots in *Amoris Laetitia*," September 19, 2016, www.ncregister.com/news/four-cardinals-formally-ask-pope-for-clarity-on-amoris-laetitia, especially no. 2.

precepts and prescriptions," and the insufficiency of the "norms of the law" (nos. 49; 58; 59; 104; 134). The main task is to open for believers a breach in the middle of the dense "thicket" of norms that "weigh down and block" progress along the path to holiness (no. 62).

The obsession with the law can take "various shapes" (no. 62), which may sometimes lead to a selective and individualistic approach to Christian life. In chapter 3, dedicated to the Beatitudes, Francis identifies the tendency to focus exclusively on a few moral issues and ignore many others of no less importance, especially in social matters, as one of the "ideological errors" which distort the ethical meaning of the Gospel:

> The other harmful ideological error is found in those who find suspect the social engagement of others, seeing it as superficial, worldly, secular, materialist, communist, or populist. Or they relativize it, as if there are other more important matters, or the only thing that counts is one particular ethical issue or cause that they themselves defend. Our defense of the innocent unborn, for example, needs to be clear, firm and passionate, for at stake is the dignity of a human life, which is always sacred and demands love for each person, regardless of his or her stage of development. Equally sacred, however, are the lives of the poor, those already born, the destitute, the abandoned and the underprivileged, the vulnerable infirm and elderly exposed to covert euthanasia, the victims of human trafficking, new forms of slavery, and every form of rejection. (no. 101)

If the point of departure in *Veritatis Splendor* is the obedience to God's law, which stresses the dynamism toward the perfection of the Beatitudes, *Gaudete et Exsultate* regards the Beatitudes as the guide to a comprehensive understanding of moral requirements, in their individual and social aspects, in the light of charity. Each of these approaches entails its own potential risks. Excessive insistence on obedience to God's law may reduce grace to a mere aid to ethical effort. On the other hand, the lack of an explicit and positive encouragement to obey the commandments, together with the multiplication of warnings about the dangers of legalism, can downplay the importance of moral norms in providing ethical content to the Beatitudes.

Francis and Intrinsically Evil Acts

The reluctance of *Gaudete et Exsultate* to include an explicit statement on the significance of the commandments suggests an intention to revisit the centrality of the doctrine of intrinsically evil acts as proposed in *Veritatis Splendor*. In this regard, *Gaudete et Exsultate* must be interpreted in continuity with the eighth chapter of

Amoris Laetitia, which deals with "irregular" situations.[5] In fact, under the title "Norms and Discernment" it says: "It is reductive simply to consider whether or not an individual's actions correspond to a general law or rule, because that is not enough to discern and ensure full fidelity to God in the concrete life of a human being" (no. 304). Francis also resorts to a traditional argument: the formulation of general norms cannot cover absolutely all situations, so that the possibility of exceptions ("failures of the principle") should always be considered (no. 304).

For Francis, the main concern clearly shifts from the defense of the absolute character of the moral requirement to the problem of how to apply moral norms in different contexts. However, in order to adopt this more sensitive approach both to the complexity of particular situations and the pastoral demands of "accompanying, discerning, and integrating weaknesses," it is necessary to resist the temptation of rigid systematization. As *Gaudete et Exsultate*, no. 44, indicates:

> In effect, doctrine, or better, our understanding and expression of it, "is not a closed system, devoid of the dynamic capacity to pose questions, doubts, inquiries. . . . The questions of our people, their suffering, their struggles, their dreams, their trials, and their worries, all possess an interpretational value that we cannot ignore if we want to take the principle of the incarnation seriously. Their wondering helps us to wonder, their questions question us."

Ethics of Spiritual Discernment

The relative silence on the commandments, the multiplication of cautious references to norms in general and the rejection of what is considered a "closed system," alien to real life, undoubtedly imply a distance from the doctrine of intrinsically evil acts as set forth in *Veritatis Splendor*.

In John Paul II's encyclical, the idea of discernment is present, firstly, as the ability of the person to know the difference between good and evil expressed in moral law, empowered by faith (nos. 2, 42, 44). However, the discernment of the faithful must take place within the framework of the discernment reserved to the magisterium of the church (nos. 5, 27–28, 30, 34, 74, 85, 110, 115), responsible for distinguishing the positive and negative aspects of the prevailing culture and the compatibility of theological theories and currents with

---

[5] Pope Francis, *Amoris Laetitia* (2016), www.vatican.va/content/dam/francesco/pdf/apost_exhortations/documents/papa-francesco_esortazione-ap_20160319_amoris-laetitia_en.pdf.

revelation, relying on the assistance of specialists in its task of guiding the faithful (nos. 112–113).

This restricted vision of discernment is based on the concept of conscience the encyclical recalls: "The application of the law to each particular case, which thus becomes for man an interior *dictum*, a call to do good in a concrete situation" (no. 59). The dignity of this rational instance and the authority of its voice and judgments derive from the truth about moral good and evil indicated by divine law, the universal and objective norm of morality (no. 60). The encyclical thus rejects what it calls the "creative" interpretation of moral conscience, which disregards the binding character of the moral law and relegates it to the role of a "*general perspective*" that guides the person in making their own "*decisions*" (i.e., no longer *applicative* judgments) in the face of the alleged unrepeatability of particular situations the general norm could never foresee (no. 55).

The contrast with *Gaudete et Exsultate* is clear, beginning with the fact that *Gaudete et Exsultate* devotes an entire chapter to the topic of discernment (chapter five). It introduces a broader concept, the habit of *spiritual* discernment, a notion of Pauline origin (Rom 12:1–3), modernly developed by the Jesuit tradition, to which all believers are called, in order to recognize the ways of the Spirit of God, whose logic contrasts with the spirit of this world (nos. 23, 62, 105, 150, 166–170, 172–175).[6] The mature Christian allows himself to be led by the Spirit of God (Gal 5:21).

As Francis states, discernment requires "obedience to the Gospel as the ultimate standard, but also to the Magisterium that guards it" (no. 173). Even so:

> It is not a matter of applying rules or repeating what was done in the past, since the same solutions are not valid in all circumstances and what was useful in one context may not prove so in another. The discernment of spirits liberates us from rigidity, which has no place before the perennial "today" of the risen Lord. The Spirit alone can penetrate what is obscure and hidden in every situation, and grasp its every nuance, so that the newness of the Gospel can emerge in another light (no. 173).

In this way, spiritual discernment opens a greater space of freedom for consideration, in light of the Spirit, of the complexity of concrete situations.

---

[6] On the implications of this method for the Synod on Synodality and Christian life, see Vimal Tirimanna, "Listening to the Voice of the Holy Spirit. The Current Synodal Process and a Few Implications for Moral Theology," *Studia Moralia* 61, no. 2 (2023): 249–278.

The tension between the rejection of "creative" conscience in *Veritatis Splendor* and the remarkable flexibility of spiritual discernment of particular situations proposed in *Gaudete et Exsultate* leads us, once more, to the problem of how to mediate between general principles and their practical application.

DISTINCTION BETWEEN DOCTRINE AND PASTORAL CARE AND THEIR RESPECTIVE DEMANDS

The new emphases of Francis's magisterium significantly alter the way of approaching so-called "pastoral solutions," shifting from the suspicion of *Veritatis Splendor*, no. 56, to the re-entry of such practices through the wide door of the Pauline doctrine of spiritual discernment. How to avoid the danger of the "double status of moral truth" about which John Paul II's encyclical warned?

For *Veritatis Splendor*, the only way to prevent the separation between the doctrinal and pastoral level is to conceive of the latter as the deductive application of the former. Once the moral requirement for the concrete case has been determined, pastoral care seeks to attenuate the impact of its rigor in the personal life of believers through practices of pastoral benignity. But mercy towards the person must be accompanied by intransigence towards evil (no. 95). The understanding of human weakness "never means compromising and falsifying the standard of good and evil in order to adapt it to particular circumstances" (no. 104).

Francis, on the other hand, invokes mercy to devote an attention to particular situations unprecedented in pontifical teaching, seeking to affirm *simultaneously* the validity of the general doctrine and the irreducible importance of each case, without giving priority to one or the other or providing any general formula to reconcile these two premises other than the case by case solution and the importance of the "small step" in the face of one's human limits (*Evangelii Gaudium*, nos. 3, 44).

However, while recognizing the hermeneutical role of mercy for decision in the concrete case, Francis's insistence on "shielding" doctrine from any possibility of revision introduces a degree of tension in various topics that threatens to disarticulate theory and practice, with negative consequences for the consistency and doctrinal authority of the magisterium.

Many examples could be cited in which Francis's magisterium introduces a strong tension between the current doctrine and the proposed pastoral approach. One of the most polemical is, undoubtedly, the one developed in the eighth chapter of *Amoris Laetitia*. In this chapter, the pope begins by confirming the church's traditional teaching on marriage (no. 292). However, he then tries to reconcile this doctrine with "the logic of integration" (no. 299) key to his pastoral view and which he considers the only possible alternative to the logic of marginalization ("casting off," no. 296).

To achieve this end, the text resorts to two different strategies. The first, as mentioned above, consists in recognizing the possibility of exceptions to the general rules due to their indeterminacy (no. 304; ST I-II, q. 94, a. 4), an argument used recurrently in the past against the doctrine of intrinsically bad acts. This could mean that there may be "irregular" situations that contradict the general formulation of the rule but, because of "particular circumstances," are not really subsumed into it and, therefore, always in an analogical sense, can be considered exceptions.

Amoris Laetitia, however, does not further explore this path, which could lead to doctrinal debates (for example, the correct interpretation of the indissolubility of marriage). It strives, instead, to clarify that "personal and pastoral discernment" can never dispense with the demands of truth and charity of the Gospel proposed by the church, since "in the law itself there is no gradualness" (no. 300).

Having closed for itself the doctrinal path suggested in the first term, this document leans towards the consideration of "extenuating circumstances" of responsibility, such as eventual ignorance of the norm or difficulty "in understanding its inherent values" (*Amoris Laetitia*, no. 301; *Familiaris Consortio*, no. 33), or even the fact that the person is "in a concrete situation which does not allow him or her to act differently and decide otherwise without further sin" (*Amoris Laetitia*, no. 301).[7] Due to these conditioning and mitigating factors, "it is possible that in an objective situation of sin—which may not be subjectively culpable, or fully such—a person can be living in God's grace, can love, and can also grow in the life of grace and charity, while receiving the Church's help to this end" (*Amoris Laetitia*, no. 305). The latter, "in certain cases, could also be the help of the sacraments" (n351). It seems that the argument of "extenuating circumstances" is considered more conducive to the purpose of widening the room of freedom for discernment.

In any case, the document fails in its attempt to avoid questioning the doctrine while offering, at the same time, a "pastoral solution" to the problem of the communion of people in "irregular" situations. According to this text, pastoral mercy, in contrast to *Veritatis Splendor*, no. 56, would make it possible to admit decisions that, while contrasting with the general norm, are *correct* (for the particular case), *or* objectively *incorrect* but subjectively conditioned. In any case, it does not foresee the possibility of mercy fulfilling any function in the

---

[7] It is not clear, in the latter case (impossibility to act otherwise), in what sense it is still possible to speak of "guilt" and "objective situation of sin."

doctrinal field, so that the danger of separation from pastoral praxis remains.[8]

FROM INTRINSIC MORALITY OF ACTS TO INTRINSIC HUMAN DIGNITY

An important novelty for overcoming the tensions mentioned above and highlighting the basic continuity between the magisterium of John Paul II and that of Francis may be found in the Declaration *Dignitas Infinita*.[9] In analyzing this declaration, it is useful to keep in mind some recent events, such as the *Synodale Weg* (2021–2024) in the German Church, the new set of *dubia* presented to the pope in 2023 regarding the blessing of same-sex couples,[10] and the publication of *Fiducia Supplicans*, which allowed "pastoral blessings" under strict conditions, and has encountered opposition from many local churches.[11] Comparing the present historical context with that of the *Syllabus of Errors* of Pius IX (1864), Bernard Brady observes: "Today the church feels itself under siege not by armies or angry crowds storming the Vatican palace, but rather by ideas about sex, sexuality, and gender—both from the wider social context and from Catholics themselves. Addressing these issues appears to be the genesis of the document."[12]

---

[8] Some ethicists believe that the anthropological and methodological developments of *Amoris Laetitia* (for example, its inductive method, appreciation for historical consciousness, culture, social conditions, etc.) may lay "the foundation for an organic development of doctrine that can effect doctrinal change" (Todd Salzmann and Michael Lawler, "*Amoris Laetitia*: Towards a Methodological and Anthropological Integration of Catholic Social and Sexual Ethics," *Theological Studies* 79, no. 3 [2018]: 634–652, 651, doi.org/10.1177/0040563918784772). For the reasons mentioned above, the pope seems to have ruled out this path.
[9] Dicastery for the Doctrine of the Faith, Declaration *Dignitas Infinita*, August 4, 2024, press.vatican.va/content/salastampa/en/bollettino/pubblico/2024/04/08/240408c.html.
[10] "Dubia" of two Cardinals (July 10, 2023) and "Responses" of the Holy Father (July 11, 2023), www.vatican.va/roman_curia/congregations/cfaith/documents/rc_con_cfaith_risposta-dubia-2023.pdf.
The full text of the responses was released by the Vatican on October 2, 2023. See also footnote no. 20.
[11] Dicastery for the Doctrine of the Faith, Declaration *Fiducia Supplicans*: On the Pastoral Meaning of Blessings, December 18, 2023, www.vatican.va/roman_curia/congregations/cfaith/documents/rc_ddf_doc_20231218_fiducia-supplicans_en.html. The negative reactions to this text were followed by a "Press Release Concerning the Reception of *Fiducia supplicans*," January 4, 2024, www.vatican.va/roman_curia/congregations/cfaith/documents/rc_ddf_doc_20240104_comunicato-fiducia-supplicans_en.html, and a clarification by Pope Francis in his address to the Plenary Session of this Dicastery, on January 26, 2024, www.vatican.va/content/francesco/en/speeches/2024/january/documents/20240126-plenaria-ddf.html.
[12] Bernard V. Brady, "*Dignitas Infinita*. A Syllabus of Errors for the 21st Century?," *Journal of Moral Theology* 13, no. 2 (2024): 7.

The unresolved debate on the doctrine of intrinsically evil acts, frequently restricted to personal ethics in spite of the social sins mentioned in *Gaudium et Spes*, no. 27, and *Veritatis Splendor*, no. 80, lurks beneath all these problems. In fact, it was only thanks to Francis's personal intervention that the initial drafts of *Dignitas Infinita*, which focused on sex and gender issues, were followed by others applying the foundational concept of human dignity to broader contemporary social issues. The need to revisit the doctrine of intrinsically evil acts, its meaning and extension, may account for the special importance the pope ascribed to the document. This importance is perceptible in the document's lengthy drafting process[13] and the degree of the pope's direct involvement.

For example, as the preface of the declaration indicates, *Dignitas Infinita* develops the anthropological foundations of human dignity in the first three sections and seeks to clarify its true meaning. It begins with a historical approach and describes the "gradual awareness" of the unique dignity of each human being in classical antiquity (no. 10), the Bible (nos. 11–12), Christian thought, and the present era (nos. 14–16). The second section presents the proclamation of the church, expressed in a "threefold conviction:" the dignity of every human being comes from their creation in the image of God (no. 18), their elevation through the Mystery of the Incarnation of Christ (no. 19), and His Resurrection, which reveals our ultimate destiny (nos. 20–21). The third section explores how this dignity becomes the objective basis for human freedom, with its rights and duties (no. 25) in relation to others (no. 26) and the "creaturely goodness of the rest of the cosmos" (no. 28), although freedom needs to be liberated from "negative influences in the moral and social spheres," such as moral relativism or social injustice, which may compromise its exercise (nos. 29–32). Finally, the fourth section indicates some current situations in which this dignity is not sufficiently recognized.

Overall, on the one hand, *Dignitas Infinita* intends to reaffirm the doctrine of moral absolutes stated in *Veritatis Splendor*. This explains why the declaration goes to great lengths to highlight its continuity with the magisterium of John Paul II. His name appears nineteen times

---

[13] An initial draft of the text was prepared in 2019 but rejected and replaced by another one elaborated *ex novo* and presented on October 4, 2021. The latter, in an amended version, was approved in November 2023. Afterwards, at the pope's request, "a new and significantly modified version" followed and was finally approved in February 2024. According to the prefect, Víctor Fernández, "the five-year course of the text's preparation helps us to understand that the document before us reflects the gravity and centrality of the theme of dignity in Christian thought. The text required a considerable process of maturation to arrive at the final version that we have published today." This long preparation stands in stark contrast to the hasty drafting process of *Fiducia Supplicans*.

throughout the text. The "infinite" character of human dignity is taken from an informal remark of that pope during an apostolic visit to Germany, although it undoubtedly constitutes a hyperbole and must be understood in a relative sense.[14] The declaration also stresses the coincidence between Francis and his predecessor regarding the importance of the *Universal Declaration of Human Rights* and its foundation in human dignity (nos. 23, 64). Moreover, it is no coincidence that the declaration was presented on April 2, 2024, on the nineteenth anniversary of St. John Paul II's death. This insistence is relevant to understand Pope Francis's intentions.

On the other hand, *Dignitas Infinita* introduces an important epistemological and methodological development of the notion of human dignity as the anthropological foundation of Catholic moral teaching. The document begins by saying: "An infinite dignity, which is inalienably grounded in his own being, belongs to every human person, beyond all circumstances and in whatever state or situation he may find himself" (no. 1). The ontological dignity of the human person, accessible to reason and confirmed by revelation, is the foundation of the church's commitment to the weakest and her insistence "on the primacy of the human person and the defense of his dignity beyond all circumstances" (no. 1).

The idea of the ontological dignity of every human being, which "is indelible and remains valid beyond any circumstances" (no. 7), is repeated insistently throughout the document. The expression "beyond all circumstances" and its equivalents are repeated sixteen times; the dignity of the person "regardless," or "independent of," any other consideration appears fourteen times. Whereas the adjective "intrinsic" in *Veritatis Splendor always* relates to acts, it is *exclusively* referred to human dignity in *Dignitas Infinita*.

This shift may seem irrelevant at first glance since John Paul II resorts to analogous terms to render the idea of the unconditionality of human dignity (*Veritatis Splendor*, nos. 90, 92, 97), and both popes believe that the exceptionless evil nature of certain acts is determined

---

[14] Pope John Paul II, "Angelus with the Disabled in the Cathedral Church of Osnabrück," November 16, 1980, www.vatican.va/content/john-paul-ii/it/angelus/1980/documents/hf_jp-ii_ang_19801116.html. Francis had already quoted these words in *Evangelii Gaudium*, no. 178. According to Edward Feser, "John Paul II's remark was merely a passing comment made in the course of a little-known informal address of little magisterial weight that was devoted to another topic. It was not a carefully worded formal theological treatment of the nature of human dignity, specifically" ("Two Problems with *Dignitas Infinita*," April 11, 2024), edwardfeser.blogspot.com/2024/04/two-problems-with-dignitas-infinita.html. In any case, the incomparable and unique dignity of the human person has been one of the central themes of the magisterium of John Paul II from its inception in *Redemptor Hominis*.

by their incompatibility with that dignity. Nevertheless, the fact that *Dignitas Infinita* aims to provide a list of acts that must be considered illicit regardless of the circumstances while carefully avoiding any reference to the traditional expression "intrinsically evil acts" which pervades previous moral teachings and doctrinal debates should not be overlooked. There are reasons to think that the declaration, by systematically reserving the term "intrinsic" to the human person and its dignity, hints at the intention to reconsider some aspects of these notions and their relevance for the foundation of ethical norms. As a result, as we shall see in what follows, the existence of evil acts without exceptions is confirmed but, at the same time, more clearly framed within an enriched doctrine of human dignity, which must be respected without exception. This probably represents the long overdue response to a widespread concern about Francis's magisterium.[15]

HUMAN DIGNITY AS A FOURFOLD CONCEPT

The concept of human dignity, despite its basic continuity with the previous magisterium, is deepened and enhanced in this declaration. In fact, it conceives human dignity as a multilayered concept. In the first place, the human person, created in the image and likeness of God and endowed with a "rational" nature (which includes the capacity to understand and love, and the corporeal functions closely related to it) has, as stated above, an *ontological* dignity (nos. 9, 11–13). But human dignity also includes other dimensions: *moral* dignity, referred to "how people exercise their freedom" before the demands of the law of love (no. 7); *social* dignity, that is, "the quality of the person's living conditions," impacted by social structures (no. 8), and *existential* dignity, "implied in the ever-increasing discussion about a 'dignified' life and one that is 'not dignified'" (no. 8). In one sense, human dignity is equal in all human beings and cannot be lost (ontological dignity); in other senses, it could be deeply compromised, either by one's own actions (moral dignity), by the doings of others or unfortunate circumstances (social and existential dignity).[16] As Todd Salzmann states: "The epistemological and methodological interrelationship between ontological dignity and the three other dignities, moral,

---

[15] According to Marciano Vidal, one of the purposes of this systematization of Francis's teaching was dispelling "doubts" and "misinterpretations": "A look at *Dignitas Infinita* from Moral Theology," *Vida Nueva Digital*, April 12, 2024, www.vidanuevadigital.com/tribuna/una-mirada-a-dignidad-infinita-desde-la-*teologia*-moral-marciano-vidal/. *Dignitas Infinita* may be considered a positive and constructive response to those difficulties after the harsh reaction to *Gaudete et Exsultate*, chapter 2.
[16] In the evaluation of this complex notion of human dignity, I don't fully agree with the idea that human dignity should be unconditional in an unqualified sense, as proposed by Brady, "*Dignitas Infinita.*"

social, and existential (MSE), are central in defining human dignity and the doctrines derived from that definition."[17]

Veritatis Splendor also grounds its teaching on intrinsically evil acts in human dignity (nos. 41, 80, 100), and "fundamental human rights" (nos. 27, 98). However, in this encyclical, human dignity and rights are bound to a particular interpretation of natural law, which has been much debated. As mentioned above, according to *Veritatis Splendor*, absolute norms derived from human nature and considered as already known must be applied in a deductive way regardless of the particular circumstances, significantly restricting the room for personal discernment.[18]

Even *within* the Thomist tradition of natural law, a more nuanced approach is possible. As Eberhard Schockenhoff states, there are gradations of practical reason with their increasing latitude and diminishing degree of certainty. Following this "law of diminishing certainty," natural law should no longer be understood as a fixed system of individual normative affirmations, but rather "a system of supreme coordinates which is articulated into a concrete ethos by the practical reason, bearing in mind the historical and contingent existential situations of the human person."[19] This does not imply that the existence of intrinsically evil acts should be excluded: "A mode of conduct must always be considered as intrinsically evil and incompatible with the personal dignity of another human being, when it attacks the irreducible minimum conditions for his human existence, which must

---

[17] Todd A. Salzmann and Michael G. Lawler, "*Dignitas Infinita*. Anthropologically and Methodologically Consistent?," *Marriage, Families, and Spirituality* 30, no. 1 (2024): 143–153.

[18] For a critique of John Paul II's "Thomistic personalism," seen as a continuation of the deductivism of traditional moral teaching, which does not take sufficient account of human experience, history, and science, see Todd A. Salzmann and Michael G. Lawler, *The Sexual Person: Toward a Renewed Catholic Anthropology* (Georgetown University Press, 2008), 88–92; Salzmann and Lawler, "*Amoris Laetitia*," 641–644. In defense of John Paul II's phenomenological conception of natural law, as skillfully integrating human subjectivity, personal experience, and freedom, see Janet E. Smith, "Natural Law and Personalism in *Veritatis Splendor*," in Veritatis Splendor*: American Responses*, 194–207.

[19] Eberhard Schockenhoff, *Natural Law and Human Dignity: Universal Ethics in an Historical World* (The Catholic University of America Press, 2003), 170. Commenting approvingly on Schockenhoff's thesis, James Keenan remarks that "this more modest assertion of our understanding of nature in an historical context is shared today by most theological ethicists." According to this view, nature is "a complex and unfolding system whose finality, development, and ways of interacting are grasped only partially—though not arbitrarily—by human insight" (*A History of Catholic Moral Theology in the Twentieth Century: From Confessing Sins to Liberating Consciences* [Continuum, 2010], 174–175).

be protected in order to give him the possibility of free ethical self-determination."[20]

As we have already indicated regarding *Amoris Laetitia*, Francis clearly recognizes the relevance of contingency in the application of general moral principles (nos. 300–305). This recognition, according to the same text, stresses the importance of practical discernment, which cannot be reduced to the consideration of the correspondence of an individual's actions to a general rule (no. 304). In this regard, *Amoris Laetitia*, no. 305, quotes a document of the International Theological Commission, which states: "Natural law could not be presented as an already established set of rules that impose themselves *a priori* on the moral subject; rather, it is a source of objective inspiration for the deeply personal process of making decisions."[21] In comparison with *Veritatis Splendor*, therefore, we may say that in *Amoris Laetitia* a broader conception of the interpretative role of practical reason is at work. In *Dignitas Infinita*, the expansion of the concept of human dignity allows *in principle* for this more inductive process of normative interpretation, although, as we shall see below, it is not always consistently applied in this same document.

Moreover, our comprehension of human nature is never complete. *Dignitas Infinita* stresses "the growing awareness of the centrality of human dignity" throughout history and the progressive development by the church's magisterium of "an ever-greater understanding of the meaning of human dignity, along with its demands and consequences" (no. 16). This suggests a deepening of historical consciousness, the recognition that moral doctrine and its application to contemporary ethical issues are subject to evolution.[22] For these reasons, even when in *Dignitas Infinita* the concept of "ontological" dignity occupies a central place, we should not presuppose that its content and implications are simply identical to those of "human nature" as used in *Veritatis Splendor*. The analysis of concrete examples may clarify the interplay of continuity and discontinuity between both magisterial documents.

VIOLATIONS OF HUMAN DIGNITY

The fourth section of *Dignitas Infinita* presents a non-comprehensive set of topics related to the different facets of human dignity that might

---

[20] Schockenhoff, *Natural Law*, 201–202.
[21] International Theological Commission, *In Search of a Universal Ethic: A New Look at Natural Law* (2009), no. 59, www.vatican.va/roman_curia/congregations/cfaith/cti_documents/rc_con_cfaith_do c_20090520_legge-naturale_en.html.
[22] See Salzman and Lawler, "*Dignitas Infinita*," 145.

be obscured in many people's consciousness. The declaration comes closer to John Paul's mindset as regards the "sexual difference," considered as "foundational" for human's dignity and identity (nos. 58–59). In other respects, however, it mainly relies on the broader notion of human dignity we have mentioned above.[23] The metaphysical core of the latter is spelled out in the universal language of human rights and duties,[24] apt to overcome the rigidities of the traditional doctrine of intrinsic evil acts without endorsing a purely teleological method exclusively concerned with consequences and evaluation of goods.[25]

Based on this approach, the declaration descends from general statements to concrete conduct, denouncing "some grave violations of human dignity" (nos. 33–62). Although the list of such "violations" is heterogeneous, most of them refer to concrete acts, considered unlawful without exception, and not simply *"ut in pluribus,"* by application of the same principle, i.e., human dignity. As regards the list of condemnations, many of them are non-controversial: the travail of migrants (no. 40), human trafficking (no. 41), sexual abuse (no. 43), violence against women (no. 44), marginalization of people with disabilities (no. 53), and digital violence (no. 61). Others show a traditional bent. Some of them reaffirm the official teaching on bioethics: abortion (no. 47), euthanasia, assisted suicide (no. 51) and surrogacy, which contradicts "the dignity of the conjugal union and of human procreation" (no. 49).

The criticism of "gender theory" (no. 55) and the rejection of sex change (no. 60), based on the link between personal dignity and the dignity of the body (nos. 18–19) and its biological sex (no. 59), seems aimed at dispelling doubts about the pope's orthodoxy in these matters. The treatment of these topics constitutes an isolated instance of a deductive conception of natural law, inconsistent with the multidimensional human dignity described in the same declaration and Francis's more nuanced approach to other sexual issues (as will be shown below regarding contraception and "irregular" situations).

---

[23] This ambiguity between the natural, prevalent in sexual matters, and the personal, better integrated in social matters, raises concerns about the methodological coherence of this document (Salzmann and Lawler, *"Dignitas Infinita,"* 145–153).

[24] *Dignitas Infinita* mentions "right/rights" sixty-eight times, considering them to be an expression of the primacy and ontological dignity of the person, as shown authoritatively by the *Universal Declaration of Human Rights*, which mentions "dignity" five times, in strategic places: in the *Preamble* and *Article One* (*Dignitas Infinita*, no. 3). In Francis's view, this declaration has therefore programmatic importance: it is "a master plan, from which many steps have been taken, but many still need to be made" (no. 63).

[25] Schockenhoff, *Natural Law*, 202.

On the other hand, there are some hints of development. "The drama of poverty" (no. 36) is ranked in the first place, probably to indicate that absolute prohibitions, when understood as violations of human rights, are not restricted to the realm of personal ethics, but must be extended to personal responsibility regarding social issues.[26] The condemnation of "all wars" as violations of human dignity (no. 38) seems to be more restrictive than the precedent teaching regarding the traditional doctrine of "just war."[27] The text also mentions one of the most striking developments in moral doctrine of this pontificate: the teaching on death penalty.

DIGNITAS INFINITA AND DEATH PENALTY

With the reform of the *Catechism*, no. 2267, the death penalty has been arguably incorporated to the list of evil *in se* acts, as "inadmissible" without exception, being "an attack on the inviolability and dignity of the person."[28] Cardinal Ladaria's "Letter to the Bishops," which accompanies the rescript, invokes a change of historical circumstances to justify the pope's decision, namely, the more efficient detention systems possessed by the modern state, which make death penalty unnecessary as protection for the life of innocent people (nos. 2, 7).[29] The decisive factor is, nevertheless, "the clearer

---

[26] According to the presentation of Cardinal Fernández, the pope himself asked, when approving the second corrected version, "that the document highlight topics closely connected to the theme of dignity, such as poverty, the situation of migrants, violence against women, human trafficking, war, and other themes." Brady correctly points out the significance of this admission ("*Dignitas Infinita*," 7).

[27] The text quotes *Fratelli Tutti*, no. 258: "It is very difficult nowadays to invoke the rational criteria elaborated in earlier centuries to speak of the possibility of a 'just war.'" In the same paragraph, this encyclical, although recognizing the right to legitimate defense, rejects its extension to preventive war, still admitted in the *Compendium* albeit under strict conditions (no. 502).

[28] In opposition to this view, attributing this evolution mainly to a change in historical conditions, see Barrett Turner, "Pope Francis and the Death Penalty: A Conditional Advance of Justice in the Law of Nations," *Nova et Vetera* 16, no. 4 (2018): 1041–1050. According to Edward Feser, *Dignitas Infinita* confirms Francis's position that no circumstances can ever justify capital punishment ("Two Problems with *Dignitas Infinita*"), but it contradicts what has in fact been taught infallibly by Scripture and the Tradition of the church. See also Edward Feser and Joseph Bessette, *By Man Shall His Blood Be Shed: A Catholic Defense of Capital Punishment* (Ignatius, 2017). E. Christian Brugger, on the other hand, considers that the death penalty is intrinsically evil as an instance of intentional killing and admits the possibility of changes in the magisterium on this subject as a case of valid development of "non-irreformable moral doctrines" (*Capital Punishment and the Roman Catholic Moral Tradition*, 2nd ed. [University of Notre Dame Press, 2014], 158–163).

[29] Congregation for the Doctrine of the Faith, "Letter to the Bishops Regarding the New Revision of Number 2267 of the *Catechism of the Catholic Church* on the Death Penalty," press.vatican.va/content/salastampa/en/bollettino/pubblico/2018/08/02/180802b.html.

awareness of the Church for the respect due to every human life" (no. 1), as well as "the increasing understanding that the dignity of a person is not lost even after committing the most serious crimes" and "the deepened understanding of the significance of penal sanctions applied by the State" (no. 2), that is, rehabilitation and social reintegration of the criminal (no. 7), both unattainable by capital punishment. Death penalty, regardless of the means of execution, entails a "cruel, inhumane, and degrading treatment" (no. 6).[30]

The papal address quoted in the last paragraph further elaborates on the lack of *humanitas* necessarily implied in this kind of punishment, reminding of "the prior anguish to the moment of execution and the terrible waiting between the dictating of the sentence and the application of the punishment, which usually lasts many years, and, in the waiting-room of death, not rarely leads to sickness and madness." Then he adds: "In the course of history, different mechanisms of death have been defended to reduce the suffering and agony of the condemned. However, there is no humane way of killing another person." Finally, the "Letter to the Bishops" includes the pope's reference to "the defective selectivity of the criminal justice system" and the possibility of judicial error (no. 6).

Dignitas Infinita confirms this new doctrine on death penalty with its unqualified rejection ("regardless of the circumstances"), because "if I do not deny that dignity to the worst of criminals, I will not deny it to anyone" (no. 34; *Fratelli Tutti*, no. 269). Even admitting that John Paul II had pushed his reservations about capital punishment to the very limit of its absolute prohibition, it is difficult to deny that Francis's arguments quoted above, absent in the previous magisterium on the subject, contributed to this final step. As Salzmann and Lawler state: "Methodologically, the ongoing dialogue between, and integration of, ontological and MSE (i.e., moral, social, and existential) dignities have promoted a nuanced understanding of ontological dignity and promoted an organic development of doctrinal teaching on death penalty."[31]

The case of death penalty illustrates the possibilities of the declaration's methodological approach. In general terms, the list of fundamental and always-inadmissible violations against human dignity offered by *Dignitas Infinita* coincides with John Paul's absolute norms. As we said before, one of the main intentions of the declaration is precisely to stress this continuity. Nevertheless, the traditional catalog of evil *in se* acts might be confirmed, rectified, or

---

[30] Francis, "Letter to the President of the International Commission Against the Death Penalty," *L'Osservatore Romano*, March 20–21, 2015, 7, www.vatican.va/content/francesco/en/letters/2015/documents/papa-francesco_20150320_lettera-pena-morte.html.
[31] Salzmann and Lawler, *"Dignitas Infinita,"* 147–149.

qualified according to the notion of human dignity as stated in this document. According to Bernard Brady, "Applying social dignity and existential dignity, particularly in its social form, would have offered a more constructive and developed interpretation of moral issues."[32] Nothing prevents this development from taking place in the future.

DIGNITAS INFINITA AND "PASTORAL SOLUTIONS"

The possibility of development is not restricted to doctrine. *Dignitas Infinita* should not be interpreted as Francis's renunciation of the originality of his pastoral approach, which seeks to open new paths for the faithful whose lives are in tension with official teaching, paying attention to particular and complex situations, and encouraging spiritual discernment to overcome the strictures of legalism. In light of *Dignitas Infinita*, this practical discernment must take into account not only ontological human dignity, or a generic notion of the "goods of the person," but also the concrete social and existential dimensions of that dignity, allowing for a deeper sensitivity to context and avoiding at the same time the risk of postulating "a double status of moral truth" (*Veritatis Splendor*, no. 56) or a "double standard" (*Amoris Laetitia*, no. 300).

As explained earlier, one of the most important "pastoral solution(s)" of his pontificate admits the possibility of an access to the sacraments for couples in "irregular" situations (*Amoris Laetitia*, no. 305), even for those who have decided not to live "as brothers and sisters" (decision which could "endanger faithfulness," n. 329). This solution raises concerns about its consistency with previous moral doctrine as stated in *Familiaris Consortio*, no. 84 and *Veritatis Splendor*, no. 22. According to Francis, "It is true that general rules set forth a good which can never be disregarded or neglected, but in their formulation, they cannot provide absolutely for all particular situations," which demand instead practical discernment, whose judgments, however, "cannot be elevated to the level of a rule" (*Amoris Laetitia*, no. 304).

For the same reason, the multi-dimensional notion of human dignity allows a more contextual and nuanced approach to contraception, taking into account social and existential circumstances considered merely accidental in the traditional Catholic teaching. In the moral magisterium of John Paul II, *Humanae Vitae* occupied a central place, as can be seen in his "Theology of the Body," where the incompatibility of "any act" of contraception (*Humanae Vitae*, no. 14) with the structure and meanings of the conjugal act, natural law, and

---

[32] Brady, "*Dignitas Infinita*," 14.

moral order established by God and the dignity of the person are pointed out insistently. Francis, on the other hand, does not characterize contraception in those terms, nor mention its intrinsically evil nature, although he adheres to *Humanae Vitae* in an explicit albeit general way, reaffirming "the intrinsic bond between conjugal love and the generation of life" (*Amoris Laetitia*, no. 68). His criticisms are aimed not against discrete acts but rather at "a mentality against having children and promoted by the world politics of reproductive health" (nos. 42, 82, 222).

Therefore, as is the case with capital punishment or irregular situations, further evolution in this matter is not unthinkable. For instance, in environments of social vulnerability, where promiscuity and sexual violence are frequent, the recourse to contraception might be, for women whose needs and wishes are ignored, an act of sexual responsibility rather than a violation of their own dignity. In the same way, the interpretation of official teaching in the context of the fight against sexually transmitted diseases could be revisited.[33]

Moving forward along this path, Francis's magisterium could achieve a more coherent moral vision, which reconciles the recognition of a wider room for discernment of the relevant aspects of each context and situation with a clearer indication of the limits that must not be transgressed under any circumstances.

CONCLUSION

When comparing the magisterium of Francis with that of John Paul II in *Veritatis Splendor*, it is evident that they confront two different concerns. The latter faces the moral crisis provoked by the relativization of the commandments, which makes it necessary to reaffirm the existence of intrinsically evil acts. For Francis, on the other hand, the main challenge lies in the absolutization of the commandments and the danger of applying them without considering the specificity of the different situations together with the limits and difficulties of those who face them.

The unresolved tension between both approaches has reignited, almost from the very beginning of the current papacy, the controversy over the doctrine of moral absolutes. So far, the pope has decided not to address it directly, perhaps with the aim of avoiding endless

---

[33] For an antecedent, see Jacques Suaudeau, "Prophylactics or Family Values? Stopping the Spread of HIV/AIDS," *L'Osservatore Romano*, weekly edition, April 19, 2000; Jon D. Fuller and James F. Keenan, "Tolerant Signals: The Vatican's New Insights on Condoms for H.I.V. Prevention," *America*, September 23, 2000, www.americamagazine.org/issue/381/article/tolerant-signals. Monsignor Jacques Suaudeau was at that time a member of the Pontifical Council for the Family.

conflicts which could become an obstacle for a more attentive pastoral care devoted to "accompanying, discerning, and integrating frailty" (*Amoris Laetitia*, no. 291).

Veritatis Splendor, an encyclical in many ways admirable, sought to restore a reasonable level of certainty and clarity for the Christian moral life, but at the risk of falling into a certain methodological rigidity and unduly narrowing the scope of personal discernment. *Gaudete et Exsultate* compensates for this difficulty by recognizing the exercise of spiritual discernment as an essential part of the Christian life and its call to holiness; yet it may underestimate the need for every Christian to be guided not only by inspiring exhortations, but also by clear and reliable criteria.

However, these contrasts do not preclude the *possibility* of a complementarity of perspectives in the face of the opposing dangers of rigorism and relativism. *Veritatis Splendor* does not simply identify holiness with obedience to the commandments; it is centered on the call of Jesus Christ to perfection. For its part, *Gaudete et Exsultate* develops this last dimension in dialogue with the difficulties and concerns of every believer, but without implying a relativization of the Law of God.

By pointing out "certain grave violations of human dignity" illicit "beyond all circumstances" (no. 34), the declaration *Dignitas Infinita* clearly shows that the idea of moral absolutes will continue to be valid, albeit in a way that allows a more holistic, historically conscious, and inductive approach, opening new possibilities for an organic and coherent development of Catholic moral teaching and practice.[34]

The unilateral insistence either on doctrinal guidance which ignores the complexity of reality or on "pastoral solutions" which leave the current official teaching unaffected, will never be enough. To address these shortcomings, it is necessary to further explore the relationship between doctrine and pastoral care. Pastoral care is not a mere deduction of doctrine, nor is doctrine a mere *a posteriori* expression of pastoral praxis. Nor are they separate and parallel levels, reflecting a "double truth." Rather, doctrine and pastoral care must be linked in a hermeneutical circle that prevents doctrine from becoming a "closed system" far removed from life, and pastoral care from degenerating into a pragmatism in which human weakness supplants holiness as the supreme ethical criterion.

---

[34] Consequently, none of the above suggests that the moral teaching of Francis constitutes a radical departure from the preceding magisterium. It is rather "a combination of continuity and discontinuity at different levels" evaluated in the light of what Benedict XVI called "the hermeneutics of reform" ("Address to the Roman Curia," December 22, 2005).

Gustavo Irrazábal is an Argentinian lawyer, Catholic priest, and theologian. After earning a law degree in 1984, he was ordained a priest for the Archdiocese of Buenos Aires in 1991. He obtained a doctorate in moral theology from the Pontifical Gregorian University in Rome in 1999. He serves as a professor of moral theology, specializing in fundamental ethics, Catholic social teaching, and social ethics, at the Faculty of Theology of the Catholic University of Argentina (UCA).

The Splendor of Freedom in Theory and Practice: The Complementary Moral Theologies of John Paul II and Francis

Conor Kelly

Abstract: Freedom is a central issue in *Veritatis Splendor*, with John Paul II particularly concerned about freedom's proper relationship to truth in contrast to a relativistic vision of freedom as complete license. In defending this position, John Paul II emphasizes the theoretical ideal of freedom as the abiding human capacity to do what is right, with the help of grace. This profound vision of freedom is best honored and preserved when joined in conversation with the understanding of freedom found in Francis's moral theology, which complements John Paul II's emphasis on the theoretical ideal by accounting for the challenges moral agents face in their efforts to put this ideal into practice. Recent developments in the concept of structural sin in Catholic theology help to explain how both John Paul II's and Francis's interpretations of freedom can be read in continuity with one another, yielding a more comprehensive vision of freedom that does justice to the already and not yet of Christian eschatology, ensuring that this crucial component of the legacy of *Veritatis Splendor* can continue to guide the church.

FREEDOM IS AT THE HEART OF MORAL THEOLOGY. FROM THE scriptural reflections of the Pauline Epistles, which wrestled with the constraints of sin on free will and stressed the renewal of moral agency in Christ (e.g., Romans 6–7), to Thomas Aquinas's decision to highlight the voluntariness of human actions at the outset of his moral treatise in the *Summa Theologiae* (ST I-II, q. 6, a. 1), and even to contemporary contextual theologies' efforts to lift up the agency and autonomy of the marginalized, the question of freedom is crucial to the work of the moral theologian.[1] Few were

---

[1] For two prominent examples of these concerns in contextual theologies, see Ada María Isasi-Díaz, "Defining Our *Proyecto Histórico*: *Mujerista* Strategies for Liberation," in *Feminist Ethics and the Catholic Moral Tradition*, Readings in Moral Theology, no. 9, ed. Charles E. Curran, Margaret A. Farley, and Richard A. McCormick (Paulist, 1996), 120–135; M. Shawn Copeland, *Enfleshing Freedom: Body, Race, and Being* (Fortress, 2010). Notably, while freedom is always central to the work of moral theology, it is not the starting place for every moral theologian. See

surprised, then, that John Paul II's encyclical on moral theology, *Veritatis Splendor*, prioritized freedom—and especially freedom's "essential and constitutive relationship to truth" (no. 4)—as one of its chief concerns.[2] An adequate evaluation of the legacy of the encyclical thus requires a careful examination of its teachings on freedom.

One valuable resource for this examination is a comparison between the encyclical's teachings on freedom and the subsequent reflections on the topic offered by John Paul II's current successor, Francis. While working in continuity with John Paul II, Francis nevertheless stresses different dimensions in his presentation of freedom and moral agency, reflecting both his own pastoral sensitivities and developments in Catholic theological ethics since 1993. By putting John Paul II and Francis in dialogue around freedom, a sharper picture of the priorities of *Veritatis Splendor* and the implications of its legacy emerges. More specifically, this comparison highlights John Paul II's commitment to developing a thorough understanding of the abstracted ideal of freedom in order to stress the full power of freedom in the moral life. This approach stands in contrast to Francis's efforts to evaluate the practical constraints on freedom experienced in the concrete particularities of ordinary life in a fallen world. Read together rather than against each other, the reflections of these two popes reveal the totality of freedom by exploring the concept both in theory and practice.

DEFENDING THE POWER OF FREEDOM: *VERITATIS SPLENDOR*'S THEORETICAL IDEAL

According to observers, there were multiple reasons spurring John Paul II to issue an encyclical on moral theology in the early 1990s, but one of the most pressing—at least according to the emphases of the encyclical itself—was a concern about the increasing cultural influence of moral relativism, a theory which suggests that moral judgments are relative to the individual and not truly universalizable.[3]

James F. Keenan, *Moral Wisdom: Lessons and Texts from the Catholic Tradition* (Rowman and Littlefield, 2017), 10–14.

[2] In his freedom-centered analysis of *Veritatis Splendor*, Avery Dulles explained that "the rootedness of freedom in the truth has been a constant and central theme in the writings of John Paul II" ("The Truth About Freedom: A Theme from John Paul II," in Veritatis Splendor *and the Renewal of Moral Theology*, ed. J. A. DiNoia and Romanus Cessario [Scepter, 1999], 129).

[3] For some illustrations of the various interpretations of the underlying motivations behind *Veritatis Splendor*, which ranged from a concern about the erosion of the Magisterium's teaching authority to an effort to reject the positions of specific moralists to a desire to propose a model for doing moral theology with closer connections to Scripture, see Servais Pinckaers, "An Encyclical for the Future:

This concern was not strictly cultural, as the encyclical responded to specific theological positions it described as emblematic of a relativist turn in moral theology. The encyclical explicitly critiques *"teleological ethical theories (proportionalism, consequentialism)"* (no. 75, emphasis original) as part of its challenge to relativism. Observers at the time were quick to read these labels as indictments of contemporaneous theologians' scholarly positions, even as the recipients of this criticism insisted that the encyclical's description did not apply to their work.[4] This historical context is significant, because the positions rejected in *Veritatis Splendor*—whether they can be neatly attributed to individual theologians—establish some clear parameters for what it means to be in continuity with the encyclical's teaching, a point that influences how John Paul II's and Francis's reflections on moral theology are read in conversation with each other.

Given the importance of continuity in Catholic teaching, it is not surprising that John Paul II would choose to use an encyclical, one of the most authoritative forms of papal writing, to respond to the threat of relativism, which opens the door to discontinuity in morality.[5] What is striking in the text, however, is the way John Paul II links the rise of relativism back to a corresponding embrace of "an individualist ethic, wherein each individual is faced with his own truth, different from the truth of others" (*Veritatis Splendor*, no. 32).[6] Due to this connection, freedom becomes an overarching concern for the encyclical, because disagreement about the degree to which each individual is free to determine what is right explains the disconnect between a growing moral relativism, on one hand, and the Catholic

---

Veritatis Splendor," in DiNoia and Cessario, Veritatis Splendor *and the Renewal of Moral Theology*, 12–17; Richard A. McCormick, "Some Early Reactions to *Veritatis Splendor*," *Theological Studies* 55, no. 3 (1994): esp. 505–506, doi.org/10.1177/004056399405500303. For the encyclical's explicit references to the dangers of relativism, see *Veritatis Splendor*, nos. 1, 33, 48, 84, 101, 106, 112.

[4] Russell Hittinger, "The Pope and the Theorists: The Oneness of Truth," *Crisis* 11 (1993): 31–36, crisismagazine.com/vault/the-pope-and-the-theorists-the-oneness-of-truth; and Ralph McInerny, "Locating Right and Wrong: *Veritatis* v. Muddled Moralizing," *Crisis* 11 (1993): 37–40, crisismagazine.com/vault/locating-right-and-wrong-veritatis-v-muddled-moralizing; Charles E. Curran, "*Veritatis Splendor:* A Revisionist Perspective," in Veritatis Splendor: *American Responses*, ed. Michael E. Allsopp and John J. O'Keefe (Sheed and Ward, 1995), 233–238; Richard A. McCormick, "*Veritatis Splendor* and Moral Theology," *America* 169, no. 13 (October 30, 1993): 8–11.

[5] The importance of continuity can be seen in the care used to address obvious changes in moral teaching. See John T. Noonan, Jr., "Development in Moral Doctrine," *Theological Studies* 54, no. 4 (1993): 662–677, doi.org/10.1177/004056399305400404.

[6] See also Lois Malcolm, "Freedom and Truth in *Veritatis Splendor* and the Meaning of Theonomy," in *Ecumenical Ventures in Ethics: Protestants Engage Pope John Paul II's Moral Encyclicals*, ed. Reinhard Hütter and Theodor Dieter (Eerdmans, 1998), 159.

Church's promotion of unchanging objective moral norms, on the other.[7] In defending the latter position, John Paul II promotes a particular vision of "genuine freedom" in *Veritatis Splendor*, arguing that human freedom is most fully realized not in people's ability "to do anything they please" (no. 34), but in choosing to align one's actions with what is truly good, as revealed in God's law (no. 17).

John Paul II's account of freedom thus prioritizes the individual's unceasing ability to choose to do what God's law commands, no matter the circumstances, in order to preserve the universal objectivity of God's law (contra relativism) without undermining human freedom. Consequently, the discussion of freedom in *Veritatis Splendor* can be interpreted as an analysis of the theoretical ideal of freedom, in the Platonic sense of an ideal, or true form, which is properly "mind-independent" (i.e., not just something a thinking being creates on a whim) and therefore "immutable, timeless, unitary, . . . and knowable."[8] To be clear, this is not to say that John Paul II was a Platonist; he was, after all, most closely associated with phenomenology, an altogether separate philosophical school. Rather than trying to place John Paul II firmly within Platonism, then, the appeal to Platonic idealism here is best understood as a heuristic and not typological category that helps illuminate the primary concerns about freedom explored in *Veritatis Splendor*.[9]

The argument for employing this heuristic is twofold. First, there is a genuine affinity between John Paul II's commitments to objectivity (certainly in a moral sense, but also in theology more broadly), which was a consistent feature of his approach to phenomenology, and the objective claims found in Platonic idealism, which stresses the unity and thus objective reality of each ideal.[10] It is thus not unreasonable to explore John Paul II's thought while considering a Platonic perspective. Second, Platonic idealism is regularly defined in contradistinction to Aristotelian realism (sometimes dubbed "naturalism" or "empiricism"), reflecting a discernible debate between Plato and his student, Aristotle, on the epistemological

---

[7] This notably was not a novel dispute in 1993, although the contours of the debate were still distinct at the time as relativism gained cultural influence. Dulles, "The Truth about Freedom," 129; McCormick, "Some Early Reactions," 502–503.

[8] Tom Rockmore, "Idealism, Platonic Idealism, and the New Way of Ideas," in *Kant and Idealism* (Yale University Press, 2017), 25.

[9] These caveats are particularly appropriate given the limits of "Platonic idealism" as a coherent typological category in philosophy (Rockmore, "Idealism," 24).

[10] On objectivity as a distinguishing feature of John Paul II's philosophical commitments, see David Schindler, "Catholic Personalism up to John Paul II," in *The Oxford Handbook of Catholic Theology*, ed. Lewis Ayres and Medi Ann Volpe (Oxford University Press, 2015), 746. For objectivity and realism in Platonic idealism, see Rockmore, "Idealism," 25–27.

question of how best to understand the reality of any given thing. Offering one interpretation, Platonic idealism presumes that the fullest expression of reality is in the ideal, which exists beyond immediate evidence, and therefore promotes a contemplative process to understand reality in the theoretical realm. Aristotelian realism, meanwhile, insists that the universal reality represented in an ideal is only discernible through the particular manifestations of that concept in the real world and thus stresses empirical analysis of the world to develop an understanding of reality.[11] Even here the distinctions remain primarily heuristic, but they nevertheless reflect an identifiable set of assumptions about how best to proceed when a concept, like freedom, is subject to scrutiny.

The pairing of these two schools is particularly valuable in the analysis of *Veritatis Splendor*, because just as there is a defensible connection to Platonic idealism in John Paul II's concerns about objectivity and his appeals to universals, there is a case to be made that Francis adopts a more Aristotelian approach in his theology, attending first and foremost to the particular.[12] As a heuristic device, then, Platonic idealism and Aristotelian realism together provide a tool for interpreting the different emphases found in John Paul II's and Francis's reflections on freedom, showing that John Paul II is more intent on evaluating human freedom in its abstract reality while Francis relies more on the practical matter of how freedom is used in ordinary life to identify what freedom can achieve. The heuristic helps to sharpen these differences and also serves as a reminder of the search for unity, because Plato and Aristotle, despite their competing claims, had much in common and sought similar ends. However, before exploring the comparison with Francis this heuristic opens, it is crucial to evaluate John Paul II's vision of freedom in *Veritatis Splendor* on its own terms.

In a careful exegesis of *Veritatis Splendor*, the Lutheran systematic theologian Lois Malcolm has argued that there are fundamentally three features to the text's explication of freedom: freedom's inherent orientation to truth, freedom's expression in conscience, and

---

[11] For one account of these distinctions and their implications, see Duane H. D. Roller, "Science and the Fine Arts: Reflections of Platonic Idealism and of Aristotelian Naturalism," *Leonardo* 13, no. 3 (1980): 192–194, doi.org/10.2307/1577816.

[12] Analysis of Francis's implicit Aristotelianism is still underdeveloped in theological scholarship, but for two illustrations exploring the links with Aristotle in Francis's thought, see Yaakov Mascetti, "The 'Dictatorship of Relativism' Revisited: Platonism vs. Pneumatology in the Vatican," *Common Knowledge* 24, no. 2 (2018): doi.org/10.1215/0961754X-4362313; and Conor M. Kelly, "Pope Francis: Virtue Ethicist?," in *The Moral Vision of Pope Francis: Expanding the US Reception of the First Jesuit Pope*, ed. Conor M. Kelly and Kristin E. Heyer (Georgetown University Press, 2024), 52.

freedom's impact on the self-determination of the personal moral agent.[13] This is a succinct summary of the encyclical's most explicit discussion of freedom found in the letter's second chapter and encompassing three sections titled, "Freedom and Law" (nos. 35–53), "Conscience and Truth" (nos. 54–64), and "Fundamental Choice and Specific Kinds of Behavior" (nos. 65–70). The real significance of these different points, however, lies not in what any one of these features reveals about freedom in isolation but in the way the three work together to convey John Paul II's more fundamental vision of human freedom as a whole. Read in this way, the central thread uniting the different features of freedom presented in *Veritatis Splendor* is an underlying argument that freedom remains ever at the service of objective morality. This interpretation not only makes sense of the three explicit elements of freedom identified in Malcolm's analysis but also accounts for the larger structure of the encyclical, which introduces its discussion of freedom (in chapter two) "sandwiched between two chapters presenting an ascetical view of Christian life."[14]

The essential link between freedom and objective morality is easiest to see in the first section of chapter two, which explores freedom's relationship with truth. Stressing that the determination of good and evil lies with God, not humans (no. 35), John Paul II proclaims, "God's plan poses no threat to man's genuine freedom; on the contrary, the acceptance of God's plan is the only way to affirm that freedom" (no. 45). For John Paul II, then, freedom is less the ability to choose between as many options as possible and more the power to choose to pursue the good and do what is right. Scholars sometimes describe this approach as a vision of "freedom for excellence," or the ability to pursue the fullness of flourishing without constraints that would divert one's desires, intention, or will away from their proper telos.[15] This vision also creates a compelling alignment with Augustine's view of freedom, which locates the fullness of freedom in liberation from slavery to sin that constitutes

---

[13] Malcolm, "Freedom and Truth," 166.
[14] John J. O'Keefe, "No Place for Failure? Augustinian Reflections on *Veritatis Splendor*," in Allsopp and O'Keefe, *American Responses*, 19. In fairness, Malcolm's account is not oblivious to the ways the vision of freedom in chapter two interacts with other portions of the text, but she mainly uses the discussion of asceticism—and especially martyrdom—to explain a tension between a "natural law" account of freedom and a "personalist" account in *Veritatis Splendor*. I maintain, however, that the structure of the encyclical and its argument makes martyrdom a crucial hermeneutic for interpreting freedom and not just one feature among many. See Malcolm, "Freedom and Truth," 161–162, 174.
[15] Servais Pinckaers, "An Encyclical for the Future," 39. For more on the category, see Servais Pinckaers, *The Sources of Christian Ethics*, 3rd ed., trans. Mary Thomas Noble (The Catholic University of America Press, 1995), 354–378.

the human condition after the Fall and undermines one's ability to pursue what is good.[16] In these accounts, humans are free when they are not simply self-determining—the decision to do what is wrong is actually a corruption of human freedom that misuses this gift—but when their self-determination is properly ordered to achieving the good.[17]

Notably, for John Paul II, the good at which freedom is supposed to aim truly is singular. Following Jesus's guidance in his response to the rich young man in Matthew 19—the scriptural text framing *Veritatis Splendor*—John Paul II stresses that "*to ask about the good, in fact, ultimately means to turn towards God*, the fullness of goodness" (no. 9, emphasis original). On this basis, a clear link between freedom and universal morality emerges, as the God whom Christians identify as one serves as the sole source of moral truth, setting a standard that is both objective and universal in stark contradistinction to moral relativism. Nowhere is this opposition with relativism clearer than in John Paul II's discussion of the natural law, which he presents, in good Thomistic fashion, "as the human expression of God's eternal law" (no. 43).[18]

For John Paul II, the natural law explains how human reason can know what God commands, creating a universal way of accessing the singular, objective moral truth all humans are supposed to use their freedom to pursue. This mechanism, specifically as interpreted through the richly theological vision of the natural law found in the work of Thomas Aquinas (see no. 44), allows John Paul II to state that the "positive precepts" of the natural law—the norms that explain what humans *should do* to pursue the good—"are universally binding; they are 'unchanging,'" and that the "*negative precepts*" of the natural law—the norms that articulate what one *must not do* in order to avoid undermining the good by choosing evil—"are universally valid. They oblige each and every individual, always and in every circumstance" (no. 52, emphases original). There is thus a consistent vision of what the good requires common to all humans and which, significantly, can also be known by all humans via the natural law. More importantly,

---

[16] O'Keefe, "No Place for Failure?," 27. For more on the Augustinian conception of freedom, see Jesse Couenhoven, *Stricken by Sin, Cured by Christ: Agency, Necessity, and Culpability in Augustinian Theology* (Oxford University Press, 2013), esp. 59–106.

[17] Dulles makes this point by presenting a contrast between the "lower level" freedom found in the "absence of physical constraint" and the "higher level" freedom that also includes the "absence of psychological compulsion." From this perspective, "if we reject the true good, we inevitably yield to the passions and instincts of our lower nature and thereby undermine our authentic freedom" ("The Truth about Freedom," 130, 132).

[18] See also ST I-II, q. 91, a. 2, cited in *Veritatis Splendor*, no. 43, n. 82.

there is simultaneously a definitive set of rules humans must not violate, establishing a truly objective standard for morality.

This vision for objective morality, accessible through the natural law, puts a pivotal parameter on human freedom. There are, according to this vision, certain things the human person must not use their freedom to choose. In a world where freedom is frequently (mis)understood as license, this claim appears to represent an arbitrary constraint on freedom. John Paul II, though, quickly dismisses this interpretation as flawed by insisting, "The natural law . . . does not allow for any division between freedom and nature. Indeed, these two realities are harmoniously bound together, and each is intimately linked to the other" (no. 50). In his evaluation, the "nature" behind the natural law is the "proper and primordial . . . 'nature of the human person'" (no. 50). The precepts of the natural law thus orient the human person to the fullness of their flourishing *as a human being*, allowing each person to become what they are meant to be in the order of creation (see nos. 38–41). The natural law's negative norms are thus not a despotic restriction on freedom, but a guardrail that helps direct human freedom to its fullest expression, proactively forestalling detours down the pathways that lead to sin so that each moral agent can follow the road of life to its ultimate destination of union with God.

As discussed so far, then, John Paul II's presentation of freedom in *Veritatis Splendor* includes two essential claims: freedom is oriented to the human person's flourishing, and there are objective standards that constitute this flourishing and thereby establish limits for how freedom can be properly exercised to achieve its proper end. John Paul II advances additional corollary claims about freedom in the encyclical, including the notion that conscience has a primary role in helping the moral agent discern what God's objective vision for flourishing demands in particular situations (nos. 54, 61) and the claim that a person's individual choices in those particular situations have a formative effect on the person's very being, to the point of defining their standing before God (nos. 65–67). These claims reflect the second and third features Malcolm identified in her overview of John Paul II's account of freedom, but it is worth noting that they remain corollary claims, because they are at the service of John Paul II's more fundamental assertion that freedom is ordered to flourishing and arrives at this end by observing objective moral norms. Significantly, while freedom can follow this pathway to flourishing by actively working to embody the prescriptive norms that encourage good behaviors (positive moral precepts), the encyclical puts its strongest onus on the obligation to steadfastly adhere to "the negative moral precepts, those prohibiting certain concrete actions or kinds of behavior as intrinsically evil" because these "do not allow for any legitimate exception" (no. 67). The interrelationship of these two obligations deserves further discussion because this is both a nuanced and pivotal point in the encyclical that elucidates key dimensions of John Paul II's presentation of human freedom.

To begin, while there is a greater stress on obedience to the negative moral norms in *Veritatis Splendor*, this does not mean that the negative precepts have greater primacy than positive ones in the moral life. Indeed, the encyclical insists, "The fact that only the negative commandments oblige always and under all circumstances does not mean that in the moral life prohibitions are more important than the obligation to do good indicated by the positive commandments" (no. 52). The encyclical attends more fully to the negative moral norms, however, precisely because they speak to the issue of universality and moral objectivity more fully. By their very nature, the positive precepts constantly call for more because they promote a closer union with God. There is no "higher limit" to this aim (no. 52), no threshold at which one is suddenly "close enough" to God that all attempts at progress can be abandoned. Consequently, exactly what it means to follow the positive precepts is a question that requires discernment in practice and admits variation to account for differences in circumstance (no. 67). The positive precepts therefore are not the most useful part of the moral law to which one could appeal when building an argument about moral objectivity to counteract the dangers of relativism, both across the Catholic theological landscape and in the broader culture. That honor falls on the precepts that explicate the "kinds of behavior which can never, in any situation, be a proper response" to the demands of the moral life. Thus, the negative moral norms receive more attention in *Veritatis Splendor* as a means of defending moral objectivity in the face of relativism.

In the encyclical's argument, the most important aspect of the negative precepts is their exceptionless nature. This is evident when examining how the letter responds to the "teleological ethical theories" it associates with relativism. Offering a detailed analysis of this section of the text, the theological ethicist James Gaffney notes that "the crucial issue for the pope seems therefore to be the admission of at least the possibility of formulating negative moral norms that admit absolutely no exceptions."[19] Further comparing the generic criticism of consequentialism and proportionalism in the encyclical with the actual positions of the Catholic theologians who would self-identify with at least one of these schools, however, Gaffney explains that a total denial of the *possibility* of exceptionless moral norms was not a genuine position of Catholic moralists at the time. As a result, he

---

[19] James Gaffney, "The Pope on Proportionalism," in Allsopp and O'Keefe, *American Responses*, 63.

concludes—not unreasonably—that the real issue in this instance is ultimately "the denial that certain familiar and traditional moral prohibitions, as they are usually stated, admit no exceptions."[20] In effect, the encyclical's discussion of negative moral norms is meant to protect both the category of "intrinsically evil acts" and its use as a tool to proscribe specific actions in all circumstances (nos. 79–83).[21]

The thrust of this argument and the contours of the debate it enters are both significant for clarifying John Paul II's assertions about freedom. Because John Paul II works to preserve the category of intrinsic evil as a means of solidifying the foundation of exceptionless moral norms in the face of relativism, *Veritatis Splendor* presumes not simply that intrinsically evil acts exist but also that they are knowable as such. Indeed, the debate with the theories the encyclical criticizes centers on the clarity with which specific intrinsic evils can be identified, and *Veritatis Splendor* maintains that the Catholic tradition—particularly through the guidance of the Magisterium—has the tools to define these acts. The relevant question for human freedom, then, is not how to exercise freedom in the discernment of whether a particular action constitutes an intrinsic evil but rather how to act freely once one has realized that an exceptionless prohibition is in force. How can one use their freedom to pursue the moral good and flourish when confronting something they fundamentally must not do? With its more Platonic attention to the ideal of freedom, *Veritatis Splendor* finds a compelling answer in martyrdom, arguing that while "it is always possible that man, as the result of coercion or other circumstances, can be hindered from doing certain good actions . . . he can never be hindered from not doing certain actions, especially if he is prepared to die rather than to do evil" (no. 52).

Ultimately, the turn to the witness of the martyrs in chapter three of *Veritatis Splendor* represents a logical extension of the encyclical's presentation of freedom's orientation to flourishing and its alignment with absolute moral prohibitions. More specifically, martyrdom highlights that in the Catholic understanding of theological anthro-

---

[20] Gaffney, "The Pope on Proportionalism," 64.
[21] Gaffney is not alone in suggesting that a defense of the category of intrinsically evil acts is at the heart of the encyclical's claims. See Joseph A. Selling, "The Context and the Arguments of *Veritatis Splendor*," in *The Splendor of Accuracy: An Examination of the Assertions Made by* Veritatis Splendor, ed. Joseph A. Selling and Jan Jans (Eerdmans, 1995), 49; and Martin Rhonheimer, "Intrinsically Evil Acts and the Moral Viewpoint: Clarifying a Central Teaching of *Veritatis Splendor*," in DiNoia and Cessario, *The Splendor of Truth*, 161–193. Additionally, for one productive account of how the category is employed in *Veritatis Splendor vis-à-vis* the broader Catholic moral tradition, see Jean Porter, "The Moral Act in *Veritatis Splendor* and in Aquinas's *Summa Theologiae*: A Comparative Analysis," in Allsopp and O'Keefe, *American Responses*, 278–295.

pology, humanity's creation in the image and likeness of God means that flourishing is exemplified not in self-preservation but through sacrifice. As the Second Vatican Council proclaimed, "This likeness reveals that man, who is the only creature on earth which God willed for itself, cannot fully find himself except through a sincere gift of himself" (*Gaudium et Spes*, no. 24). John Paul II builds on this conviction to provide a Christological description of freedom's fullest expression in flourishing. "*The Crucified Christ reveals the authentic meaning of freedom*," the pope explains; "*he lives it fully in the total gift of himself*" (*Veritatis Splendor*, no. 85, emphasis original). This gift of self is understood quite literally, in Christ's very "crucified flesh," which for John Paul II "reveals the unbreakable bond between freedom and truth" because it shows Christ's willingness to suffer the ultimate price for his "total obedience to the will of God" (no. 87). The martyrs bear witness to this same fullness of freedom and flourishing. "Martyrdom is also the exaltation of a person's perfect 'humanity' and of true 'life,'" John Paul II proclaims, because "martyrdom, accepted as an affirmation of the inviolability of the moral order, bears witness both to the holiness of God's law and to the inviolability of the personal dignity of man, created in the image and likeness of God" (no. 92). In this manner, martyrdom reiterates that human freedom must be aligned with the objective requirements of the moral law and affirms "the absoluteness of the moral order" (no. 91), by showing that humans can always use their freedom to observe the demands of that moral order, even when faced with extreme costs for doing so.

That John Paul II completes his discussion of freedom with a reflection on martyrdom is no accident. His account of freedom's relationship to human flourishing and sense of the objective nature of that flourishing as defined by God's commandments and contained in the precepts of the natural law—particularly exceptionless negative norms—demands the martyrs' witness. Without their sacrifices, a logical inconsistency in John Paul II's appeals to objectivity emerges, as one could rightly question whether the human person would always be capable of using their freedom to honor the demands of the objective moral order. By presenting Christ's crucifixion as the highest example of freedom and appealing to the martyrs to show that Christ's example is not unattainable for the rest of humanity, John Paul II has a rational response to this potential inconsistency. Even when it appears that there are no good options left, one at the very least remains free to refuse to violate the absolute norms that set the boundaries for what one must not do, even if the cost is death. Or, as John Paul II puts in somewhat understated terms, "Certainly, maintaining a harmony between freedom and truth occasionally demands uncommon sacrifices, and must be won at a high price: it can even involve martyrdom" (no. 102).

While John Paul II argues that martyrdom is a form of ultimate "witness to moral truth . . . to which relatively few people are called" (no. 93), he nevertheless stresses that all Christians are, in fact, called to share in Christ's model of total self-gift displayed on the cross (no. 85). Similarly, he argues that "there is nonetheless a consistent witness which all Christians must daily be ready to make, even at the cost of suffering and grave sacrifice" (no. 93). As a result, the *possibility* of martyrdom is decisive for John Paul II's account of freedom, allowing him to maintain that human freedom never loses its capacity to remain in alignment with the will of God, the objective standard of morality. Recalling the Platonic heuristic, what John Paul II is most keen to preserve is the theoretical ideal of freedom as the ability of the moral agent to choose the good. By establishing martyrdom as the pinnacle of human freedom, John Paul II can assert that this theoretical capacity remains an option at all times, for even when one does not actually give their life for the objective moral truth, their freedom is preserved by the simple fact that they could.

Importantly, two nuances are necessary to yield a full picture of John Paul II's conception of freedom. First, John Paul II does not present the theoretical ideal of freedom as a simple achievement of the human will; grace is a requisite component. From the very beginning of the encyclical, the pope notes that the necessity of grace for the moral life is one of the most important conclusions supported by the account of the rich young man in Matthew 19 (nos. 17, 21–24). He then doubles down on this point when discussing the witness of the martyrs, arguing that the call "to a sometimes heroic commitment" is encountered "with the grace of God invoked in prayer" (no. 94). His ultimate point is that the observance of God's commands is never easy—hence, again, the paradigm of martyrdom—but the theoretical ideal of freedom remains and God's grace makes it possible to exert this capacity to follow the law (no. 103).[22]

Second, John Paul II is aware that moral agents often confront constraints in their efforts to put the power of their theoretical freedom into practice in the real world. The most obvious constraints are ignorance (no. 70) and concupiscence (no. 86) which, respectively, can make it difficult to know the right thing to do and challenging to do the right thing once it is known. At the same time, John Paul II also acknowledges larger external forces, including "the enormously complex and conflict-filled situations present in the moral life of individuals and society today" (no. 95), that pose obstacles for anyone seeking to use their freedom to observe the objective moral law. He

---

[22] For more on the way *Veritatis Splendor* builds on Jesus's conversation with the rich young man to draw out the necessity of grace in support of the demands of the moral life, see Pinckaers, "An Encyclical for the Future," 34–37.

similarly accepts the insights of "a number of disciplines, grouped under the name of the 'behavioral sciences,' [which] have rightly drawn attention to the many kinds of psychological and social conditioning which influence the exercise of freedom" (no. 33), suggesting an awareness of the way external pressures, and not just internal obstacles like ignorance and concupiscence, can condition human freedom. What he refuses to abide, however, is the notion that these constraints erode that freedom. Given his absolutization of freedom in its theoretical ideal, John Paul II rejects the claim that any of these constraints result in a determinism that would force someone to choose to act against the demands of the moral order (no. 33) or somehow make those norms obsolete for a particular individual (no. 81). He can accept, in a claim that has clear resonance across the Catholic moral tradition, that these internal and external forces might mitigate subjective culpability, but they will never, in his estimation, shift the demands of the moral law itself, which remain objective and universal (nos. 63, 81–82, 95).[23] Freedom, at least at the theoretical level, always persists.

Even with these nuances, John Paul II's primary emphasis on the theoretical ideal of freedom remains. The fundamental vision of freedom that emerges from *Veritatis Splendor* is thus a capability that, as a result of grace, every human being preserves even in the face of the strongest countervailing forces. This vision is valuable for its clear defense of the dignity of the human person, who always and everywhere retains the possibility of honoring the demands of God's law. This approach likewise provides a staunch defense of moral objectivity, justifying the claim that morality is not a relativistic code that shifts with changing circumstances but rooted in a universal vision of the good that applies to all people in all times and places. Helpfully, the nuances to John Paul II's vision of freedom also underscore the role of grace in the moral life, with his acknowledgment of external and internal constraints confirming both the necessity of grace and its transformative power.

Despite these genuine assets, John Paul II's decision to emphasize the theoretical ideal of freedom also presents some liabilities for those searching for a complete understanding of human freedom. Chief among them is the way the idealization of freedom's absolute power in theory can seem at odds with the human experience of feeling the limited power of one's own agency, particularly in a fallen world. One patristic theologian, John J. O'Keefe, has articulated this liability in Augustinian terms, arguing that while the encyclical clearly embraces Augustine's account of moral freedom as fundamentally freedom

---

[23] For more on the role of these claims in the broader theological tradition, see *Catechism*, no. 1735; ST I-II, q. 6, a. 8; q. 18, a. 10.

from sin, it nevertheless fails to appreciate the ways Augustine's eschatology made this form of freedom inherently incomplete in this life.[24] Put another way, one might say John Paul II's emphasis on the theoretical ideal of freedom puts too much stress on the "already" to the detriment of the "not yet" in Christianity's eschatological convictions. O'Keefe's assessment is not out of place, as one can see a similar trend in other areas of John Paul II's moral theology. Consider his work in sexual ethics, for example, where his influential theology of the body has faced criticism for an overly optimistic view of the capacities of married couples and insufficient attention to the breadth of real-life human experiences of love and sexuality.[25] There is, of course, an acknowledgment of fallenness in John Paul II's work—his theology of the body notes the dangers of lust, for instance, and *Veritatis Splendor* accounts for the "weakness" of concupiscence noted above. Acknowledgment in the abstract, however, is not the same as dealing with the pervasiveness of this fallen nature and its effects, which John Paul II is at times too quick to dismiss. One result of this insufficient attentiveness to the fallenness of the world is a potential disconnect between John Paul II's staunch, and necessary, emphasis on the theoretical ideal of freedom, and the limitations this freedom encounters in real life. Helpfully, this fallenness is a point Pope Francis seems keen to recognize and address in his descriptions of freedom, making his contributions to the theology of freedom a vital complement to John Paul II's reflections in *Veritatis Splendor*.

ACCOUNTING FOR CONSTRAINTS ON FREEDOM: FRANCIS'S PRACTICAL PERSPECTIVE

Much, of course, has been made of the distance between the theologies of John Paul II and Francis, but for all the perceived conflict, one cannot deny that Francis, at least in his explicit statements, adamantly insists that he views his pontificate in continuity with his predecessors.[26] For example, in a letter to a

---

[24] O'Keefe, "No Place for Failure?," 17, 23, 27.
[25] Cristina L. H. Traina, "Papal Ideals, Marital Realities: One View from the Ground," in *Sexual Diversity and Catholicism*, ed. Patricia Beattie Jung and Joseph Coray (Liturgical Press, 2011), 269–288; Luke Timothy Johnson, "A Disembodied 'Theology of the Body': John Paul II on Love, Sex, and Pleasure," *Commonweal* 128, no. 2 (January 26, 2001): 12–13, 14, 15–16, www.commonwealmagazine.org/disembodied-theology-body.
[26] The most famous illustration of allegations about Francis's departure from the teachings of John Paul II is the *Dubia* submitted by four cardinals in late 2016 to question the interpretation of teachings found in *Amoris Laetitia*. For the text of the *Dubia* as well as a defense of a greater continuity between John Paul II and Francis, see James Bretzke, "*Responsum ad Dubia*: Harmonizing *Veritatis Splendor* and

Catholic author preparing a book about *Amoris Laetitia*, Francis insisted that the teaching in the exhortation emerges from "the magisterial hermeneutic of the Church, always in continuity (without ruptures), yet always maturing."[27] Taking Francis at his word, this continuity challenges the church to engage both Francis and the tradition more fully, militating against reductionistic readings that put the two in opposition and instead inviting an analysis that must reconcile any superficial disconnect with a deeper appreciation of the shared concerns that unite even Francis's most dramatic claims with the tradition preceding him.

Of course, not all scholars are ready to read Francis with this hermeneutic of continuity. Some wish to stress a dramatic departure in Francis's theology, either as a rationale for condemning his teachings as an inauthentic exercise of magisterial authority or an argument for inaugurating more dramatic changes across the Catholic Church.[28] I believe a reading that presumes continuity while acknowledging the possibility for development is preferable, however, for two reasons. First, this is not only how Francis presents his own teaching but also how the Catholic Church envisions the broader relationship between popes.[29] Presuming continuity thus offers a decidedly Catholic way of reading the papal magisterium in general, not just for this specific pontificate. Second, in the particular case of this pontificate, the search for continuity amidst any development helps to make sense of what Francis is doing because it brings certain interpretations to the forefront more readily. This is not insignificant, because Francis's theological style is much more pastoral than systematic, leaving room for ambiguity and heightening the need for

---

Amoris Laetitia through a Conscience-Informed Casuistry," *Journal of Catholic Social Thought* 15, no. 1 (2018): doi.org/10.5840/jcathsoc201815111; for other theologians criticizing potential discontinuities between Francis and John Paul II, see John Finnis and Germain Grisez, "The Misuse of *Amoris Laetitia* to Support Errors Against the Catholic Faith," *Catholic Culture*, November 21, 2016, www.catholicculture.org/culture/library/view.cfm?recnum=11463; Nicholas J. Healy, "Interpreting Chapter Eight of *Amoris Laetitia* in Light of the Incarnation," *Journal of Moral Theology* 10, no. 2 (2021): 144–159, jmt.scholasticahq.com/article/25767.

[27] Francis, "Preface," in Stephen Walford, *Pope Francis, the Family, and Divorce: In Defense of Truth and Mercy* (Paulist, 2018), xi.

[28] Richard A. Spinello, "*Amoris Laetitia*: A Ticking Moral Time Bomb," *Crisis*, June 8, 2022, crisismagazine.com/opinion/amoris-laetitia-a-ticking-moral-time-bomb; Todd A. Salzman and Michael G. Lawler, "*Amoris Laetitia*: Has Anything Changed?," *Asian Horizons* 11, no. 1 (2017): 62–74; Emily Reimer-Barry, "*Amoris Laetitia* at Five," *Theological Studies* 83, no. 1 (2022): 115–122, doi.org/10.1177/00405639211070199.

[29] See *Catechism of the Catholic Church*, no. 77.

interpretive analyses.³⁰ Continuity can help with this interpretive task, often yielding insights that might otherwise be overlooked.³¹

On the specific matter of Francis's account of freedom there is a particular type of continuity at work. Here, the continuity is less about extending or expanding what has already been said and more about adding a complementary perspective that, together with those previous reflections, can produce a more complete picture of freedom. The complements largely emerge due to Francis's pastoral instincts, which give him a distinct perspective on the challenges that arise when the faithful try to put the theoretical ideal of freedom championed by John Paul II into practice in their own lives. Following the heuristic mentioned earlier, Francis embodies a more Aristotelian approach that gives primary attention to the concrete particulars of the intersections between the theoretical potency of freedom and the constraining forces of a world marred by sin. Consequently, Francis evaluates freedom with a different emphasis than the one employed by John Paul II, prodding the church toward a more complete vision of freedom that can build on the strengths of the model found in *Veritatis Splendor* to help more people identify the genuine freedom championed by John Paul II as a viable capacity in their lives.

The first thing to note about Francis's reflections on freedom is that they are not nearly as systematic as John Paul II's. Francis has not authored an entire encyclical on moral theology in which he expounds upon the theme of human freedom. He has, however, dealt with the question consistently throughout his pontificate, but one must read through multiple texts to appreciate the content of his claims about freedom. One implication of these different teaching styles is that exploring the theme of freedom in John Paul II and Francis is not strictly an "apples to apples" project. Whereas *Veritatis Splendor*, as a single document, offers a relatively comprehensive account of John Paul II's view of human freedom, Francis's views on the same topic must be drawn out of disparate texts crafted for different audiences and distinct purposes and representing varied levels of authority. This is not inherently a problem, but it bears acknowledging that the process of identifying Francis's contributions to the question of

---

³⁰ For one discussion of how this unsystematic approach plays out in ethics, see Conor M. Kelly and Kristin E. Heyer, "Introduction," in Kelly and Heyer, *Moral Vision of Pope Francis*, 3–4.

³¹ Elsewhere, for instance, I have argued that this hermeneutic of continuity reveals ways that Francis's teachings on the specific topic of the theology of the family manifest not an invitation to disruption but rather a call to a fuller embrace of impulses found in John Paul II's pontificate. Conor M. Kelly, "From John Paul II to Francis: The Widening Pastoral Trajectory of the Catholic Theology of Family," in *Alegria et Misericórdia: A teologia do Papa Francisco para as famílias*, ed. Miguel Almeida (Frente e Verso, 2020), 133–156.

freedom requires more constructive analysis and is thus inevitably open to more interpretation.

When embarking on this constructive project, one of the most important points to emerge is the number of overlapping concerns Francis shares with John Paul II. Francis endorses the vision of Christian freedom as a freedom from sin that allows the human person to pursue the fullness of their flourishing (*Christus Vivit*, nos. 119–123). Consequently, he too insists that freedom is only fully realized when exercised in accordance with God's plans (*Gaudete et Exsultate*, no. 32). Indeed, with words that would not have been out of place in *Veritatis Splendor*, Francis argued in his first Apostolic Exhortation that "some people think they are free if they can avoid God; they fail to see that they remain existentially orphaned, helpless, homeless" (*Evangelii Gaudium*, no. 171). Furthermore, just like John Paul II, Francis pinpoints the roots of this erroneous conflation of "true freedom" (no. 171) with complete license in the loss of moral objectivity and the rise of an individualistic moral relativism. "Ultimately," he writes, "it is easy nowadays to confuse genuine freedom with the idea that each individual can act arbitrarily, as if there were no truths, values and principles to provide guidance, and everything were possible and permissible" (*Amoris Laetitia*, no. 34; see also *Laudato Si'*, no. 6).

In crucial ways, then, Francis embraces the theoretical ideal of freedom championed by John Paul II. He accepts that freedom is properly exercised in accordance with God's will and rejects the idea that the constraints of the moral law are somehow a restriction on freedom. Notably, Francis even endorses John Paul II's fundamental claim that this theoretical ideal of freedom always remains a possibility in the moral life, allowing one to honor the demands of the moral law at all times. In reflecting on the damage humanity's misuse of freedom has wrought in *Laudato Si'*, for instance, Francis insists, "Yet all is not lost. Human beings, while capable of the worst, are also capable of rising above themselves, choosing again what is good, and making a new start despite their mental and social conditioning. We are able to take an honest look at ourselves, to acknowledge our deep dissatisfaction, and to embark on new paths to authentic freedom" (no. 205). Like John Paul II, he also stresses that grace is the requisite ingredient that facilitates this transformation. In *Gaudete et Exsultate*, Francis cites the Argentinian theologian Lucio Gera to underscore that "our freedom is a grace" (no. 55) and explain that the human person's ability to use their freedom to transform themselves is properly not an independent act of the person but a form of cooperation in the work of God (nos. 52–56). Despite these clear alignments, however, the shared recognition of the necessity of grace in empowering human freedom is also the point at which Francis's account of freedom begins to depart from John Paul II's, introducing new insights that sharpen John Paul II's theoretical account of freedom and make it approachable for the faithful in a new way.

There are, in essence, two key developments Francis adds to John Paul II's account of freedom, both of which invite deeper reflections on the practical implications of the freedom *Veritatis Splendor* presents in more theoretical terms. Significantly, both developments reflect renewed attention to the impact of the fallen state of the world on human agency, offering a response to the overly sanguine eschatology that at times influences John Paul II's promotion of a more Platonic ideal of freedom. In keeping with that heuristic framing, Francis's insights on these matters emerge from his keener attention to the particular, an Aristotelian trait that has been a common thread across Francis's theological reflections and reflects his pastoral, rather than academic, background.[32]

The first development is Francis's insistence that the particulars matter in the moral life, leading to the notion that one crucial exercise of freedom is to determine how to meet the demands of the moral law in the concrete contexts of a person's own life. Of course, John Paul II hardly opposed this idea. In *Veritatis Splendor* he stressed, for instance, that the positive precepts of the natural law "are applied to particular acts through the judgment of conscience" (no. 52) and championed the traditional description of the work of conscience itself as "the application of the law to a particular case" (no. 59). Francis embraces the same principles but suggests that their application extends more broadly than John Paul II's presentation of human freedom would seem to imply. There is a difference in degree alongside an agreement in kind.

Consider the most prominent example of the appeal to the particular in Francis's moral theology, the question of the pastoral response to couples in "irregular" situations explored in chapter 8 of *Amoris Laetitia* (nos. 291–312). While the exact nature and significance of *Amoris Laetitia*'s "solution" to the specific question of communion for the divorced and remarried is open to interpretation, as ongoing scholarly disputes demonstrate, one point is very clear: the exhortation creates room for a plurality of answers, presuming that the proper decision can and will vary according to the particulars of different couples' circumstances.[33] Stressing "the immense variety of concrete

---

[32] Lisa Sowle Cahill, "The Moral Theology of Pope Francis: Contextual, Collaborative, Charitable, and Not Always Clear," in Kelly and Heyer, *The Moral Vision of Pope Francis*, 16–20.

[33] On the debated interpretations, see, for instance, Matthew Levering, *The Indissolubility of Marriage: Amoris Laetitia in Context* (Ignatius, 2019); James F. Keenan, "Receiving *Amoris Laetitia*," *Theological Studies* 78, no. 1 (2017): 193–212,

situations" in which couples find themselves, Francis rejects the articulation of "a new set of general rules ... applicable to all cases" and instead offers "a renewed encouragement to undertake a responsible personal and pastoral discernment of particular cases" (no. 300). Should this process yield different outcomes for different couples, Francis maintains that such plurality will not amount to "any kind of relativism," because "to show understanding in the face of exceptional situations never implies dimming the light of the fuller ideal, or proposing less than what Jesus offers to the human being" (no. 307). Instead, it reflects "a pastoral discernment filled with merciful love" (no. 312), which accepts that "a general law or rule" in isolation "is not enough to discern and ensure full fidelity to God in the concrete life of a human being" (no. 304). For Francis, there is good to be found in giving moral agents the freedom to discern their response to God.

In significant ways, Francis's emphasis on the particular and his corresponding tolerance for plurality embodies a willingness to take the fallenness of the human condition seriously. He resists the pursuit of constant uniformity and absolute certainty because he does not want the narrow confines of humanity's finite, creaturely understanding to limit the "unruly freedom" of the infinite God (*Evangelii Gaudium*, no. 22). "By thinking that everything is black and white," he cautions, "we sometimes close off the way of grace and of growth, and discourage paths of sanctification which give glory to God" (*Amoris Laetitia*, no. 305). Thus, in his first major interview, Francis articulated his conviction that "if one has all the answers to all the questions—that is the proof that God is not with him. It means that he is a false prophet using religion for himself."[34] Counteracting this temptation, Francis promotes freedom for discernment and accepts the corollary possibility of ambiguity as a corrective to the arrogance that haunts humanity's fallen condition, ensuring that no one presumes to define the will of God in advance.

This position neither requires nor implies a rejection of any of John Paul II's claims about the universal applicability of moral norms (as explored in more detail below), but it does represent a shift in emphasis away from the identification of the norm and toward the use of freedom to discern its applicability in particular circumstances. One way to recognize the shift is to consider how Francis's guidelines for

---

doi.org/10.1177/0040563916681995; Gerhard L. Müller, "What Can We Expect from the Family?," trans. Matthew Sherry, *Chiesa*, April 5, 2016, chiesa.espresso.repubblica.it/articolo/1351294bdc4.html?eng=y.

[34] Francis in Antonio Spadaro, "A Big Heart Open to God: The Exclusive Interview with Pope Francis," *America* 209, no. 8 (September 30, 2013), 30, www.americamagazine.org/faith/2013/09/30/big-heart-open-god-interview-pope-francis.

accompanying divorced and remarried couples compare to John Paul II's treatment of the same issue. In *Familiaris Consortio*, John Paul II proposed that divorced and remarried couples who "for serious reasons . . . cannot satisfy the obligation to separate" could be readmitted to the Eucharist under certain conditions, which he then explicated in detail: when they "live in complete continence, that is, by abstinence from the acts proper to married couples" (no. 84). In *Amoris Laetitia*, Francis likewise argues that divorced and remarried couples who might be "in an objective situation of sin" can nevertheless "also grow in the life of grace and charity, while receiving the Church's help to this end," including, according to a now famous footnote, "in certain cases . . . the help of the sacraments" (no. 305n351). While some have argued that these statements are merely references to John Paul II's original solution, Francis himself has indicated that the resolution in *Amoris Laetitia* is not so narrowly confined.[35] Regardless of the interpretation, the mere fact of this disagreement demonstrates the larger point, which is that Francis has not outlined one specific remedy in the same way John Paul II did in *Familiaris Consortio*. Whereas John Paul II took pains to articulate *the* path forward in order to help steer the freedom of moral agents toward its proper end in these matters, Francis moved away from such specificity entirely, preferring instead to encourage moral agents to exercise their freedom in the work of discernment.

To appreciate how these distinct emphases can be complementary rather than contradictory, consider again the matter of negative precepts and exceptionless moral norms. John Paul II closely connected these categories with the notion of intrinsic evil and stressed the clarity with which certain actions could be universally prohibited based on the object of the act (*Veritatis Splendor*, nos. 79–80). Francis has given far less attention to the category of intrinsically evil acts, but he certainly accepts the notion. Indeed, the one reference to the idea in his encyclicals to date occurs in a quotation from *Veritatis Splendor* offered as part of a rejection of relativism (*Fratelli Tutti*, no. 209, quoting *Veritatis Splendor*, no. 96). Francis's own writings, meanwhile, contain emphatic condemnations of various immoral behaviors, from "unbridled consumerism" in *Evangelii Gaudium* (no. 60) to environmental degradation in *Laudato Si'* and the death penalty

---

[35] Angel Perez-Lopez, "*Veritatis Splendor* and *Amoris Laetitia*: Neither Lamented nor Celebrated Discontinuity," *Nova et Vetera* 16, no. 4 (2018): 1183–1214, doi.org/10.1353/nov.2018.0044; Gerald O'Collins, "The Joy of Love (*Amoris Laetitia*): The Papal Exhortation in Its Context," *Theological Studies* 77, no. 4 (2016): 918–919, doi.org/10.1177/0040563916666823; Andrea Tornielli, "Pope Francis on the Correct Interpretation of *Amoris Laetitia*," *La Stampa*, September 12, 2016, www.lastampa.it/vatican-insider/en/2016/09/12/news/pope-francis-on-the-correct-interpretation-of-the-amoris-laetitia-br-1.34803710/.

in *Fratelli Tutti* (nos. 263–270). These and similar judgments show that Francis is not averse to the kind of clarity John Paul II sought to emphasize in his discussion of intrinsic evil and universal moral norms. By giving less weight to general categories, however, Francis presents these indictments as particular conclusions rather than abstract norms. Thus, the rejection of capital punishment hinges both on the observation that "the death penalty is inadequate from a moral standpoint and no longer necessary from that of penal justice" (*Fratelli Tutti*, no. 263), signaling an evaluation that, in a more Aristotelian fashion, reflects an understanding born of a particular time and place. The implication for freedom is that moral agents must exercise their freedom not only in determining what to do after a norm has been identified—the point at which John Paul II's consideration of martyrdom became so important—but also in deciding which norm truly applies. In effect, John Paul II's and Francis's distinct approaches to freedom can be merged sequentially: Francis stresses freedom's responsibility to discern whether an intrinsic evil is involved and define the relevant norm in a given situation, and John Paul II stresses freedom's power to adhere to the norm once defined.

If the first development in Francis's analysis of freedom accounts for the epistemic effects of the Fall, by tolerating plurality and ambiguity as a hedge against false certitude about the ineffable ways of God, the second development attends to the fallen nature of the world more broadly. Reflecting the same Aristotelian impulse that spawned his attention to particularity in discernment, Francis is much quicker than John Paul II to take the impact of worldly constraints on freedom into account and reshape the discussion about the shift from the theoretical ideal of freedom to its practical embodiment in real life accordingly. Whereas John Paul II was willing to acknowledge that there can indeed be external (and internal) influences on the moral agent that would impact their *perceived* degree of freedom (see again *Veritatis Splendor*, no. 33), he appealed to the witness of martyrs to insist that the agent's actual freedom—at the level of its Platonic ideal—can never be diminished.

Francis, on the other hand, in his more Aristotelian fashion, appears skeptical of the degree to which this theoretical ideal is encountered in practice, particularly in this fallen world. "Situated freedom, *real freedom*," he declares, "is limited and conditioned. It is not simply the ability to choose what is good with complete spontaneity.... A person may clearly and willingly desire something evil, but do so as the result of an irresistible passion or a poor upbringing. In such cases, while the decision is voluntary . . . it is not free" (*Amoris Laetitia*, no. 273, emphasis added). Here one can see an appreciation of the imperfections of the "not yet" that received less attention in the implicit eschatology shaping John Paul II's discussion of freedom, as

Francis incorporates the influence of a fallen world as a constraint on the practice of moral agency in a way John Paul II's focus on the theoretical power of freedom could not fully recognize. Francis's appeals to freedom in discernment make sense as a response to this problem, granting each moral agent the room to meaningfully pursue the good even as they navigate the particular web of intersecting influences that conspire to constrain their practical ability to exercise the full potential of the freedom John Paul II outlined as a theoretical ideal.

Although Francis is not especially clear about the mechanisms by which freedom "is limited and conditioned" in its translation from theory to practice, one plausible explanation can be found in recent developments in Catholic moral theology surrounding the concept of structural sin. The turn to these developments is justifiable for three reasons. First, the idea of structural sin has already received magisterial recognition, making the category relevant for interpreting Francis's magisterial teaching.[36] Second, Francis has explicitly noted the way economic structures (*Fratelli Tutti*, no. 108), social institutions (*Laudato Si'*, no. 142), and "cultural factors" (*Amoris Laetitia*, no. 33) serve as constraining influences on freedom, bringing a decidedly structural perspective to his ethical analyses.[37] Because these are all relevant elements in the theological discussion of structural sin, this concept has added value as an interpretative tool for the claims Francis is making.[38] Finally, the understanding of structural sin currently advocated by Catholic moral theologians does justice to Francis's insistence that even when freedom is limited, it remains "real freedom." In fact, the desire to find a "non-deterministic" explanation that can both "appreciate the radical character of human freedom . . . [and] recognize the constraints on that freedom which individuals face in their daily life within social structures" has been a driving force in the refinement of the theological understanding of structural sin for

---

[36] For more on the incorporation of this concept into magisterial teaching (before Francis), see Margaret Pfeil, "Doctrinal Implications of the Magisterial Use of the Language of Social Sin," *Louvain Studies* 27, no. 2 (2002): 132–152, doi.org/10.2143/LS.27.2.932. For the ways Francis has embraced a "structuralist approach," see Thomas Massaro, *Mercy in Action: The Social Teaching of Pope Francis* (Rowman and Littlefield, 2018), 28–33.

[37] Kristin E. Heyer, "Walls in the Heart: Social Sin in *Fratelli tutti*," *Journal of Catholic Social Thought* 19, no. 1 (2022): 25–40, doi.org/10.5840/jcathsoc20221913.

[38] Notably, social structures, institutions, and culture are all central elements in the specific analysis of structural sin that has the most prominence in Catholic moral theology today. See Daniel K. Finn, ed., *Moral Agency Within Social Structures and Culture: A Primer on Critical Realism for Christian Ethics* (Georgetown University Press, 2020).

Catholic ethicists.[39] This priority means that the contemporary Catholic theological analysis of structural sin is particularly helpful for the task of reading Francis's views on freedom in continuity with John Paul II's, because its non-deterministic account of social constraints on freedom allows Francis's depiction of "situated freedom" that is "limited and conditioned" to coexist with John Paul II's theoretical ideal.

In the intervening years since the publication of *Veritatis Splendor*, Catholic moral theologians have developed this non-deterministic account of the operation of structural sin through the incorporation of insights found in critical realist sociology. Broadly speaking, critical realism defends the idea that society is organized in such a way that the connections between people create "social structures" that have a real impact in the world. These social structures exert their influence through the incentives and restrictions they impose on the people who interact with the structures. Thus, a corporation is a structure that emerges from the relationships that link a company's employees to their bosses and the corollary relationships that then link all these workers to the customers. Within the corporate structure, certain behaviors are incentivized (behave this way and you may see a promotion) and others are restricted (behave that way and you will be fired), exerting an influence on the people who interact within the structure. The critical realist argument that Catholic moral theologians have appropriated contends that these incentives and restrictions have a tangible effect on the decisions people make as they navigate the structures in their lives. These structures never *make* somebody do something, because each agent remains free to ignore the incentives and accept the consequences for violating the restrictions, but the structures do have a causal impact by shifting the costs associated with certain behaviors. Indeed, if the incentives are particularly high or the restrictions particularly severe, then fewer people will buck the trend and many (or most) will choose to work within the system.[40]

The upshot of the recent Catholic theological appropriation of this critical realist description of social structures is that Catholic theologians have a way of explaining how an individual moral agent can simultaneously preserve the freedom of self-determination while nevertheless facing real constraints that may make the exercise of that

---

[39] Daniel K. Finn, "What is a Sinful Social Structure?," *Theological Studies* 77, no. 1 (2016): 143, doi.org/10.1177/0040563915619981.

[40] For an explanation of the critical realist account of social structures that gives attention to its potential compatibility with Catholic theology, see Finn, "What is a Sinful Social Structure?," 151–154. See also Daniel J. Daly, *Structures of Virtue and Vice* (Georgetown University Press, 2021); and Daniel K. Finn, "Social Structures," in *Moral Agency Within Social Structures and Culture*, esp. 31–32.

freedom difficult to achieve. This approach provides, in other words, a way of affirming Francis's claims about the limited, conditional nature of "real freedom" without denying John Paul II's insistence that freedom retains its full power as a theoretical ideal. Yes, all options remain on the table, but some options are much more viable than others.

The critical realist account of the structural conditioning of freedom used in Catholic moral theology helps to make sense of Francis's famed assertion in *Amoris Laetitia* that "conscience can do more than recognize that a given situation does not correspond objectively to the overall demands of the Gospel. It can also recognize with sincerity and honesty what for now is the most generous response which can be given to God . . . amid the concrete complexity of one's limits, while not yet fully the objective ideal" (no. 303). Two points from this quotation bear emphasis in the context of the discussion of freedom and constrained agency.

First, Francis appeals to "the concrete complexity of one's *limits*" to make the case that conscience can come to terms with an agent's regrettable but nevertheless real distance from what ought to be. In this manner, Francis accounts for the fact that human freedom is often constrained in ways that are not strictly traced back to an agent's own culpable failures. This suggests a contrast, to a degree, with John Paul II, who had a tenuous relationship with the concepts of structural and social sin as a result of his interest in their diagnostic power (see *Sollicitudo Rei Socialis*, no. 36) alongside a fear that they could be used to undermine personal responsibility (see *Reconciliatio et Paenitentia*, no. 16). Francis is more convinced by the former and less concerned with the latter, resulting in a willingness to attend to the structural forces shaping and constraining human freedom.[41] Indeed, his earlier comments in *Amoris Laetitia* about the influence of mitigating factors (nos. 301–302) indicate that Francis not only acknowledges the possibility of these forces in the abstract but also attends to their power in practice. Quoting the final Synod document with approval, Francis insists that "under certain circumstances people find it very difficult to act differently. Therefore, while upholding a general rule, it is necessary to recognize that responsibility with respect to certain actions or decisions is not the same in all cases" (no. 302). What he suggests, then, is that the lofty ideal may not be immediately attainable to the same degree for every moral agent, a conviction easiest to understand if one appreciates the critical realist notion that agency can be meaningfully constrained—but, again, not

---

[41] Heyer, "Walls in the Heart," 30–31; see also Kristin E. Heyer, "'Hearts of Flesh': Structural Sin and Social Salvation," *Proceedings of the Catholic Theological Society of America* 78 (2024): esp. 59–69, ejournals.bc.edu/index.php/ctsa/article/view/18527.

altogether eliminated—by structural factors. Francis's attentiveness to the limits of freedom in practice therefore offers a compelling nuance to John Paul II's emphasis on the persistent power of freedom in its theoretical ideal.

The second point from the quotation, which concerns Francis's appeal to the "objective ideal," helps to explain how this nuance functions alongside rather than in opposition to John Paul II's account of freedom. Assuming genuine continuity with John Paul II, Francis's recognition of an individual agent's distance from the objective ideal along with his insistence that conscience can accept this distance as "the most generous response which can be given" cannot amount to the license to dispense with moral norms nor to the suggestion that different rules apply to different people. Instead, reflecting the "law of gradualness" John Paul II outlined in *Familiaris Consortio* (no. 34), the same objective ideal remains in effect and establishes expectations for the individual who recognizes that the best they can offer in a given situation still falls short of that ideal.[42] This is the significance of the caveat that such a recognition applies "for now." As the same section in *Amoris Laetitia* goes on to explain, "This discernment is dynamic; it must remain ever open to new stages of growth and to new decisions which can enable the ideal to be more fully realized" (no. 303). Francis has opened the door for the freedom to discern that one might not be able to achieve all the good the objective ideal found in a general norm promotes, but this cannot be a static state of affairs. One is constantly called to moral growth. To accept that such growth is genuinely possible, however, one must maintain that the moral agent's deepest, existential freedom retains its potential to shape the agent and empower their choice to pursue the good no matter the circumstances. This claim, of course, is precisely what John Paul II's account of freedom stressed, meaning that Francis's reminders about the limitations on human freedom in practice need the complementary reinforcement of John Paul II's promotion of the absolute power of freedom in theory to avoid a reductionistic determinism that portrays every agent as nothing more than a product of their circumstances.

What the continuity of John Paul II and Francis provides, then, is a critical reminder that the moral question must not be reduced to an either/or choice between realizing the ideal no matter the cost and giving up on the ideal altogether. The fallenness of the human condition means that everyone needs a degree of humility in their efforts to discern the best path toward the objective ideal and also that some will face more limitations than others in their pursuit of the ideal.

---

[42] On the various uses of gradualism and its presence in the Synod that shaped *Amoris Laetitia*, see Jason King, "Which Gradualism? Whose Relationships," *Horizons* 43 (2016): 87–98, doi.org/10.1017/hor.2016.4.

Francis's reflections on freedom help to call attention to both these features of life in the already but decidedly not yet, offering a dose of Aristotelian realism to complement the Platonic idealism found in John Paul II's defense of freedom.

CONCLUSION

Fundamentally, what this article has asserted is that there is a productive tension that emerges when reading the legacy of *Veritatis Splendor*'s teachings on freedom in light of developments in Francis's subsequent reflections on the same theme. There are, indeed, distinctions between John Paul II's prioritization of the theoretical ideal of freedom, as the perennial capacity to cooperate with the unfailing power of grace and choose what is good, and Francis's assertion that *real* freedom is always conditioned. Yet, nevertheless, these two constructions of freedom can functionally coexist and, in fact, must do so for Catholics to avoid two equally dangerous poles. On one hand, a complete embrace of John Paul II without Francis would suggest that there is only ever one way to follow the demands of God, robbing the Christian moral life of its dynamism and making the summons to discipleship seem hopelessly unattainable for people who feel the burden of structural injustices most fully. On the other hand, a wholesale decoupling of Francis from John Paul II would imply that there is no reason to work against unjust structural constraints, inviting a form of complacency that would dismiss Jesus's assurance that "I came that they may have life, and have it abundantly" (John 10:10). Happily, by honoring the productive tension that emerges from keeping both John Paul II and Francis together, Catholics can evade these pitfalls and pursue a bold vision for the fullness of freedom, as a theoretical ideal already possible through grace, while grappling with the numerous structural constraints that mean its full realization is not yet a reality in practice. M

Conor M. Kelly, PhD, is associate professor in the Department of Theology at Marquette University. His research and teaching address moral discernment in ordinary life with an applied ethics focus on health care and Catholic social thought. His publications include *The Fullness of Free Time* (Georgetown University Press, 2020), *Racism and Structural Sin* (Liturgical Press, 2023), and the co-edited volumes *Poverty: Responding Like Jesus* (Paraclete, 2018, with Kenneth R. Himes) and *The Moral Vision of Pope Francis* (Georgetown University Press, 2024, with Kristin E. Heyer).

Divine Authority and Absolute Moral Norms

Anthony Hollowell

Abstract: According to the Doctors of the Church, God is a divine Lawgiver who may give a command that overrides an absolute moral norm. In this paper, some of the modern and ancient scenarios in which absolute moral norms are superseded by divine authority will be explored and discussed. This article will also consider Francis's description of how conscience can generate such "exceptions" through a process of personal and pastoral discernment in the concrete lives of specific persons. In conclusion, the article considers the Magisterium's articulation of how moral norms and conscience are not destined to contradict each other but rather converge as mutual and complementary representatives of divine authority.

IN THE THIRTY YEARS SINCE THE PUBLICATION OF *VERITATIS Splendor*, papal comments about exceptions to absolute moral norms have proven difficult to interpret. These difficulties, which some critics describe as "confusion," are well documented in the pontificate of Francis, but Benedict XVI also stirred up this tension during his pontificate. One of the more "confusing" remarks came after Benedict XVI stated in a published interview that the use of a condom by a male prostitute with AIDS could represent "a first step in the direction of a moralization, a first assumption of responsibility, on the way toward recovering an awareness that not everything is allowed and that one cannot do whatever one wants."[1] Benedict XVI did state that condoms are not "a real or moral solution" to the problem of AIDS, but he did repeat his belief that, "in this or that case" and for "some individuals," the use of a condom in a sexual act (specifically that of a male prostitute infected with AIDS) would be, to some undefined and ambiguous extent, morally tolerable, so long as there was "the intention of reducing the risk of infection."[2]

The reaction to such a papal declaration was swift and decisive, for *Veritatis Splendor* affirms the existence of absolute moral norms that prohibit intrinsically evil acts "*semper et pro semper*, that is, without exception" (no. 82). Since the use of contraception is considered

---

[1] Benedict XVI, *Light of the World: The Pope, the Church, and the Signs of the Times*, trans. Michael Miller and Adrian Walker (Ignatius, 2010), 119.
[2] Benedict XVI, *Light of the World*, 119.

intrinsically evil, many wondered how it is coherent to teach that the use of a condom by "some individuals" is tolerable in any way. Is Benedict XVI teaching that absolute moral norms sometimes admit of exceptions?

As is often done in situations of "confusion," the DDF issued a clarifying statement. Referencing *Veritatis Splendor* (nos. 75–77), the DDF noted that "those involved in prostitution who are HIV positive and seek to diminish the risk of contagion by the use of a condom may be taking the first step in respecting the life of another—even if the evil of prostitution remains in all its gravity. This understanding is in full conformity with the moral theological tradition of the Church."[3] According to the DDF, Benedict XVI's statement in *Light of the World* is fully compatible with *Veritatis Splendor*, not on the basis of some revised understanding of absolute moral norms, but because of a "first step" in a morally-positive direction, even while performing an intrinsically evil act like contraceptive sexual intercourse among prostitutes.

With the publication of *Amoris Laetitia*, this same tension between absolute moral norms and alleged exceptions reached a new level of intensity. This escalation is due in part to the context, for Benedict XVI's comments had a colloquial and not a magisterial context, whereas Francis has insisted that the controversial teachings in *Amoris Laetitia* are to be understood as part of his Magisterium. This has created a perceived (or actual) conflict between fundamental principles in *Veritatis Splendor* and *Amoris Laetitia*, giving moral theologians some work to do in reconciling the perceived (or actual) difficulty.

To date, there have been a few approaches to resolving the difficulties. One approach has been to suggest, as the DDF did for Benedict XVI, that it is permissible to allow a "first step" by the acting person in these intrinsically evil situations.[4] Another approach has been to consider, from a normative perspective, the ways in which circumstances impact the species of a moral act, transforming the

---

[3] Dicastery for the Doctrine of the Faith, "Note on the Banalization of Sexuality Regarding Certain Interpretations of *Light of the World*," December 22, 2010, www.vatican.va/roman_curia/congregations/cfaith/documents/rc_con_cfaith_doc_2 0101221_luce-del-mondo_en.html.

[4] *Amoris Laetitia*, no. 305, citing *Evangelii Gaudium*, no. 44. See also Philippe Bordeyne, *Portare la legge a compimento:* Amoris Laetitia *sulle situazioni matrimoniali fragili* (Libreria Vaticana, 2018), 99–106; Francesco Cardinal Coccopalmerio, *Il Capitolo Ottavo della Esortazione Apostolica Post Sinodale* Amoris Laetitia (Libreria Vaticana, 2017), 27–30, 37–42; Gianfranco Girotti, Amoris Laetitia: *L'importanza della coscienza, del discernimento e il ruolo del confessore* (Libreria Vaticana, 2021), 53–60.

intrinsically evil act into something else entirely.[5] In this paper, I will discuss a third approach, appealing to the authority of God. This third approach, neither equivalent nor unrelated to the others, will be presented because it is found specifically in *Amoris Laetitia* and is one of the important ways Francis thinks the difficulties can be resolved.

To explore this third approach, the first section will consider situations in which an absolute moral norm seems to admit of an exception because of divine authority. The next section will consider when and how conscience functions as a faculty for discerning a divine judgement of moral acts which seem to contradict an established moral norm, focusing especially on norms that appear to be contradicted in *Amoris Laetitia*. The final section will consider some objections raised by John Finnis and Robert Spaemann which reveal the complementary, not contradictory, interaction between conscience and absolute moral norms, as envisioned by the Magisterium.

THE AUTHORITY OF GOD AND MORAL ACTS

This first section will begin with a description of *Veritatis Splendor*'s appeal to the authority of God, not moral systems, as the primordial and essential foundation of moral action. Then, several examples from Aquinas will be considered which illustrate and contextualize this teaching, especially as it applies to situations in which an absolute norm appears to be superseded by divine authority. In closing, this section will consider the role of divine authority in a process of "personal and pastoral discernment" of moral acts, as described in *Amoris Laetitia*.

According to *Veritatis Splendor*, there is a recurring tendency to reduce moral theology to ethical systems which, despite their value, do not and cannot serve as the end of moral action. This tendency towards systems-thinking is heavily critiqued in *Veritatis Splendor*, which dedicates a significant portion of its commentary to describing the flaws of ethical systems like proportionalism, consequentialism, and many other "-isms." This critique leads to the statement that "the Church's Magisterium does not intend to impose upon the faithful any particular theological system, still less a philosophical one" (no. 29). Rather than proposing a complete system of rules or even a theory that would address every moral problem, "the encyclical will limit itself to

---

[5] Giovanni del Messier, "Quando le circostanze mutano la specie intrinsecamente illecita: Considerazioni *a latere* di *Amoris laetitia*," *Studia Moralia* 60, no. 2 (2022): 305–323; Anthony Hollowell, "Moral Impossibility and Communion to the Divorced and Remarried," *Journal of Moral Theology* 13, no. 2 (2024): 18–43, doi.org/10.55476/001c.121938.

dealing with *certain fundamental questions regarding the Church's moral teaching*, taking the form of a necessary discernment about issues being debated by ethicists and moral theologians" (no. 5). From beginning to end, *Veritatis Splendor* understands itself as a text limited in scope, choosing to focus on the theological and philosophical limitations of moral systems by engaging in "a necessary discernment" of how these systems interact with other elements in the church's moral tradition.[6]

This critique of systems-thinking culminates in *Veritatis Splendor*'s affirmation that "*Following Christ is thus the essential and primordial foundation of Christian morality*" (no. 19). According to *Veritatis Splendor*, the goal of moral theology is not to produce a premeditated set of rules that answer all moral questions, but "that each person may be able to find Christ" (no. 7). This obligation to follow Christ is not some pious goal of moral action; rather, it is a moral imperative because the divine authority of Christ is the final criterion of moral acts, an idea found not only in *Veritatis Splendor* but also in the works of many Doctors of the Church. Thomas Aquinas is one Doctor who consistently advances this idea, and we will present three examples from his writings which manifest how following divine authority is the final criterion of moral acts in the Thomistic tradition.

In *De Malo*, Aquinas tries to understand God's command to the prophet Hosea to "take a harlot wife and beget of her a harlot's children" (q. 15, a. 1, obj. 8).[7] Because he views sexual intercourse with a harlot as fornication and thus a mortal sin, Aquinas wants to understand how this command of God can be considered licit. Aquinas responds with the following logic: "The copulation that would otherwise have been fornicacious was not such because of the authority of God himself, who is superior to the law of marriage" (q. 15, a. 1, ad obj. 8). For Aquinas, the resolution of this "confusing" command to Hosea is simple, not because of Aquinas's strict allegiance to the absolute moral norm that forbids adultery, but because the judgment of God is more authoritative than this norm, even a norm connected to something as critical as marriage.

Aquinas provides a second instance of this logic when he argues for the moral liceity of "theft" by the Israelites against Egypt: "What would otherwise have been theft was not theft (*fuisset furtum fuit non*

---

[6] For a detailed account of how one theologian experienced *Veritatis Splendor* as magisterial suppression of a moral system which permits contraception, see Bernard Häring, "A Distrust that Wounds," in *Understanding* Veritatis Splendor, ed. John Wilkins (SPCK, 1994), 9–13; for another theologian who celebrates *Veritatis Splendor* as magisterial support for a system of "exceptionless moral norms," see John Finnis, "Beyond the Encyclical," in *Understanding* Veritatis Splendor, 69–76.

[7] Thomas Aquinas, *De Malo*, trans. Richard Regan (Oxford University Press, 2001). All English translations of *De Malo* in this article come from this translation.

furtum) for the children of Israel when they despoiled the Egyptians, as Exodus 12:35–36 relates, because of the command of God, to whose power all things belong (*in cuius potestate sunt omnia*)" (q. 15, a. 1, ad obj. 8). Once again, the factor which changes a norm ("thou shall not steal") into a permissible act is divine authority. There is also a broadening of scope when compared to the previous example, for Aquinas states that God is superior, not just to the law of marriage, but to "all" (*omnia*).

A third recurrence of this logic appears in Aquinas's discussion of killing innocent persons. Aquinas states that it is always sinful to kill an innocent person, and yet he simultaneously teaches that "anyone who kills an innocent person in obedience to God's command commits no sin (*ille qui mandato Dei occidit innocentem, talis non pecca*), since God whose order he is executing commits no sin; on the contrary, he is showing his fear of the Lord thereby" (ST II-II, q. 64, a. 6, ad 1).[8] In this passage, Aquinas is trying to rationalize how God could command Abraham to kill his son Isaac, which he interprets to mean that God could command someone to kill an innocent person. For Aquinas, the explanation of such a scriptural and moral paradox was rooted in the authority of God, not the authority of the decalogue.

It is necessary to reflect briefly on these statements by Aquinas. In each scenario, Aquinas makes a distinction between the form and species of a moral act. Considered from the perspective of form, these persons committed sinful acts, but once the moral judge (in this case, Aquinas) factors in the command of God, the formal description of the act becomes inadequate for describing the species of the act. Thus Hosea can only be accused of the form of adultery but not the sin of adultery, for the command of God has made the "harlot" a licit "wife"; the Israelites committed the formal act of theft, but this "was *not* theft" (and thus a different moral act) because of divine authority; Abraham can be accused only of the form of murder but not the sin of murder because of this same authority.[9] This recurring distinction between the form and species of a moral act provides a poignant demonstration of

---

[8] Thomas Aquinas, *Summa Theologiae*, trans. Marcus Lefébure (Eyre and Spottiswoode, 1975). Such a teaching, found not only here in Aquinas but also in the writings of other Doctors, makes it difficult to give absolute allegiance to the belief that "the Church's tradition, authoritatively interpreting revelation, has constantly and most firmly taught as a truth to be held definitively by every Catholic [that] it is always wrong to choose to kill the innocent, whatever the circumstances" (John Finnis, "Beyond the Encyclical," 70).

[9] Even if Abraham did kill Isaac, Aquinas says that it would not have been murder "because his son was due to be slain by the command of God, Who is Lord of life and death," and any person following such an order "would be no murderer any more than God himself would be" (ST I-II, q. 100, a. 8, ad 3., trans. Fathers of the English Dominican Province [Benziger, 1947]).

how there is no ethical system that can ever replace divine authority as the supreme authority for defining the species of a moral act.[10] For Aquinas, even the norms of the decalogue are incapable of providing a definitive judgment for every personal moral act because only the voice of God has such all-encompassing authority over the definition of such acts, a logic that derivatively applies to the moral norms in *Veritatis Splendor* and any other magisterial document. While a theologian or a moral system may possess quasi-complete knowledge of the form of a moral act, a final determination of the species of *every* moral act must include the will of God, at least in the Thomistic tradition.[11]

Furthermore, these "exceptions" did not erode the validity of the decalogue for Aquinas; rather, they illustrate the authority undergirding the decalogue, which is God, not an ethical system. If Aquinas could provide such notable exceptions to the commandments without eroding their authority, it is at least theoretically possible that some papal "exceptions" will not erode the role of absolute moral norms in the Magisterium.[12]

---

[10] Jean Porter argues that moral systems (like consequentialism) provide more certainty about the species of a moral act than can ever be found in the Thomistic tradition: "It is not the case that Aquinas's analysis brings more certainty to individual moral judgments than does consequentialism; to the contrary, most consequentialists would assert what Aquinas more than once denies, namely, that we can arrive at a certain moral judgment about every specific moral act" ("The Moral Act in *Veritatis Splendor* and in Aquinas's *Summa Theologiae*," in Veritatis Splendor: *American Responses*, ed. Michael Allsopp and John O'Keefe [Sheed and Ward, 1995], 293).

[11] A similar idea appears in Thomas's description of the possibility for error among the angels. Thomas says that both angels and demons intuit perfectly the essences among the natural order ("by merely intuiting an essence they know all that can be said about it"), but error is possible for the demons because of their "unconditional judgments" (*judicant absolute*) that neglect an account for the supernatural order ruled by the wisdom of God (ST I, q. 58, a. 5, resp., trans. Kenelm Foster [Eyre and Spottiswoode, 1968]). One commentator notes that, for the angels who remain good, "all their thought about the universe is ultimately conditional—conditioned by reverence. In the fallen angels this condition, this brake is removed; hence they are liable to dogmatize, and so to err" (ST I, trans. Kenelm Foster [Blackfriars], 160, n. 4). Unconditional judgments of *every* moral act, among angels as well as among moral theologians, are liable to error because the supernatural order (according to Aquinas) sometimes generates anomalies that are unique "exceptions" to the natural order.

[12] Aquinas connects these normative "exceptions" to the logic of miracles, noting that some complex cases are not "a contradiction to the principles which God has implanted in nature, but an exception to them (*nec tamen talis dispensatio datur contra rationes quas Deus naturae inseruit, sed praeter eas*), because those principles are not intended to apply to all cases but to the majority," and that "it is not contrary to nature when certain occurrences take place in natural things miraculously" (ST *Supplementum*, q. 65, a. 2, ad 2, trans. Fathers of the English Dominican Province; see also *De Potentia*, q. 6, a. 2; ST III, q. 43, a. 1, resp.). Kevin Flannery interprets Aquinas as one who thinks that "these seeming 'exceptions' to the moral law as

Presuming the validity of Aquinas's understanding of the above scriptural paradoxes, his same logic will now be applied to more contemporary situations. In a way that echoes Aquinas's provocative thought above, Francis has expressed ongoing concern about ethical systems that supersede God as the final and primordial authority of moral acts. Thus he says that "it is reductive simply to consider whether or not an individual's actions correspond to a general law or rule, because that is not enough to discern and ensure full fidelity to God in the concrete life of a human being" (*Amoris Laetitia*, no. 304). Despite the appearance of a lack of concern for norms or rules, Francis is drawing attention to what *Veritatis Splendor* calls the primordial foundation of Christian morality, which is fidelity to the Lawgiver, not moral equations. This fidelity to God has created numerous paradoxes in moral theology, and while Aquinas has provided several examples of such paradoxes, Francis does not think they are the last examples.

In *Amoris Laetitia*, this appeal to the authority of God is applied specifically to sacramental norms for those who are divorced and remarried, creating a wave of confusion for many theologians who considered these situations resolved normatively (and therefore definitively) by Francis's predecessors.[13] But the Doctors of the Church would not have been offended by Francis's appeal to "full fidelity to God in the concrete life of a human being" as a foundation from which could arise a judgment that diverges from strict application of the normative protocol guiding the divorced and remarried. When a law for the divorced and remarried comes into conflict with the will of God, Francis thinks that the Lawgiver, not the

---

formulated are not exceptions at all but fall within the scope of the moral law as intended by the legislator (God)" ("Conscience and the Moral Law," *The National Catholic Bioethics Quarterly* 23, no. 4 [2023]: 613). A thorough discussion of how, exactly, Aquinas and other theologians and Doctors explained these exceptions is presented in John Dedek, "Intrinsically Evil Acts: An Historical Study of the Mind of St. Thomas," *The Thomist*, 43, no. 3 (1979): 385–413, doi.org/10.1353/tho.1979.0023.

[13] A variety of documents expressing confusion are presented in *Defending the Faith Against Present Heresies*, ed. John Lamont and Claudio Pierantoni (Arouca, 2021). The following is a brief selection of moral commentaries on this topic, in chronological order: Alain Thomasset and Jean-Miguel Garrigues, *Une morale souple mais non sans boussole* (Cerf, 2017); Stephan Goertz and Caroline Witting, eds., Amoris Laetitia: *un punto di svolta per la teologia morale?* (San Paolo, 2017); Salvatore Cipressa, ed., *La Teologia Morale dopo L'*Amoris Laetitia (Cittadella, 2018); Angel Perez-Lopez, "*Veritatis Splendor* and *Amoris Laetitia*: Neither Lamented nor Celebrated Discontinuity," *Nova et Vetera* (English Edition) 16, no. 4 (2018): 1183–1214; Gianfranco Girotti, Amoris Laetitia: *L'importanza della coscienza, del discernimento e il ruolo del confessore* (Libreria Vaticana, 2021); Vimal Tirimanna, "Moral Norms/Principles and Lived Reality: Does *Amoris Laetitia* re-echo the Pastoral Moral Theological Spirit of St. Alphonsus?," *Studia Moralia* 59, no. 2 (2021): 297–332; *Sui Sentieri di* Amoris Laetitia: *Svolte, Traguardi, e Prospettive*, ed. Roberto Massuro (Cittadella, 2022).

law, should determine the case. Francis is not alone in this judgment, for he has many Doctors to support him.[14]

One important way in which Francis differs from the precedent set by these Doctors is the imposition of ecclesial authority to help discern fidelity to God. Such an idea is not found in Aquinas and many of the Doctors, who acknowledged Abraham's capacity to discern God's command to kill his innocent son without consulting another person.[15] But Francis is more cautious, teaching that divorced and remarried persons should undergo a process of "personal and pastoral discernment" which involves not only the individual but also their pastor (*Amoris Laetitia*, no. 300). In essence, Francis has commanded pastors to analyze more closely some of the irregular situations in their community, helping the faithful through "a process of accompaniment and discernment which guides the faithful to an awareness of their situation before God" (no. 300). The criteria for this discernment could not be any clearer: to determine God's judgment on the specific situation, which Aquinas has shown above is not always equivalent to a norm. According to the Doctors of the Church, there are some persons who transgress an absolute moral norm "not in human delusion but under divine command, not in error but in obedience," setting an example for pastors to be alert for similar anomalies among those entrusted to their care (Augustine, *City of God*, 1.26).[16] Rightly, therefore, does Francis encourage the divorced and remarried, and the pastors who serve them, to avoid reducing the voice of Christ exclusively to a rule. These rules are an important part of this discernment, but they are not always equivalent to the voice of Christ; to better hear this Lawgiver's voice, Francis thinks accompaniment and discernment should be as normative for the divorced and remarried as the norms themselves.

THE CHRISTONOMOUS CONSCIENCE

In the previous section, examples were provided, both in the early and contemporary Church, of "exceptions" to absolute moral norms

---

[14] Many of these Doctors are cited in Dedek, "Intrinsically Evil Acts," 385–413. See also Ambrose of Milan, *De Virginibus*, 3.7; Jerome, *Commentary on Jonah*, 1.12; Augustine of Hippo, *The City of God*, 1.26.

[15] Regarding human law, Aquinas says that some perils can be so sudden that "the very necessity carries a dispensation with it, for necessity knows no law (*necessitas non subditur legi*)" (ST I-II, q. 96, a. 6, resp., trans. Thomas Gilby [Eyre and Spottiswoode, 1966]). Aquinas later admits of dispensations due to necessity even for divine laws (ST II-II, q. 66, a. 7), making the necessity, not ecclesial discernment, the rational basis for such a dispensation.

[16] Augustine, *City of God*, trans. William Babcock, The Works of Saint Augustine: A Translation for the 21st Century, vol. 6 (New City, 2012).

by appealing to divine authority. In the contemporary church, Francis thinks a process of "personal and pastoral discernment" may give rise to some of these exceptions, and he appeals specifically to conscience as a critical faculty for guiding this process of discernment.[17] Therefore, this section will consider conscience and its capacity to generate decisions that would supersede an absolute moral norm, focusing on the difference between an auto-nomous ("self-law") conscience and a christo-nomous ("Christ-law") conscience in moral discernment.

First, it is important to clarify what is meant by "conscience." In his reflections on conscience in *Veritatis Splendor*, John Paul II repeats the consensus opinion of the Catholic tradition that conscience involves "a dialogue of man [sic] with God," is "the sacred place where God speaks to man," and thus forms "the proximate norm of personal morality" (nos. 58, 60). John Paul II further teaches that the maturity and responsibility of these judgements of conscience "are not measured by the liberation of conscience from objective truth, in favor of an alleged autonomy in personal decisions, but, on the contrary, by an insistent search for the truth and by allowing oneself to be guided by that truth in one's actions" (no. 61). Here and throughout the encyclical, John Paul II does not reduce conscience to a purely subjective, rationalistic, and autonomous faculty; instead, conscience represents something divine, relational, and absolute. The conscience cannot achieve authoritative status in isolation; rather, it does so only through an active and living relationship with objective truth.

Cardinal Newman provides some clarifying insights into the role of objective truth in forming the conscience. His insights are particularly important because, according to Ratzinger, the treatment of conscience at the Second Vatican Council "takes its place in the line of thought deriving from Newman," thus making it both difficult and negligent to find a contemporary discussion on conscience without reference to Newman.[18] Newman explains that a primordial, isolated, and unformed conscience "is so delicate, so fitful, so easily puzzled, obscured, perverted, so subtle in its argumentative methods, so impressible by education, so biased by pride and passion, so unsteady in its flight" that it is "at once the highest of all teachers, yet the least luminous," thus requiring guidance by "the Church, the Pope, and the Hierarchy" to become an authentic and robust expression of the voice

---

[17] One commentator correctly notes that "the deeper theological question raised by *Amoris Laetitia* is the question of the place of conscience in moral discernment" (Ryan Connors, "*Veritatis Splendor* at Thirty," *The National Catholic Bioethics Quarterly* 23, no. 4 [2023]: 662).

[18] Joseph Ratzinger, "The Dignity of the Human Person," in *Commentary on the Documents of Vatican II*, ed. Herbert Vorgrimler (Herder and Herder, 1969), 134.

of God.[19] Only through a relationship with authority outside itself (in this case, the various organs of the Magisterium) can conscience attain its fullest dignity and veracity. But once this active and living relationship with objective truth is established, conscience becomes so authoritative, absolute, and binding in its judgments that it was believed by Newman hierarchically superior (or at least equivalent) to the pope himself.[20] Like Aquinas, for whom it was not scandalous to consider real instances in which the voice of God would override a rule of the decalogue, Newman was not scandalized by concluding that conscience (which he describes as the "aboriginal vicar of Christ") can lead to judgments that would override the norm of a pope.[21] This type of conscience, no longer auto-nomous but rather "christo-nomous," is not some puppet instrument of public opinion or socially-acceptable sentiment; rather, it is an active and open pathway through which Christ himself speaks. And the words he speaks are not suggestions; according to Aquinas, they are commands that bind so absolutely and definitively that to neglect such commands is to incur mortal sin.[22]

It is in the context of this tradition of giving normative authority to conscience when it is in active relationship with objective truth that

---

[19] John Henry Newman, "Letter to His Grace the Duke of Norfolk," in *Newman and Gladstone: The Vatican Decrees* (University of Notre Dame Press, 1962), 132–133. Joseph Ratzinger likewise speaks of the need for the primordial conscience to be formed by the Magisterium, and that "the Magisterium has the right to expect that the conscience will be open to it in a manner befitting the seriousness of the matter" (*On Conscience* [National Catholic Bioethics Center, 2007], 63). *Veritatis Splendor* (no. 64) likewise teaches that "Christians have a great help for the formation of conscience in the Church and her Magisterium."

[20] Newman, "Letter to His Grace," 138.

[21] Understandably, there is often some hesitancy in accepting that Newman's comments can lead to such a claim (Tracy Rowland, "Principles for a New Ressourcement in a Time of Crisis," *The New Ressourcement* 1, no. 1 [2024]: 155), but Newman cites several possible examples of this divergence, noting that a dictate of conscience "in order to prevail against the Pope, must follow upon serious thought, prayer, and all available means of arriving at a right judgment on the particular matter" ("Letter to His Grace," 135–136). Ralph McInerny says that Aquinas would agree with Newman's ordering of conscience and the papacy, "since this [ordering] means, God first, then the pope. And, when pope and Church teach infallibly, to toast them is to toast God, no conflict being possible. That is what infallibility means" ("Conscience and the Object of the Moral Act," in *Crisis of Conscience,* ed. John Haas [Crossroad, 1996], 106).

[22] Aquinas states that even if an erroneous conscience "declares that something which is indifferent or intrinsically evil (*per se malum*) is a command of God," then the acting person commits a mortal sin (*mortaliter peccat*) if this command is *not* followed, because the acting person has "decided not to observe the law of God." Here, conscience *is* the law of God for the acting person, even if conscience is in error (*Questiones Disputatae de Veritate*, q. 17, a. 4, resp., trans. James McGlynn [Henry Regnery, 1953]).

some of the apparent contradictions between *Veritatis Splendor* and *Amoris Laetitia* begin to dissolve. Specifically, Francis has taught in *Amoris Laetitia* that "priests have the duty to accompany the divorced and remarried in helping them to understand their situation according to the teaching of the Church and the guidelines of the bishop. Useful in this process is an examination of conscience through moments of reflection and repentance" (no. 300). Clearly, this examination of conscience is not some autonomous and subjectivistic exercise; rather, it places the conscience of the acting person into a relational dialogue with a pastor, the teachings of the church, and the guidelines of the bishop, which are, according to Newman, the essential ingredients for ensuring that conscience is communicating the voice of Christ, thus becoming christonomous. Admittedly, such an appeal to the christonomous conscience is not mentioned in *Familiaris Consortio*, where the only discernment necessary for the pastor is determining whether or not the irregular couple is engaging in sexual intercourse: if so, then they are in a state of mortal sin and cannot receive communion, but if they are not having sexual intercourse, then they can live as brother and sister and receive communion.[23] It is precisely this systematic, universally binding, and non-varying moral equation which Francis wants to subjugate to the living voice of Christ. While Francis teaches that this discernment "can never prescind from the Gospel demands of truth and charity, as proposed by the Church" (no. 300), so too does he state that "it can no longer be said that all those in any 'irregular' situation are living in a state of mortal sin and are deprived of sanctifying grace" (no. 301) and that such persons can receive "the help of the sacraments" (no. 305, n351).[24]

Such a statement by Francis is sometimes considered contradictory to *Familiaris Consortio* and, derivatively, *Veritatis Splendor*.[25]

---

[23] Even this moral equation is a development of praxis, for prior to *Familiaris Consortio*, an irregular couple who lived as brother and sister were still subject to the penalty of excommunication (1917 *Code of Canon Law*, c. 2356). See also Maurizio Faggioni, "La Teologia del Matrimonio in *Familiaris Consortio* e Amoris Laetitia: Aspetti Pastorali," *Studia Moralia* 60, no. 1 (2022): 149–150.

[24] Some have expressed doubt as to whether this teaching in *Amoris Laetitia* means that Communion can be given to some persons in irregular situations, and the Magisterium has continued to state explicitly that such a possibility must be discerned and not reduced to an all-encompassing rule. See *Acta Apostolica Sedis* 108, no. 10 (2016): 1071–1074; Dicastery for the Doctrine of the Faith, "Response to a Series of Questions Posed by His Eminence, Dominik Cardinal Duka, OP, Regarding the Administration of the Eucharist to Divorced People Living in a New Union," September 25, 2023, no. 4, www.vatican.va/roman_curia/congregations/cfaith/documents/rc_con_cfaith_pro_202 30925_risposte-card-duka_en.html.

[25] *Amoris Laetitia* never cites *Veritatis Splendor*, but it does cite *Familiaris Consortio* twenty-four times always to demonstrate continuity, indicating which document Francis considered most applicable to *Amoris Laetitia*.

However, Francis's teaching on conscience and discernment is intrinsically united to *Veritatis Splendor* insofar as this discernment has, as its goal, to help conscience fully realize God's will in a concrete situation, which *Veritatis Splendor* considers the deepest and primordial foundation of moral action. Newman himself articulated the way in which a christonomous conscience is hierarchically superior (or at least equivalent) to the dictates of a specific pope, and there is nothing radical in applying Newman's principle to one important norm in *Familiaris Consortio*, especially when the authority who has advocated for such a possibility includes Francis and many bishops in union with him.[26]

For Francis, one important aspect of this christonomous conscience is that it is dynamic, not static, for what God is commanding in one moment is not strictly equivalent to his future commands. Thus Francis states that conscience "can also recognize with sincerity and honesty what for now is the most generous response which can be given to God, and come to see with a certain moral security that it is what God himself is asking amid the concrete complexity of one's limits, while yet not fully the objective ideal" (*Amoris Laetitia*, no. 303). Because "what God himself is asking" may change over time, Francis wants personal and pastoral discernment to be a continual process instead of a once-and-for-all decision that determines every future act. Hence he teaches that "what is part of a practical discernment in particular circumstances cannot be elevated to the level of a rule" (no. 304). This mirrors the logic of Aquinas, who restricted God's command for Abraham to kill his innocent son to a temporary and personal obligation not to be interpreted as a rule for all, but an obligation that changed in very short time even for Abraham. According to both Aquinas and Francis, following Christ via conscience may admit of unique "exceptions" to standardized rules, but these exceptions do not redefine the rule. Even when such an exception is commanded, conscience must remain in active dialogue with God who may give orders that differ from the current obligation. Thus to be a christonomous conscience is to be an active, engaged, and ever-attentive conscience, an idea emphasized by Francis but stated in similar terms by Newman and in *Veritatis Splendor*.

---

[26] There are reasons to think that John Paul II would not be scandalized by such an application of conscience to one of his magisterial norms. For just one example, when explaining the attempt to stone the adulteress because of the law of Moses, John Paul II noted that "the discernment of good and evil engraved in the human conscience can prove to be more profound and more correct than the content of a legal norm" ("General Audience," August 13, 1980, trans. the author, www.vatican.va/content/john-paul-ii/it/audiences/1980/documents/hf_jp-ii_aud_19800813.html).

SOME OBJECTIONS

In the previous section, Francis's proposal for a process of personal and pastoral discernment was seen to rely on a christonomous ("Christ-law") conscience categorically distinct from an autonomous ("self-law") conscience. Because this process can sometimes lead to judgments that differ from the normative guidelines, this section will consider limits to such a process, for if personal and pastoral discernment can rephrase moral norms for some of the divorced and remarried, what is to stop such discernment from being applied to every magisterial and scriptural norm? Can "personal and pastoral discernment" lead a person to murder a child, steal from the poor, or commit adultery?

There are three vantage points from which we will consider this question. The first is the perspective of Aquinas, who in three short sentences overrides three different commandments (thou shall not steal, thou shall not kill, thou shall not commit adultery), noting how God himself is superior to these commandments and can direct a person to an act which, considered normatively, is an "exception" to the divine commandment. There is no good reason to believe that Aquinas thought this logic should stop with just these three commandments, for Aquinas states that God is supreme over "all" (*omnia*) and not just these three commandments.[27]

The second perspective to consider comes from John Finnis's concern for the rational consequences of allowing any exceptions to absolute moral norms. According to Finnis, if there exists a single exception in which it is licit for an innocent person to be killed, then there no longer exists any "reason" to prevent others from doing likewise; after granting a single exception, "people will make exceptions for themselves."[28] But this comment reveals that Finnis's essential concern is autonomous morality, an arbitrary world in which the only law is what people make "for themselves." This concern, for all its justifications, still has its own limits, for some "exceptions" to absolute norms (at least in the Thomistic tradition) are based not on autonomous but rather divine authority, and God is always to be obeyed because God always leads to the good. This reason for an "exception" does not translate well into the atheistic world Finnis critiques and with whom he wishes to communicate, but the difficulty in translation does not equate to this divine authority being

---

[27] Aquinas does argue that the commandments of the first tablet of the decalogue admit of no such exceptions, but the commandments on the second tablet can admit of these exceptions (*In I Sent.*, d. 47, q. 1, a. 4, resp.).

[28] Finnis, "Beyond the Encyclical," 73.

unfounded.[29] *Amoris Laetitia*'s appeal to divine authority in situations involving the divorced and remarried does not equate to Finnis's concern of allowing persons to make exceptions for themselves, for both personal *and* pastoral discernment are required to discern this divine authority.[30] Francis does state that "individual conscience" needs to be better incorporated in some situations (*Amoris Laetitia*, no. 303), but even when it is, the ultimate authority remains God, not the individual.[31]

This leads to a third vantage point to consider, the perspective of Abraham. According to Finnis, "Allowing exceptions and justifying any choice to kill an innocent person radically transforms one's attitude towards human life as such. Making and carrying out any choices . . . on the basis of that transformed attitude reshapes individual character and social practices."[32] But if a tree is known by its fruit, then the fruit of Abraham's decision to follow God's command to kill his innocent son is not nearly as disastrous as a strict interpretation of Finnis's perspective would suggest. If innocent persons ever are being killed on the basis of autonomous authority, then the fruit will lead to Finnis's portentous forecast, and there are too many historical examples to prove his point, but for Aquinas, the authority directing Abraham's moral act is not autonomy but rather divinity, and this authority will produce different fruit because, in essence, this is to consider a different tree. Throughout *Veritatis Splendor*, the fruit of absolute autonomy is always disastrous, whereas the fruit of fidelity to God is freedom (John 8:32). Scripture says that Abraham lived in this freedom, that "the Lord had blessed Abraham in all things" (Genesis 24:1), even after planning and preparing to fulfill God's command to kill an innocent person. In forecasting the fruits of papal exceptions to moral norms, this scriptural precedent should be kept in mind, as well as avoiding interpretations that would

---

[29] Francis reminds theologians that "we will never be able to make the Church's teachings easily understood or readily appreciated by everyone. Faith always remains something of a cross; it retains a certain obscurity which does not detract from the firmness of its assent. Some things are understood and appreciated only from the standpoint of this assent, which is a sister to love, beyond the range of clear reasons and arguments" (*Evangelii Gaudium*, no. 42).

[30] Francis similarly states that it is a "grave danger" to think that "any priest can quickly grant 'exceptions'" (*Amoris Laetitia*, no. 300).

[31] John Paul II similarly emphasized the role of individual conscience for irregular marriages and the Eucharist when he stated that "the judgment of one's state of grace obviously belongs only to the person involved, since it is a question of examining one's conscience" (*Ecclesia de Eucharistia*, no. 37). But this statement is not papal approval of autonomy, for John Paul II (like Francis) emphasized the role of pastors in this process, noting that such pastors "cannot fail to feel directly involved" when the matter is grave sin.

[32] Finnis, "Beyond the Encyclical," 71.

confuse autonomous trees for christonomous trees. To expect the evils of autonomy from a christonomous conscience is to either misidentify this conscience or distrust the divine authority speaking in such a conscience.

Another insightful critic who wants to limit appeals to conscience when moral norms are at stake is Robert Spaemann. He notes that the word "conscience" often serves as a sort of "black box" for some theologians, and that when a person is told to violate an absolute moral norm by following their conscience, what these theologians are really saying is that "the Church is not convinced of the truth of its own teachings."[33] Spaemann cites the situation of the divorced and remarried as an example of his opinion: "The same is true when the Catholic Church advises divorced and remarried people to receive Holy Communion as their conscience instructs them. This is another way of saying that the Church no longer believes that marriages cannot be dissolved. It would never be written that indiscriminate promiscuity while receiving communion is a matter of personal conscience. It appears that the theme of conscience is carefully introduced when one feels on shaky ground."[34] Is this what Francis has done in *Amoris Laetitia*?

According to Spaemann, the dissolution of norms is inevitable when theologians tell people to follow "their conscience," which he says is equivalent to "personal conscience." So, in these comments, Spaemann is speaking about an autonomous conscience, not a christonomous conscience; Spaemann is not speaking about a conscience formed through an active and living relationship with Christ and his Church, but rather a conscience which has become the judge of the church. Spaemann and many others rightly describe how this autonomous authority would destroy all teaching authority in the Church.[35] Although this is an error which some have accused Francis of making in his remarks about the divorced and remarried, *Amoris Laetitia* does not give conscience such complete, autonomous, and subjective authority; rather, Francis presents his vision for a process of personal *and* pastoral discernment, a path which seeks "to form consciences, not to replace them" (no. 37). What this discernment yields is not so much "their conscience" or "personal conscience" but rather the church's conscience (if it can be called such), a conscience

---

[33] Robert Spaemann, "Conscience and Responsibility in Christian Ethics," in *Crisis of Conscience,* ed. John Haas (Crossroad, 1996), 129.

[34] Spaemann, "Conscience and Responsibility," 129.

[35] "Although we must always be bound by conscience, some of the greatest crimes of our own day have been committed, and are being committed, by an appeal to individual conscience, as though there were no higher norm" (Joseph Ratzinger, *Crisis of Conscience*, xiii). In this passage, Ratzinger refers to "individual conscience," not a christonomous conscience.

that has bridged the subject and object through a living relationship, thereby overcoming autonomy without losing the individual.[36] This is a conscience that reflects the unitive principles of communion, and so long as the pastor, the normative teachings of the church, and the guidelines of the bishop are part of this communion, Francis thinks that the judgment which emerges can be trusted as the voice of Christ.[37] At least in theory, this proposal by Francis is categorically distinct from Spaemann's critique, for any exceptions to sacramental norms for the divorced and remarried that arise in a christonomous conscience have divinity, not autonomy, as the basis of such exceptions. According to Aquinas, it would be a mortal sin *not* to follow such a conscience, even when commanding an act forbidden from a normative perspective in *Familiaris Consortio*.

Too often, any exception to a moral norm by way of conscience is presented as an illustration of how conscience and moral norms are destined to end in conflict, supposing that one or the other must be chosen as the ultimate arbiter of difficult moral questions.[38] But this is not the vision of the Magisterium, for *Gaudium et Spes* states that "the more right conscience holds sway, the more persons and groups turn aside from blind choice and strive to be guided by the objective norms of morality" (no. 16). According to this theory, both "right conscience" (the terminological equivalent of a christonomous conscience) and the objective norms of morality do not diverge, but rather converge in their content.[39] There are unique exceptions (noted by Aquinas and others) in which this theory from *Gaudium et Spes* seems to be upended, but Ratzinger notes that "the seeming exception is in reality very often the symptom that shows us the insufficiency of our previous schema of order, which helps us to break open this schema and to

---

[36] Ratzinger remarks that "conscience signifies the perceptible and demanding presence of the voice of truth in the subject himself. It is the overcoming of mere subjectivity in the encounter of the interiority of man with the truth from God." Ratzinger likewise laments that the modern age does "not allow for bridges between subject and object," and the properly formed conscience is one such bridge ("Conscience and Truth," in *Crisis of Conscience*, 9, 14).

[37] The presence of these objective elements keeps *Amoris Laetitia* in alignment with Flannery's assertion that "personal conscience cannot be separated from the objective moral law" ("Conscience and the Moral Law," 605).

[38] For sustained discussion on this idea in light of *Amoris Laetitia*, see Aristide Fumagalli, "Coscienza e Norma: Due poli da coniugare," in *Sui Sentieri di* Amoris Laetitia, 142–148.

[39] Thus Ratzinger says that "the conciliar text implies that obedience to conscience means the end to subjectivism, a turning aside from blind arbitrariness, and produces conformity with the objective norms of moral action" ("The Dignity of the Human Person," 135).

conquer a new realm of reality."[40] The challenging examples suggested by Aquinas and *Amoris Laetitia* illustrate, not that conscience and moral norms are destined to end in conflict, but that both conscience and moral norms serve as instruments of a single person (Christ) in whom there is "no confusion, no change, no division, no separation."[41] Neither conscience nor absolute moral norms should be revered in themselves; rather, the object of reverence is the divine Lawgiver who communicates through these two "organs" of truth.

In *Veritatis Splendor*, this unitive theory of conscience and moral norms is maintained by teaching that conscience itself *is* a norm (specifically, a proximate norm), making it impossible to separate the concept of conscience in *Veritatis Splendor* from the concept of norms. This intrinsic unity between conscience and norms has been maintained in *Amoris Laetitia*, for any exceptions to norms for the divorced and remarried are rooted in the authority of God who, in the words of Aquinas, "is superior to the law of marriage" (*De Malo*, q. 15, a. 1, ad 8). Following Aquinas, *Amoris Laetitia* argues that a person's conscience can never be too scrupulous in aligning itself to the personal dictates, and not just the recorded decalogue, of this Lawgiver.

The above objections of Finnis and Spaemann have additional value, for they draw attention to two perennial and interrelated concerns which further illustrate the complementary, not contradictory, interaction between norms and conscience in the Catholic moral tradition.

The first perennial concern is this: while an autonomous conscience is always distrusted for reasons defended clearly by Finnis and Spaemann, autonomous moral norms are equally dangerous. When moral norms are given authority to such an extent that they refuse subordination to the voice of Christ (or to one of his vicars, either aboriginal or historical), they have become auto-nomous by relying on the voice of man and not God; they have become, in the words of *Veritatis Splendor*, a "merely 'human' morality," a type of morality with its own capacity to justify heinous acts (no. 36). Without this subordination of norms to their primordial source of authority, persons like the Pharisees would be justified in their autonomous "religious" system, thereby transforming Christ into a person who is no longer freedom's advocate but rather freedom's restrainer.[42] In

---

[40] Joseph Ratzinger, "Concerning the Notion of Person in Theology," in *Anthropology and Culture*, ed. David C. Schindler and Nicholas J. Healy (Eerdmans, 2013), 114.

[41] Council of Chalcedon, *Definition of the faith*, trans. Robert Butterworth, in *Decrees of the Ecumenical Councils*, vol. 1, ed. Norman Tanner (Sheed and Ward, 1990), 86.

[42] Spaemann notes the presence of autonomous and destructive consciences in hyper-religious environments: "All sorts of things can be concealed by the term *conscience*.

such situations, divine authority is reduced to the autonomous (though no doubt religious) minds of pharisaical rule-creators who claim authority just as potent as the "personal and pastoral discernment" envisioned by Francis. At its logical terminus, giving moral norms absolute authority over conscience would be only a smoke-screen for returning moral theology to a foundation built on autonomy and not divinity, an autonomy such moral norms had supposedly eliminated.[43] Rightly, then, does the Church defend the need for moral discernment to depend on both moral norms and conscience, refusing to reduce one to the other but rather preserving them both in a mutually enriching and convergent relationship.

The second perennial concern for the church is the dissolution of conscience by appealing to conscience itself. Such dissolution of conscience is inevitable if moral theology were to travel one of two paths: first, if an autonomous conscience were made equivalent to the voice of Christ, then "right conscience" becomes only a fanciful term for group-think and self-will, which Ratzinger decries as "the canonization of subjectivity."[44] A second path is less discussed but equally fatal to conscience, and it is traveled by those who want to give moral norms (and other systems) complete and strict equivalence to the voice of Christ, turning "right conscience" into a fanciful term for "doing what the norm/system/equation has already determined." The first path leads to the canonization of subjectivity, but the second leads to a canonization of moral systems; the first leads to a dictatorship of relativism, the second to a dictatorship of Pharisees;

Christ himself tells us this is possible: 'The hour is coming when whoever kills you will think he is offering service to God' (John 16:2). Christ was no more inclined to teach us simply to follow our conscience than was Socrates" ("Conscience and Responsibility," 117). Francis likewise notes that the Pharisees, "even when they obey the commandments and do good works, are centered on themselves; they fail to realize that goodness comes from God.... They become closed in on themselves and isolated from the Lord and from others; their lives become futile and their works barren, like a tree far from water" (*Lumen Fidei*, no. 19). For both Spaemann and Francis, religious rules can function as cloaks for autonomous, self-willed moral systems which lead to slavery, not freedom.

[43] Newman has already warned that "if the pope [were to] speak against Conscience in the true sense of the word, he would commit a suicidal act.... On the law of conscience and its sacredness are founded both his authority in theory and his power in fact" ("Letter to His Grace," 138). But if this is true for the pope, then it is true for all theologians: to "speak against" a christonomous conscience in such a way that an absolute moral norm would become more authoritative than the christonomous conscience would be equivalent to overriding the divine foundation which gives authority to such norms. Far from defending absolute norms, Newman demonstrates how such logic destroys the authority of absolute norms.

[44] Ratzinger, "Conscience and Truth," 6. He similarly notes that "it will not do to identify man's conscience with the self-consciousness of the I, with its subjective certainty about itself and its moral behavior" ("Conscience and Truth," 16).

the first leads to an abuse of conscience, the second to the neglect of right conscience, and thereby a neglect of Christ. A great anxiety over the hyper-subjectivity of the modern age has prepared the church well to avoid the first path, but such anxiety is not fully equipped to avoid the second; indeed, a hyper-fixation on avoiding the first path can lead to travelling down the second. Just like Christology after Chalcedon, moral theology after *Veritatis Splendor* is destined to journey forever along a route that is not circuitous but rather precarious.

Furthermore, an appeal to conscience is not always done in order that a theologian may "carefully introduce" subtle logic which eventually destroys the validity of absolute norms (this is Spaemann's concern) but rather to help answer specific questions the norm alone cannot resolve. The norm is helpful in the abstract, but something is needed to clarify the concrete (and thus proximate) reality, for remote concepts begin to destabilize as all persons, including popes and the Doctors of the Church, zoom into the concrete details of what, *hic et nunc*, is to be done in light of the norm. The general prohibition against contraceptive sexual intercourse is clear, but the application of this norm to a detailed and complex situation (such as the use of a condom by a male prostitute with AIDS) puts the church on "shaky ground," and even the colloquial opinion of Benedict XVI is not enough to stabilize the difficulty.[45] Similarly, the general norm prohibiting sexual intercourse between unmarried persons is clear, but the application of this norm to some situations involving the divorced and remarried is not so clear to Francis, whose magisterial statements on the matter do not appear any more influential than Benedict XVI's colloquial statements. Regardless of the degree of receptivity, both papal teachings demonstrate the Magisterium's reliance on an authority that speaks to remote realities (absolute moral norms) and another authority that speaks to proximate realities (conscience), and situations continue to arise in which it can be difficult to translate between the two.[46] Moral norms clarify questions from a distance,

---

[45] Such difficulties are a recurring theme in all of ethics and not just "situation ethics" (*Veritatis Splendor*, no. 53), illustrated well in one paper which carefully distinguishes "abortion" from "induction before viability to eliminate a grave and present danger posed by a life-threatening condition resulting from the interaction of a normally functioning placenta with diseased organs of the mother" (Ascension Health, "Medical Intervention in Cases of Maternal-Fetal Vital Conflicts: A Statement of Consensus," *The National Catholic Bioethics Quarterly* 14, no. 3 [2014]: 477–489). This difficulty of normative precision is the basis of Newman's claim that "conscience cannot come into direct collision with the Church's or the Pope's infallibility; which is engaged only on general propositions, or the condemnation of propositions simply particular" ("Letter to His Grace," 134).

[46] Jean Porter interprets Aquinas as one who would think that "there are logical limits to the certainty and the degree of consensus that can be attained in moral judgment, even among those who share the same basic moral concepts and attempt to apply them

whereas conscience clarifies questions immediately in view; moral norms can be infallible but not precise, whereas conscience is precise but sometimes errs. The conscience may not be fully reliable, but it is absolutely necessary for translating the norm into its practical expression; so necessary, in fact, that to disregard the command of conscience is a mortal sin, which is the most unstable ground of all.

Thus, the precarious journey of moral theology will always lead to some situations in which conscience must function as a sort of "black box" for moral questions. Every moral norm stands on shaky ground as that norm gets closer to the concrete realities of a particular act, sometimes transforming an act which, upon inspection by the great Doctors of the Church, should only be considered an "exception" to an established moral norm. One of the challenges for moral theologians is to make room for these anomalies without turning the exception itself into a complete moral system or a threat to a system that already exists. The legal maxim "hard cases make bad law" is important to uphold in these situations, for both Benedict XVI and Francis have advocated for complicated cases to be treated individually and not extrapolated to a broad range of erroneous systems that destroy, rather than build upon, fundamental elements of *Veritatis Splendor*.

Although the power of systems-thinking remains attractive as an absolute answer to the most difficult cases, even Aquinas abandoned some difficulties to divine and not human authority. There is nothing in *Veritatis Splendor*, nor subsequent pontificates, that encourages hard moral cases to be resolved only through norms, and divine authority will not be lacking for those tasked with discerning these hard cases.

Anthony Hollowell, STD, currently serves as pastor in the Archdiocese of Indianapolis, dean of the Tell City Deanery, and visiting professor at Saint Meinrad School of Theology. His research focuses on the development of moral doctrine and epistemology. He completed his doctoral studies at the Accademia Alphonsiana.

---

in all good faith. . . . There will always be some hard cases about which we, as individuals, just cannot judge, or about which we, collectively, cannot agree" ("The Moral Act," 287).

Veritatis Splendor After Thirty Years: Exposition and Critique

Michael G. Lawler and Todd A. Salzman

Abstract: Some thirty years ago, as an antidote to widespread dissent from Catholic sexual teaching among many theologians and faithful, Pope John Paul II published his encyclical *Veritatis Splendor*. His stated purpose was "to reflect on the whole of the Church's moral teaching with the precise goal of recalling certain fundamental truths of Catholic doctrine which, in the present circumstances [a 'new situation'] risk being distorted or denied." In this essay, we focus on John Paul's teaching on natural law in *Veritatis Splendor* and offer several critiques of it.

THE MAJORITY OF CATHOLICS AND CATHOLIC THEOLOGIANS DO not accept official teaching on many sexual ethical issues. These teachings are grounded in the Magisterium's interpretation of natural law. That dissent became very public with the publication in 1968 of Paul VI's encyclical letter *Humanae Vitae* and its claim that "each and every marital act [of sexual intercourse] must of necessity retain its intrinsic relationship to the procreation of human life" (no. 10). This particular doctrine, the encyclical continues, "is based on the inseparable connection, established by God, which man on his own initiative may not break between the unitive significance and the procreative significance which are both inherent in the marriage act [of sexual intercourse]" (no. 12).[1]

Humanae Vitae was greeted with worldwide dissent, and that dissent has not only been sustained but has also grown. In a major study by Univision Communications in 2014, some 80 percent of Catholics worldwide were ignoring its ruling. The number dissenting in France was 94 percent, in Brazil 93 percent, in Spain 90 percent, in Mexico 88 percent, and in the United States 79 percent.[2] As an

---

[1] We recognize the lack of inclusive language in the official English translation of Church documents. Although we disagree with the exclusive male-dominated language, we will follow the official translation throughout our essay.
[2] Francis X. Rocca, "After 50 Years, a Pope's Birth-Control Message Still Divides Catholics," *Wall Street Journal* (May 10, 2018), www.wsj.com/articles/after-50-years-a-popes-birth-control-message-still-divides-catholics-1525962322.

antidote to the widespread dissent on sexual morals (*Veritatis Splendor*, no. 4), John Paul II published his encyclical *Veritatis Splendor*, setting forth for the first and, indeed, the only time in a papal encyclical what he considered to be an orthodox theory of Catholic moral theology. In this essay, we present John Paul II's treatment of natural law in *Veritatis Splendor* and argue that natural law, as the Pope describes it, is not as new as he might intend and suffers from many of the same drawbacks suffered by a traditional Catholic theory of natural law.

VERITATIS SPLENDOR

John Paul II states at the very beginning of his encyclical the Catholic position that "the splendor of truth shines forth in all the works of the Creator and, in a special way, in man, created in the image and likeness of God" (*Veritatis Splendor*, Introduction). That assertion runs all through and controls the message of his encyclical. He notes, however, that "a new situation has come about within the Christian community itself, which has experienced the spread of numerous doubts and objections of a human and psychological, social and cultural, religious and even properly theological nature" (no. 4). In response to this new situation, he says, his encyclical has

> the aim of treating "more fully and more deeply the issues regarding the very foundations of moral theology," foundations which are being undermined by certain present-day tendencies. . . . Certain of the Church's moral teachings are being found simply unacceptable; and the Magisterium itself is considered capable of intervening in matters of morality only in order to "exhort consciences" and to "propose values," in the light of which each individual will independently make his or her decisions and life choices. (no. 5)

Veritatis Splendor opens with two claims that control what follows, namely, that women and men can know truth because God has shown it to them, and that the encyclical and its author, John Paul II, are setting forth Catholic moral truth. For the Pope, the splendor of the truth "enlightens man's intelligence and shapes his freedom, leading him to know and love the Lord" (no. 1). The question that has arisen throughout human history and been famously formulated by Pilate arises here too: "What is truth?" (John 19:38). There have been many answers in intellectual history to that crucial question, but here we reflect on only two, one religious and the other philosophical.

The Christian religious answer to that question is easy and straightforward. It was given by Jesus in answer to a question from his Apostle Thomas. His answer could not be clearer: "I am the way, and the truth, and the life" (John 14:6). In his life, actions, and relationships, Jesus is the truth for all to see. "The decisive answer to every one of man's questions, his religious and moral questions in particular," John Paul II argues, and we agree, "is given by Jesus Christ or rather is Jesus Christ himself" (no. 2). Man and woman, "as a result of that mysterious original sin" dwell in a "darkness of error" (no. 1). Jesus dispels that darkness by his way, his truth, and his life. "Following Christ," therefore, "is the essential and primordial foundation of Christian [truth and] morality" (no. 19). Jesus asks his followers to follow specifically along the path of love: "This is my commandment that you love one another *as* I have loved you" (John 15:12). The "*as*" in that invitation, John Paul II insists correctly, "requires imitation of Jesus and of his love" (no. 19). For that to happen, of course, Jesus must first be known and understood, and that brings us to the philosophical question of what it is to know and understand.

God, John Paul II teaches, has already given an answer to the philosophical question of what it is to know and understand by creating man and woman and wisely ordering them to their final end through the law inscribed in their nature, the natural law. This natural law "is nothing other than the light of understanding infused in us by God, whereby we understand what must be done and what must be avoided. God gave this light and this law to man at creation." He also gave it "in the history of Israel, particularly in the 'ten words,' the commandments of Sinai" (no. 12). He also gave it, as we have already noted, in the life, actions, and relationships of Jesus, his incarnate Son, who could ultimately reply to the rich young man's question, "What good must I do to have eternal life?," with the simplest of answers: "Follow me" (no. 6; see Matthew 19:16–21). Follow me in my life, actions, and relationships.

The natural law receives its name "not because it refers to the nature of irrational beings, but because the reason that promulgates it is proper to human nature" (no. 42). The human, rational creature "is subject to divine providence in the most excellent way, insofar as it partakes of a share of providence, being provident both for itself and others. Thus it has a share of the Eternal Reason . . . [and] this participation of the eternal law in the rational creature is called natural law" (no. 43). Human reason and human law are essentially subject to divine reason and law. Leo XIII appealed to the higher reason of the divine lawgiver and argued that no prescription of human reason could have "the force of law unless it were the voice and the interpreter of some higher reason to which our spirit and freedom must be subject" (no. 44). It follows that the natural law "is the same thing as the eternal law, implanted in rational creatures, and inclining them to their right action and end; and can be nothing else but the eternal reason of God, the Creator and Ruler of all the world" (*Libertas Praestantissimum*, no. 8). We are now in a position to understand the meaning of the natural law. "It refers to man's proper and primordial nature, the nature of the human person, which is the person himself in the unity of soul and body, in the unity of his spiritual and biological inclinations and of all the other specific characteristics necessary for the pursuit of his end" (*Veritatis Splendor*, no. 50). Thus understood, the natural law "does not allow for any division between freedom and nature," as is frequently argued. "Indeed, these two realities are harmoniously bound together, and each is intimately linked to the other" (no. 50).

At this point, our inclination is to deal with conscience, for "in the depths of his conscience man detects a [natural] law which he does not impose on himself, but which holds him to obedience. Always summoning him to love good and avoid evil, the voice of conscience can when necessary speak to his heart more specifically: do this, shun that" (*Gaudium et Spes*, no. 16; *Veritatis Splendor*, no. 54). Since conscience will be dealt with more specifically and extensively elsewhere in this issue, we content ourselves with one single but crucial statement for this essay: "The judgment of conscience is a practical judgment, which makes known what man must do or not do. . . . This first principle of practical reason is part of the natural law; indeed, it constitutes the very foundation of the natural law" (*Veritatis Splendor*, no. 59).

IN SEARCH OF A UNIVERSAL ETHIC

Given its foundational and essential importance in the Catholic moral theological tradition, it is critical to understand how natural law is to be understood, which is brilliantly articulated in a recent document from the International Theological Commission (ITC), *In Search of a Universal Ethic: A New Look at the Natural Law*.[3] The ITC makes the contemporary Catholic position clear from the beginning of its document, inviting those who ponder the ultimate foundations of morality "to consider the resources that a renewed presentation of the doctrine of the natural law contains. This law affirms that persons and human communities are capable, *in the light*

---

[3] International Theological Commission, *In Search of a Universal Ethic: A New Look at the Natural Law*, www.vatican.va/roman_curia/congregations/cfaith/cti_documents/rc_con_cfaith_doc_20090520_legge-naturale_en.html. We refer to this document as quasi-magisterial because of its statutory relationship to the Congregation for the Doctrine of the Faith; see John Paul II's Motu Proprio *Tredecim Anni*, w? vatican.va/content/john_paul_ii/en/motu_proprio/documents/hf_jp_ii_motu_pro prio06081982_tredecim_anni.html.

of reason, of discerning the fundamental orientation of moral action in conformity with the very *nature of the human subject* and of expressing these orientations in a normative fashion in the form of precepts or commandments" (no. 9, emphasis added).

At the beginning of this section, we wish to draw attention to the use of two words throughout *In Search of a Universal Ethic*, for these words both point to the ITC's presentation of natural law as something dynamic, "far from a static given" (no. 64). The words are *inclination*, including the verb *incline*, and *orientation*, including the verb *orient*. *Inclination* and *incline* are used thirty-one times in the English version of the document, and *orientation* and *orient* twenty-four times.[4] There can be no doubt, therefore, how important both words are for the document's authors. We agree with William Mattison III that *inclination* "is used primarily to refer to those 'givens' discerned by practical reasoning."[5] Human persons are morally inclined to, or actively inclined toward, certain givens discerned as the result of a rational search of practical reasoning, and those givens are part of the natural law. The word *orient* is used in a more active sense, as something moving a person towards her fulfillment. "By the dynamisms that the Creator Word has inscribed in the innermost part of beings, he orients them to their full realization. This dynamic orientation is none other than the divine government that realizes within time the plan of divine providence, i.e., the eternal law" (no. 69).

"Every creature," the document continues, "in its own manner, participates in the *Logos*. Man, since he is defined by reason or *logos*, participates in it in an eminent manner. In fact, by his reason, he is capable of interiorizing the divine intentions manifested in the nature of things. He formulates them for himself under the form of a moral law that inspires and orients his actions" (no. 70). This reason-as-nature approach is the ancient Catholic approach to morality recovered. The ITC details the roots of this approach in the older moral tradition (chapter 1) but, given space restrictions, we choose to begin our analysis in the medieval world. The Scholastics, in general, consider reason to be the human characteristic *par excellence* and frequently speak of the natural law as being tantamount to reason. Aquinas, for instance, argues that what is distinctive about the human person is the capacity for rational self-direction (ST I-II, q. 1, a. 6) and

---

[4] See William C. Mattison III, "Part of the 'New Look' at the Natural Law: The Use of 'Orientation' Alongside 'Inclination,'" in *Searching for a Universal Ethic: Multidisciplinary, Ecumenical, and Interreligious Responses to the Catholic Natural Law Tradition*, ed. John Berkman and William C. Mattison III (Eerdmans, 2014), 284n6 and 287n13.

[5] Mattison, "Part of the 'New Look' at the Natural Law," 285.

that, while every creature acts in accordance with rational principles established by the Creator, only rational creatures are capable of following rational principles (ST I-II, q. 91, a. 2, ad 3). This Thomistic stance, which Jean Porter correctly describes as broadly Scholastic, is encapsulated in the phrase "reason as nature, which appears to have been first used by Philip the Chancellor."[6] Around 1188, the distinguished medieval canonist, Huguccio of Ferrara, sums up this stance. "The natural law is said to be reason, that is to say, a natural power of the soul by which the human person distinguishes between good and evil, choosing good and rejecting evil. And reason is said to be a law because it commands, also because it binds." It is said to be natural "because reason is one of the natural goods, or because it agrees with the highest nature, and does not dissent from it."[7] To embrace reason as a source of moral wisdom, Huguccio judges, is to embrace the natural law, and this is precisely what most contemporary Catholic natural law theologians do with, however, "a new look."

Jean Porter argues that, in contradistinction to the neo-Thomists of the eighteenth and nineteenth centuries, medieval natural law theorists, including Aquinas, "did not attempt to derive moral principles from a supposedly self-evident and fixed conception of human nature."[8] For them, "the natural law in its primary sense was identified either with reason or with the most basic principles of action, which were in turn linked to the image of God, that is, the capacity for moral judgment found in all men and women."[9] Germain Grisez and John Finnis, the founders of what is called the New Natural Law Theory, agree, teaching that nature, understood as what is pre- or non-rational, stands in contrast to reason and that moral terms are derived from reason alone.[10] Already sixteen years ago, we argued that "God has created an orderly universe, and every created thing within that universe participates in the eternal law according to its nature. Natural law is the participation of humans in the eternal law through reason."[11] In *Veritatis Splendor*, John Paul II agrees, arguing that thus the rational creature "has a share of the Eternal Reason, whereby it

---

[6] Jean Porter, *Natural and Divine Law: Reclaiming the Tradition for Christian Ethics* (Eerdmans, 1999), 87.
[7] Odon Lottin, *Le droit naturel chez saint Thomas D'Aquin et ses prédécesseurs*, 2nd ed. (Beyart, 1931), 109.
[8] Porter, *Natural and Divine Law*, 17.
[9] Porter, *Natural and Divine Law*, 17.
[10] See John Finnis, *Natural Law and Natural Rights*, 2nd ed. (Oxford University Press, 2011); Germain Grisez, "The First Principle of Practical Reason: A Commentary on *Summa Theologiae* Ia IIae, q. 94, a. 2," in *Natural Law Forum* 10 (1965): 162–201.
[11] Todd A. Salzman and Michael G. Lawler, *The Sexual Person. Toward a Renewed Catholic Anthropology* (Georgetown University Press, 2008), 62.

has a natural inclination to its proper act and end. This participation of the eternal law in the rational creature is called natural law" (no. 43).

Catholic moral theory, as the ITC document lays out, has largely moved away from a focus on a fixed "human nature" to an evolving "rational human person" (nos. 113–115). The once narrow, classicist understanding of human nature and natural law is in the process of being transformed into a broader, historically conscious, rational, and personalist understanding. The former defines the morality of acts based on the physical structure of those acts; sexual intercourse, for instance, is moral only when it is for procreation within a marital relationship. The latter defines the morality of acts based on the meaning of those acts for persons in relationship. Sexual intercourse, for instance, is moral when it is to celebrate and enhance the love between two partners, even when procreation is impossible, as it is for most of the life of every human female. Although Catholic moral theology has moved beyond physicalism and theoretically embraces personalism, there continues to be an epistemological distinction and ontological prioritization in various personalist accounts. Whereas John Paul II's personalism prioritizes the biological over the personal in his "ontological complementarity,"[12] we and other personalists prioritize the personal over the biological. In the former, the biological genitalia, penis and vagina, are the *sine qua non* for personal complementarity; in the latter, the personal looks at the human person holistically, including sexual orientation, to discern the appropriate genitalia, penis-vagina, penis-penis, or vagina-vagina, depending on a person's sexual orientation, for realizing truly human sexual acts.[13] Despite claims that John Paul II's theology of the body or official magisterial sexual teaching is not physicalist, both prioritize the biological over the relational in the absolute sexual doctrines that prohibit any non-reproductive marital sexual acts.

The ITC rejects a most important and, for some, much-contested fact, namely, that reason *deduces* "the precepts of the natural law, beginning from the definition of the essence [nature] of the human being." In reality, we have no access to unembellished pure nature; we experience nature only as interpreted and socially constructed by rational, social beings.[14] When we derive moral obligations from nature, we are actually deriving them from our interpretation of nature. Porter, therefore, is correct in her judgment that "a contemporary

---

[12] John Paul II, *Letter to Women*. See also, Pontificium Consilium Pro Laicis, *Men and Women: Diversity and Mutual Complementarity*.

[13] See chapter four in Salzman and Lawler, *The Sexual Person*. We note here that the ITC distinguishes John Paul II's perspective from physicalism, a different interpretation from ours (*In Search of a Universal Ethic*, no. 79).

[14] Porter, *Nature as Reason*, 117.

appropriation of the Scholastic concept of the natural law would undoubtedly go beyond the Scholastics in recognizing the element of human construction in the development of social practices and mores."[15] The ITC does precisely that and highlights its reason for doing so. "Oriented by the persons who surround him, permeated by the culture in which he is immersed, the person recognizes certain ways of behaving and of thinking as values to pursue, laws to observe, examples to imitate, visions of the world to accept. Social and cultural context exercises a decisive role in the education in moral values" (no. 38). In plain language, the human, rational construction of natural law is culturally and historically influenced.

Every moral norm derived from natural law is not neutrally derived from a static human nature but interpreted from an evolving understanding of human nature perceived and understood through historical and/or cultural perspectives. The ITC is correct: "in morality, pure deduction by syllogism is not adequate. The more the moralist confronts concrete situations, the more he must have recourse to the wisdom of experience, an experience that integrates the contributions of the other sciences and is nourished by contact with men and women engaged in the action" (no. 54). The specification of natural law does not, indeed cannot, take place through syllogistic deduction but through a communal reflection on human experience and tradition.

It is inevitable that different groups of equally rational but historically and culturally diverse human beings may arrive at different interpretations of nature and the moral obligation deriving from nature, on the one hand, and that any given interpretation may be either right or wrong, on the other. This fact has been demonstrated time and again in history, including Catholic theological and ethical history (no. 53).[16] *In Search of a Universal Ethic* observes "convergences" in the wisdom traditions of Hinduism, Buddhism, China, Africa, and Islam (nos. 13–17). The social scientific enterprise known as the sociology of knowledge also forefronts the origin of human knowledge in human culture, history, and experience. One of the founders of that discipline, Alfred Schutz, presents its taken-for-granted principle: "It is the *meaning* of our experiences and not the ontological [physical] structure of the objects that constitute [human] reality."[17] "The potter, and not the pot," Alfred North Whitehead adds

---

[15] Porter, *Natural and Divine Law*, 307.
[16] See Michael G. Lawler, *What Is and What Ought to Be* (Continuum, 2005), 127–129; Todd A. Salzman, *What Are They Saying About Catholic Ethical Method?* (Paulist, 2003).
[17] Alfred Schutz, *Collected Papers* (Martinus Nijhoff, 1964–1967), 230. See also Peter L. Berger and Thomas Luckmann, *The Social Construction of Reality: A Treatise in the Sociology of Knowledge* (Doubleday, 1966).

judiciously and metaphorically, "is responsible for the shape of the pot."[18] The uninterpreted experience of nature, as of every other objective reality, is restricted to the mere noting of its facticity and is void of meaning, a quality that does not inhere in nature but is assigned to it by rational beings in interpretive acts. The decisive criterion for the meaning of any human action, including any moral action, is the project of the actor. Meaning is what is meant by the *actor*, always to be understood not as an Enlightenment individual but an Aristotelian-Thomistic social being. The Catholic natural law tradition is fully committed to a universalist, objectivist ethic grounded in human nature, reason, and creation. Yet, it also recognizes the particularity of these foundations, influenced by history, culture, communities, familial relations, and power structures.[19]

The sociology of knowledge reveals that individuals and the society in which they live are not two completely separate and independent realities but rather conjoined realities in an ongoing dialectic of interdependence. Human society, with its symbols, meanings, and values, is a human product and nothing but a human product. "Despite the objectivity that marks the social world in human experience, it does not thereby acquire an ontological status apart from the human activity that produced it."[20] And yet this humanly produced social world, including the natural law, constantly acts back on its producers, conforming them to itself and controlling their understanding, judgment, and action. Thus, in their life expressions, humans are simultaneously social products and actors who modify and give new form to the society that produced them. The ITC is seeking to articulate something similar regarding the natural law. The relationship between men and women, the producers, and the social world, their product, is dialectical. Social reality is a product of human activity and humans, in their social and personal reality, are products of social reality. The dialectic tension between humans and society has three moments: a moment of externalization, a moment of objectivation, and a moment of internalization.

Humans do not have a given relationship to the world that is out, there, now, and real; they must establish one. In the process of establishing this relationship, they simultaneously produce both a *human* world and themselves as social beings in this world. The world produced is called, broadly, culture, the totality of human products,

---

[18] Alfred North Whitehead, *Symbolism: Its Meaning and Effect* (Putnam's, 1959), 8.
[19] Todd A. Salzman, "Natural Law and Basic Goods: Particular to Someone Everywhere," in *Moral Theology: New Directions and Fundamental Issues*, ed. James Keating (Paulist, 2004), 252.
[20] Berger and Luckmann, *The Social Construction of Reality*, 60.

both material and non-material.[21] Men and women produce tools of every kind. They also produce language and, via this language, complex constructions of meaning that permeate every aspect of their lives. They produce, in Schutz's terminology, complex and finite provinces of meanings;[22] in Lonergan's terminology, they produce perspectives,[23] a concept we shall return to at the end of this essay. Society is part of that complex of meanings, the part that structures men's and women's ongoing relations with their fellow men and women. Humans define themselves, and are socially defined, through the opportunities and constraints others set before them as either socially appropriate and right or socially inappropriate and wrong. "It is human nature," David Martin asserts, "to grow real in the mirror of other people's eyes."[24] As an element of the cultural meaning complex, society fully shares in culture's character as a human product. Society and its citizens are both constituted, socially constructed, and maintained by the activity of human beings and have no meaningful reality apart from such activity.

Social reality, like natural law, then, is an externalized product of the human animal. To speak, however, of an externalized product is already to imply that the product achieves a certain autonomy from its producer. The process of transformation of human products into a world that not only derives from humans but also confronts them as an objective reality apart from them is called objectivation. The product of objectivation becomes something as out, there, now, and real as any physical object, endowed with the status of objective reality. For the material products of human activity, that objectivity is readily grasped. Men and women construct automobiles, computers, houses, and cakes, and by their actions, increase the totality of physical objects that confront them as out, there, now, and real, independent of them. So it is, too, with the human products they produce. They construct a language and then find that their verbal communication is controlled by that language and its rules of syntax. They construct laws, natural and civil, and then feel guilty when they contravene them. They fashion structures of meaning and institutions that then confront them as powerful forces in the external world apart from their activities. Institutions such as family, education, politics, economics, and religion; meaning structures such as mythology, philosophy,

---

[21] The use of "culture" in this broad sense to refer to the totality of human products is adopted from the discipline of American cultural anthropology. Sociologists tend to use it in a sense restricted to symbolic spheres. The broader sense is more appropriate to the argument of this essay.
[22] Schutz, *Collected Papers*, I: 230.
[23] Bernard J. F. Lonergan, *Method in Theology* (University of Toronto Press, 1990), 217.
[24] David Martin, *Reflections on Sociology and Theology* (Clarendon, 1997), 48.

theology, and science; roles and identities such as parent, child, theologian, and scientist; all these are apprehended as out, there, now, and real phenomena in the social world apart from human activity, though both they and the social world are nothing but the products of creative human activity.

Morality, the ITC asserts, "deals with contingent [objectivated, human] realities that evolve over time" (*In Search of a Universal Ethic*, no. 53). Moral reflection, then, "must descend into the concreteness of action to throw its light on it. But the more it faces concrete and contingent situations, the more its conclusions are affected by a note of variability and uncertainty" (no. 53). Thomas Aquinas recognized this contingent character of morality. Practical reason, he wrote, "deals with contingent realities, about which human actions are concerned. Therefore, although there is some necessity in the general principles, the more we descend to particular matters, the more we encounter indeterminacy." The devil, Aquinas is arguing in his academic language, is always in the details. The variety of particular matters and actions in both history and culture means that "truth or practical rectitude is not the same for all in its particular applications, but only in its general principles. . . . And here, the more one descends to particulars the more the indeterminacy grows" (ST I-II, q. 94, a. 4).[25] Different objectivated particularities and concreteness will present themselves to different historical and cultural actors, and those different actors living in different historical and cultural worlds may define the meaning of an action in radically different ways. A question then arises: which action is true and moral? Common sense suggests that something is the same for each and every historically and culturally different actor, but common sense cannot determine how that sameness is to be understood.

The divinely created goodness of human nature, a fact that should never be ignored or forgotten in any discussion of natural law, is undoubtedly the ultimate ground for human morality but, in Porter's apposite articulation, human nature also "under-determines morality." Porter articulates what many Catholic moralists, including ourselves, have pointed out, namely, that there can be "more than one natural morality. Indeed, there are many such, because every indigenous moral tradition should be considered as a distinctive form of natural morality."[26] Common sense cannot determine which of these moral traditions and actions is really true and moral. Only rational research

---

[25] For the first time ever in an official magisterial document, Francis approvingly cites this passage from Aquinas in *Amoris Laetitia* (no. 304), recognizing the importance of the particular historical, cultural, and relational context when discerning if, or how, a norm applies in a particular situation.

[26] Porter, *Natural and Divine Law*, 308.

and examination can, we suggest, an approach affirmed by the ITC (*In Search of a Universal Ethic*, no. 61).[27] The human subject "must discover the 'right rule of acting' and establish an adequate norm of action." The "right rule follows from preliminary principles. Here one thinks of the first principles of practical reason, but it also falls to the moral virtues to open and connaturalize both the will and the sensitive affectivity with regard to different human goods, and so to indicate to the prudent person the ends to be pursued in the midst of the flux of everyday events" (no. 57). The ITC goes on to insist that "prudence is indispensable to the moral subject because of the flexibility required to adapt universal moral principles to the diversity of situations" (no. 58). From both nature and serious research on nature, reliable moral norms can be constructed, especially in open dialogue.[28] Any discussion of moral norms, therefore, must include radical research, both scientific and theological, careful attention and interpretation, and open and honest dialogue, such as the synodal process initiated by Francis, between the supporters of different interpretations of nature and the moral norms derived from it.

We summarize the contemporary Catholic approach to natural law in four statements. First, there is a meta-ethical level of nature that provides first principles known by "an innate intellectual disposition called *synderesis*" (ST I, q. 79, a. 12; see *In Search of a Universal Ethic*, no. 39). Second, there is a normative moral level on which these meta-ethical first principles are concretized by rational human persons in different times and cultures into specific moral norms. Third, flowing from both the meta-ethical and normative ethical levels, there is a level of concrete moral judgments made by rational human beings in concrete life situations. Fourth, the judgment of conscience, as John Paul II asserts, "states 'in an ultimate way' whether a certain particular kind of behavior is in conformity with the [natural] law; it formulates the proximate norm of the morality of a voluntary act, 'applying the objective law [norm] to a particular case'" (*Veritatis Splendor*, no. 59). This Catholic perspective on the natural law, the ITC states, "gives an account of the historicity of the natural law, whose concrete applications can vary over time. At the same time, it opens the door to the reflection of moralists, inviting them to dialogue and discussion. This is all the more necessary because in morality pure deduction by

---

[27] See Lisa Sowle Cahill, "Natural Law, Global Justice, and Equality," in *Searching for a Universal Ethic*, 239–249.

[28] See Lisa Sowle Cahill, *Sex, Gender, and Christian Ethics* (Cambridge University Press, 1996), 14–72; also "Feminist Ethics, Differences, and Common Ground: A Catholic Perspective," in *Feminist Ethics and the Catholic Moral Tradition*, ed. Charles E. Curran, Richard A. McCormick, and Margaret A. Farley (Paulist, 1996), 184–204.

syllogism is not adequate. The more the moralist confronts concrete situations, the more he must have recourse to the wisdom of experience" (*In Search of a Universal Ethic*, no. 54). We second that invitation to moral dialogue and discussion and urge that it be the honest and open kind of dialogue consistently advocated by Francis.

RELATIVISM VS. PERSPECTIVISM

Early in *Veritatis Splendor*, John Paul II identifies relativism as the intellectual issue at work in what he calls a "new situation" within the Church. According to him, such a situation has caused and promoted widespread dissent from traditional moral doctrine and constitutes a distorted understanding of, and fundamental challenge to, natural law (nos. 1, 4). John Paul II does not treat relativism in depth in *Veritatis Splendor*, though he hints at it regularly. Both he and Benedict XVI, however, continually raise concerns over relativism, which denies the existence of universal truth, like objective natural law, and fundamentally threatens the human search for truth. In his homily at the opening of the 2005 papal conclave, Cardinal Joseph Ratzinger, soon to be Benedict XVI, spoke of the "dictatorship of relativism" that "does not recognize anything as definitive and whose ultimate standard consists solely of one's own ego and desires."[29] In this section, we will be specifically concerned with moral relativism, which denies the existence of universal, objective moral truth. Such truth is necessary, the Magisterium argues, as the foundation for absolute norms asserting that certain acts—contraceptive and homosexual acts, for example—are intrinsically evil and can never be morally justified regardless of intent or circumstance. Concern about relativism is undoubtedly warranted in the twenty-first century, but the Magisterium fails to discern the difference between *relativism*, which rejects all objective moral truth, and *perspectivism*. The latter acknowledges that there is objective moral truth we can grasp reliably and adequately but affirms that we can only attain it partially. Accordingly, for perspectivism, moral truth is always in need of further clarification. The Magisterium also fails to discern legitimate theological pluralism, which the ITC's recent document, "Theology Today,"[30] advances as an essential criterion for Catholic theology. Neither moral nor theological pluralism is to be unquestionably equated with the relativism John Paul II warned the Church about. To

---

[29] Joseph Ratzinger, "Homily for the Pro Eligendo Romano Pontifice Mass," April 18, 2005, www.vatican.va/gpII/documents/homily-pro-eligendo-pontifice_20050418_en.html.
[30] International Theological Commission, *Theology Today: Perspectives, Principles, and Criteria*, www.vatican.va/roman_curia/congregations/cfaith/cti_documents/rc_cti_doc_20111129_teologia-oggi_en.html.

demonstrate this point, we consider the difference between relativism and what we name perspectivism in some detail.

In modern times, moral relativism has been the subject of much magisterial concern. As far back as 1952, Pius XII condemned "situation ethics," which he believed to be a form of relativism that denies universal moral truth.[31] Paul VI warned of moral relativism that claims that "some things are permitted which the Church had previously declared intrinsically evil," and that this vision "clearly endangers the Church's entire doctrinal heritage."[32] In *Veritatis Splendor*, John Paul II warns that, since the Second Vatican Council, "there have developed certain interpretations of Christian morality [like relativism] that are not consistent with 'sound doctrine'" and that "the Magisterium has the duty to state that some trends of theological thinking and certain philosophical affirmations are incompatible with revealed truth" (no. 29). Some Catholic moralists complain that in *Veritatis Splendor* John Paul II falsely accused them of "canonizing relativism."[33] Cardinal Ratzinger often warned of the dangers of a relativism that denies the existence of objective truth, calling it "the gravest problem of our time."[34] Concern with relativism and its impact, especially in the area of morality, continued to be a central concern of his pontificate as Benedict XVI.

With Bernard Lonergan, we prefer to speak of *perspectivism* rather than relativism. "Where relativism has lost hope about the attainment of truth, perspectivism stresses the complexity of what the historian is writing about and, as well, the specific difference of historical from mathematical, scientific, and philosophic knowledge."[35] While relativism concludes to the falsity of a judgment, perspectivism concludes to its *partial* truth. According to Lonergan, perspectivism in human knowledge arises from three factors. First, human knowers are finite; the information available to them is incomplete, and they do not attend to or master all the data available. Second, the knowers are

---

[31] See Pius XII, "Allocution to the Fédération mondiale des jeunesses féminines catholiques," January 18, 1952, *Acta Apostolicae Sedis* 34: 413–419 (henceforth *AAS*); "Radio Message About the Christian Conscience," March 23, 1952, *AAS* 34: 270–278; and "Instruction of the Holy Office," February 2, 1956, in *Enchiridion Symbolorum*, ed. Henry Denzinger and Adolf Schönmetzer, 33rd ed. (Herder, 1965), no. 3918.
[32] Paul VI, "Address to Members of the Congregation of the Most Holy Redeemer," *AAS* 59: 962.
[33] Maura Anne Ryan, "Then Who Can Be Saved?: Ethics and Ecclesiology in *Veritatis Splendor*," in Veritatis Splendor: *American Responses*, ed. Michael E. Allsopp and John J. O'Keefe (Sheed & Ward, 1995), 11.
[34] Joseph Cardinal Ratzinger, "Christ, Faith, and the Challenge of Cultures," March 3, 1993, www.vatican.va/roman_curia/congregations/cfaith/incontri/rc_con_cfaith_19930303_hong-kong-ratzinger_en.html.
[35] Lonergan, *Method in Theology*, 217.

selective, given their past socialization, personal experience, and range of data offered. Third, knowers are individually different, and we can expect them to make different selections of data. The theologian trained in the philosophy of Plato, Augustine for instance, will attend to different data, achieve different understanding, make different judgments, and act on different decisions from the theologian trained in the philosophy of Aristotle, Aquinas for instance. They produce different theologies, both of which will be necessarily incomplete explanations and partial portrayals of a very complex divine mystery. They are like two viewers respectively at the fourth-story and twelfth-story windows of a skyscraper; each gets a different, but no less partial, view of the total panorama that unfolds outside the building.

Every judgment of truth, including, perhaps especially, every judgment of theological truth, is a limited judgment and commitment based on limited data and understanding.[36] "So far from resting on knowledge of the universe, [a judgment] is to the effect that, no matter what the rest of the universe may prove to be, at least *this* is so."[37] It is precisely the necessarily limited nature of human, socio-historical sensations, understandings, judgments, and conceptual knowledge that leads to perspectivism, which is, to repeat, not a source of falsity but of partial truth.

True "objective" knowledge, therefore, is a *tertium quid*, a third thing that results from the dynamic interaction of the out, there, now, and real object, on the one hand, and the attending, understanding, judging, and deciding subject, on the other. It does not derive from objective structure alone but from the interaction of object and intelligent human subjects, who socially construct reality, meaning, value, and truth. What is frequently called *objective* reality by non-critical common sense is more properly called *social reality* or reality humanly invested with *social existence, meaning, and truth*. Objective knowledge is "an arbitrary construct in which a given society in a given historical situation has invested its sense of meaningfulness and value."[38] Such an approach to the relationship of being, meaning, and truth in the human world precludes the absolute connection of meaning and truth with objective being alone and explains why plural meanings and truth about the "same" reality abound in the human world. Plural meanings and truth, deemed objective by the actors who

---

[36] On limit language, see David Tracy, *Blessed Rage for Order: The New Pluralism in Theology* (Seabury, 1975); *The Analogical Imagination: Christian Theology and the Culture of Pluralism* (Crossroad, 1987); *Plurality and Ambiguity: Hermeneutics, Religion, and Hope* (Jossey-Bass, 1987).
[37] Bernard J. F. Lonergan, *Insight: A Study of Human Understanding* (Longmans, 1957), 344, emphasis added. See also *Method in Theology*, 217–219.
[38] Theodore Roszak, *The Making of a Counter Culture* (Doubleday, 1969), 215.

subscribe to them, derive inevitably from the plural socio-historical perspectives that abound in the human world.

Objectivist meta-ethical theories, such as natural law, claim both that moral terms do have meaning and that their meaning can be justified.[39] In Catholic moral theology, the moral terms *good* and *right* are defined in relation to human dignity and human fulfillment, or some such formulation. What is good or right facilitates human dignity and fulfillment; what is bad or wrong frustrates human dignity and fulfillment. The great religions of the world all agree with the Golden Rule in the wisdom tradition of Israel: "And what you hate, do not do to anyone" (Tobit 4:15; see Matthew 7:12; see also, *In Search of a Universal Ethic*, nos. 12–21). Virtually every Catholic moralist espouses such an objectivist meta-ethic and defines the human good or right on the basis of what facilitates human dignity and fulfillment. There are among them, however, a variety of theological anthropologies and understandings of human dignity. Perspectivism is an epistemological theory that explains this variety and the different formulations and justifications of norms facilitating or frustrating human dignity and fulfillment.[40]

When facing a question about moral principles, norms, or actions, there must be a first step towards an answer. That first step, moralist James Sellers suggests, is the stance the person takes *vis-à-vis* the question,[41] a notion even the distinguished Catholic moral theologian Charles Curran adopts.[42] Instead of the metaphor of stance, we prefer the visual metaphor of *perspective* introduced by James Gustafson, which suggests that the way we look at something puts everything about it into focus.[43] John Paul II also prefers the metaphor of perspective in *Veritatis Splendor*, where he notes, "In order to be able to grasp the object of an act which specifies that act morally, it is therefore necessary to place oneself *in the perspective of the acting person*" (no. 78, emphasis original). The analogy we offer to clarify the notion of perspective is that of a man in a multi-story building. The perspective he gets when he looks out a first-floor window is quite different from the perspective from a twentieth-story window. The two

---

[39] William K. Frankena, *Ethics*, 2nd ed. (Prentice Hall, 1973), 97–102. Robert Veatch distinguishes four types of absolutist theories: Supernatural, Rationalist, Intuitionist, and Empirical ("Does Ethics Have an Empirical Basis?," *Hastings Center Studies* 1 [1973]: 50–65). Catholic natural law is considered an empirical absolutist theory. See David F. Kelly, *Contemporary Catholic Health Care Ethics* (Georgetown University Press, 2004), 81–85.
[40] See Cahill, "Natural Law, Global Justice, and Equality."
[41] James Sellers, *Theological Ethics* (Macmillan, 1968), 34–38.
[42] Charles E. Curran, *The Catholic Moral Tradition Today: A Synthesis* (Georgetown University Press, 1999), 30–55.
[43] James M. Gustafson, *Christ and the Moral Life* (Harper and Row, 1968), 240–247.

perspectives, though different, put into reliable and adequate focus what really lies outside the windows.

Perspectivism applies to questions about natural law in that different perspectives on nature and norms that derive from nature result from different perspectives or ways of looking at nature. The perspectives from two different windows lead the man to different but reliably and adequately true views of what truly lies outside his building. Similarly, the approach to questions about human nature from two different perspectives lead to two different but reliably and adequately true answers to questions about nature and natural law and the principles and norms that facilitate or frustrate its attainment. This perspectival approach confronts magisterial charges of relativism aimed at those who disagree with some of its absolute norms and shows that they are not sustainable. Relativism concludes to the falsity of a judgment; perspectivism concludes to its partial but reliable and adequate truth. Again, this does not mean that anything goes. For any perspective to be moral, there still remains the judgment about how it contributes to human dignity and fulfillment.

Every human judgment of truth, including every judgment of moral truth, is a limited judgment and decision based on limited data and understanding. In Bernard Lonergan's words, "So far from resting on knowledge of the universe, [a judgment] is to the effect that, no matter what the rest of the universe may prove to be, at least *this* is so."[44] Relatedly, the moral judgment of a well-informed conscience is to the effect that, no matter what the rest of the universe may prove to be, at least *this action* is to be done and *that action* is to be avoided. It is precisely the necessarily limited nature of human understanding and judgment that leads to perspectivism, not as to a source of falsity but of partial, reliable, and adequate truth. We offer here an analogy between moral knowledge and the systematic theological knowledge of God, whom "no one has ever seen" (John 1:18). Restating earlier Greek theologians, Augustine expresses the basic Christian approach to truth about God in a famous declaration: "*Si comprehendis non est Deus*," if you have understood what you have understood is not God.[45] Aquinas expresses the same truth in his mature doctrine: "Now we cannot know what God is but only what God is not; we must, therefore, consider the ways in which God does not exist rather than the ways in which God does exist" (ST I, a. 3, Preface). Theologian Karl Rahner writes in the same vein: "Revelation does not mean that the mystery is overcome by gnosis bestowed by God. . . . On the

---

[44] Lonergan, *Insight*, 344, emphasis added. See also *Method in Theology*, 217–219.
[45] *Sermo* 52, 16, *Patrologia Latina* 38, 360; and ITC, *Theology Today*, no. 97. For a detailed analysis, see Victor White, *God the Unknown* (Harper, 1956) and William Hill, *Knowing the Unknown God* (Philosophical Library, 1971).

contrary, it is the history of the deepening perception of God *as mystery*."⁴⁶ The God whom Christians believe in is always *Deus absconditus*, a hidden God.

Human nature is inarguably not the depth of mystery that the wholly other God is,⁴⁷ but still a mystery to be plumbed, and no single natural law, objectivist definition of it can comprehensively capture either its full truth or the full truth of the dignity flowing from it. However, there are partial, reliable, and adequate truths, and perspectivism can account for their plurality. Perspectivism offers a theory of knowledge that presents human persons as human experience and praxis shows them to truly exist, selects those dimensions of the human person deemed most important for defining common human dignity, interprets and prioritizes those dimensions if and when they conflict, and formulates and justifies norms that facilitate, and do not frustrate, the attainment of human dignity. The only way for women and men to achieve universal knowledge is via perspectives that are particular.⁴⁸ It is thus necessary to focus on different particular perspectives that lead to different, partial, and reliably true definitions of human dignity and the formulation of different objective norms that facilitate or frustrate its attainment.

CONCLUSION

There is broad meta-ethical agreement within Catholic moral theology. First, it accepts meta-ethical objectivism; there *are* objective, universal definitions of human nature and dignity. Second, it defines and justifies the moral terms *good* and *right* in relation to an objective definition of human dignity. Third, it justifies the definition of human dignity through the selection, interpretation, prioritization, and integration of the sources of ethical knowledge, scripture, tradition, reason, and experience. Fourth, given different perspectives, different Catholic moral theologians can and sometimes do disagree on both the definition of universal human dignity and the formulation and justification of objective norms that facilitate or frustrate its attainment. Fifth, perspectivism, which recognizes the inherent

---

⁴⁶ Karl Rahner, "The Hiddenness of God," in *Theological Investigations*, vol. 16 (Darton, Longman, and Todd, 1979), 238. This dialogue is precisely what Francis is promoting through the Synod on Synodality.

⁴⁷ See Rudolph Otto, *The Idea of the Holy: An Inquiry into the Non-Rational Factor in the Ideas of the Divine and its Relation to the Rational*, trans. John W. Harvey (Oxford University Press, 1923).

⁴⁸ Bryan Massingale, "Beyond Revisionism: A Younger Moralist Looks at Charles E. Curran," in *A Call to Fidelity: On the Moral Theology of Charles E. Curran*, ed. James J. Walter, Timothy O'Connell, and Thomas A. Shannon (Georgetown University Press, 2002), 258.

limitations of human knowledge, helps to account for the different definitions of human nature and human dignity and the different formulations and justifications of objective norms that facilitate or frustrate its attainment. Sixth, the variability that arises from perspectivism is an essential part of an objectivism that recognizes universals, including the natural law; the good is objectively defined as human dignity. Magisterium *non-obstante*, different objective definitions of human dignity are not *eo ipso* a form of relativism that denies universal truth but simply the unavoidable outcome of defining human dignity, formulating and justifying norms, and viewing moral questions from different human perspectives or stances.

In this essay, we have shown that the meta-ethical foundation of all Catholic morality is natural law, understood in the Catholic tradition to be nature-as-reason, and that moral norms are interpreted from natural law under the influence of various cultural and historical perspectives. We have further shown that, though Catholic moral norms are magisterially acknowledged to be related to historical and cultural perspectives, they are not to be understood as untrue as in relativism but as partially, reliably, and adequately true as in what we have called perspectivism. We have also shown that moral perspectives reaching different normative conclusions than Catholic moral norms are not *necessarily* to be understood as untrue as in relativism but as possibly partially, reliably, and adequately true.

Much of what was written by John Paul II and his advisors thirty years ago in *Veritatis Splendor*, especially regarding the understanding of natural law and objective moral norms, has been superseded by the more nuanced perspectives of the ITC, Catholic moral theologians, and Francis. John Paul II's posture of suspicion and negative judgment of new theological trends and, by implication, the theologians behind those trends, has also been superseded by Francis's judgment that the vocation of a theologian is to go beyond existing doctrine because she or he is trying to make theology more explicit and relevant to people's lived experience. Francis is critical of past attempts to control theologians and emphasizes that different perspect-ives on theological and pastoral thought, "if they allow themselves to be harmonized by the Spirit in respect and love, can also make the Church grow."[49] Sound advice and a perspective to guide moral theologians beyond the restrictive theological and ethical confines of *Veritatis Splendor*.

Michael G. Lawler, PhD, is the Amelia and Emil Graff Chair Professor Emeritus of Catholic Theology at Creighton University.

---

[49] Elise Ann Allen, "Pope Charges New Doctrine Czar to Spurn 'Immoral Methods' in Defense of the Faith," *Crux* (July 1, 2023), cruxnow.com/vatican/2023/07/pope-charges-new-doctrine-czar-to-spurn-immoral-methods-in-defense-of-the-faith.

Todd A. Salzman, PhD, is Amelia and Emil Graff Chair Professor of Catholic Theology at Creighton University.

Together they have published: *The Sexual Person: Toward a Renewed Catholic Anthropology* (Georgetown University Press, 2008); *Sexual Ethics: A Theological Introduction* (Georgetown University Press, 2012); *Virtue and Theological Ethics: Toward a Renewed Ethical Method* (Orbis, 2018); *Introduction to Theological Ethics: Foundations and Applications* (Orbis, 2019); *Pope Francis and the Transformation of Catholic Health Care Ethics* (Georgetown University Press, 2021); *Pope Francis, Marriage, and Same-Sex Civil Unions: Foundations for the Organic Development of Catholic Sexual Doctrine* (Lexington, 2024); and numerous scholarly articles in *Theological Studies, Louvain Studies, Horizons, Heythrop Journal, Irish Theological Quarterly, Commonweal,* and *America*.

"He Himself Becomes a Living and Personal Law": *Veritatis Splendor*, Eating Disorders, and Misguided Moralism

Megan Heeder

Abstract: *Veritatis Splendor* is well-known for its use of the Gospel of Matthew's depiction of Christ's exchange with the rich young man seeking eternal life as the framework for understanding the moral life. It establishes relationship with Christ and one's neighbor as central to both love of God and doing moral theology, highlighting the role of connection and relationship. The Christocentric framing of *Veritatis Splendor* responds to misguided moralism's role in the development of eating disorders and the role of relationship in recovery, which has implications for moral theology's understanding of eating disorders in a social media age. Misguided moralism conceives of eating disorders as rooted in a link between eating and goodness to which relationship as a moral key is particularly responsive. Studies of eating disorder recovery in various fields indicate that strong, compassionate, hope-filled relationships are key to recovery, providing fertile ground for interconnections between *Veritatis Splendor*'s understanding of the centrality of relationship with Christ and morality within the process of eating disorder recovery.

A MOTHER'S RELATIONSHIP TO HER DAUGHTER MOTIVATED the discovery of "embodied ascetic values" related to anorexia nervosa in 2008.[1] Anthropologist Penny Esterik, whose daughter struggled with anorexia from age 13 to 16, was befuddled by young people like her daughter who reported that they wanted to make their bodies "even more perfect," while realizing the incongruence of their desire to have a "skeleton as a body" which "really is not perfect."[2] Esterik's desire to understand this paradoxical conundrum prompted her and fellow anthropologist Richard O'Connor to research "the anorexic's anorexia."[3] Contemporary medical narratives about the disease that shaped their research expectations were

---

[1] Richard A. O'Connor and Penny Van Esterik, "De-Medicalizing Anorexia: A New Cultural Brokering," *Anthropology Today* 24, no. 5 (October 2008): 6.
[2] O'Connor and Esterik, "De-Medicalizing Anorexia," 6.
[3] O'Connor and Esterik, "De-Medicalizing Anorexia," 6.

challenged by their findings: "Instead of adolescent girls literally dying for looks, we found youthful ascetics—male as well as female—obsessing over virtue, not beauty."[4] In addition, "Most had an experience of transcendence or grace" as part of that experience.[5] As they examined their data, O'Connor and Esterik realized that those struggling with anorexia possessed a pathology that reflected self-imposed asceticism quite different from desert monks' fasting. People struggling with anorexia venture into a realm beyond that of religious institutions, with an aim that differs from that of pious monastics.

More specifically, anorexia's self-imposed asceticism lacks both a community and a tradition when its roots are upended from faith-based practice. In the anthropologists' assessment, the absence of guidance from a community, tradition, or external boundaries has left anorexia to "reign in excess. Initially exhilarating, their virtuous eating and exercising eventually became addictive."[6] O'Connor and Esterik found, "Shockingly, that this is not the disease that many institutions are treating," because anorexia is about more than just eating—it is about asceticism, adolescence, exercise, and other aspects of the human person.[7] These anthropologists, lacking a theological sense of personhood, nevertheless recognize that the healthcare system's approach to treating anorexia is founded on "explanations [that] look *through* rather than *at* the anorexic as a whole person."[8] This approach appears consistent across healthcare's engagement with eating disorders: the medical system tends to treat the problem, thinking about eliminating symptoms of an eating disorder as opposed to healing a person's broken heart, soul, and being. In other words, treating eating disorders as purely medical ailments risks making the human person unidimensional; a patient with a problem to be solved, instead of an ensouled human to be beheld or seen as a "Thou." O'Connor and Esterik's study was published in 2008, but the anthropologists' observations continue to ring true over fifteen years later.

My overarching argument in this essay is that moral theology is responsive to the challenging paradigm of treating and understanding eating disorders and their complex matrix of ethical, beauty, and medical implications, in no small part because eating disorders already possess a moral dimension. This is especially true in light of O'Connor

---

[4] O'Connor and Esterik, "De-Medicalizing Anorexia," 6.
[5] O'Connor and Esterik, "De-Medicalizing Anorexia," 6.
[6] O'Connor and Esterik, "De-Medicalizing Anorexia," 6.
[7] O'Connor and Esterik, "De-Medicalizing Anorexia," 6. I would argue that this holds true to at least some degree for other types of eating disorders due in part to the ubiquity of the feminine thin-ideal and the correlation between goodness and thinness in Western culture.
[8] O'Connor and Esterik, "De-Medicalizing Anorexia," 6.

and Esterik's determination that the people with anorexia they studied functioned like "misguided moralists" whose struggles reflect the way Western culture understands food and eating to be an ethical issue:

> Witness the popular prejudice whereby fat people, seen as "letting themselves go," are stigmatized as weak or even bad, while slim people, perceived as strict with themselves, exemplify strength and goodness. Or consider how people readily judge their own eating, speaking of "sinning" with dessert, "being good" with veggies, or "confessing" a late-night binge. What is at stake here is virtue, not beauty. Over the last century or so, as the body has increasingly become a moral arena, eating and exercise have come to test our moral fibre.[9]

The assumption in contemporary Western-European culture is that thinner is better, and that one's commitment to being beautiful or attractive is acted out by the choices people make about what to eat. When people eat together, it is common (to the point of being unremarkable) to overhear people commenting about being "good" or "bad" depending on what they order off a menu. If one forgoes dessert to save on calories, their discipline is lauded; if one "caves" and orders a chocolate mousse, such a decision might be accompanied by an explanation to justify the "splurge." They may note that this is a rare treat or that the amount of air whipped into the mousse decreases the fat content and calorie count, making it a "better" choice than the lava cake.

The enactments of the so-called "virtue" of misguided moralism women with eating disorders exemplify (avoiding consuming fat, losing weight, decreasing their calorie intake, exercising) are neither objectively good nor bad themselves. In fact, there are times when they could be good, and in other instances—even on the same day—detrimental. Rather, giving moral valence to these choices reflects a taste profile imposed by cultural ideas that have been shaped by thin-idealized beauty standards. Food and exercise's existence in the realm of virtue reflects the value Western-European culture places on appearance and the belief that one's appearance can be controlled through eating, exercise, and willpower.

O'Connor and Esterik conclude that those with anorexia do not possess a cohesive self-narrative. They ask how a person can be anything but lost as they try to understand their eating disorder when the culture around them hides or incorrectly imagines their experience of having an eating disorder, highlighting society's blindness to the effects of casting food and eating in a moral light. O'Connor and

---

[9] O'Connor and Esterik, "De-Medicalizing Anorexia," 7–8.

Esterik propose a non-dualistic vision of the human person which understands the social nature of health and sickness, and humans' existence as fundamentally moral beings. Their work convincingly depicts the moral dimension of eating disorders and of food, eating, and exercise more broadly, but lacks a sense of the human person as more than just mind and body.[10] What is one who struggles with an eating disorder, or disordered eating, to do when they locate within themselves a sense of misguided moralism which might compel them to restrict their eating, or evaluate their value as a person in light of their weight or eating habits? What does this misguided moralism have to do with their soul, the spiritual dimension of their human existence?[11] And how might *Veritatis Splendor* guide a moral theological response to the moral nature of eating disorders?

The moral theological tradition, especially as communicated in *Veritatis Splendor*, offers a fundamentally relational vision of the human person, and conceives of a person's existence within the matrix of community. This wisdom pushes back against the belief that by controlling one's body via stringent eating and exercise habits one can earn goodness and value in their own eyes and those of others. In this essay I couple data from social work together with *Veritatis Splendor*'s presentation of moral theology, in order to foreground the centrality of relationships for eating disorder recovery. Relationships provide those who struggle with a sense of connection, thwarting the isolation that often accompanies eating disorders and accountability for one's commitment to recovery when it feels impossible, or the temptation to engage in eating disorder behaviors feels overpowering. Thirty years after its publication, *Veritatis Splendor*'s Christocentric moral frame responds to misguided moralism's role in the

---

[10] Feminist philosopher Susan Bordo also discusses incidents of moral language around food and thinness, especially in advertisements over time, in *Unbearable Weight: Feminism, Western Culture, and the Body*, 10th anniversary ed. (University of California Press, 2003). A purely medical approach to eating disorders will also reflect an understanding of humans as corporeal, in contrast to theological anthropology's sense of the human person as ensouled.

[11] I do note that misguided moralism is not the only paradigm that can be used to understand the challenges people face with eating disorders, and some people with eating disorders may not relate to a sense of eating connected to virtue. Eating disorders are incredibly complex, with biological, psychological, and social influences. However, this model is grounded in the anthropologists' study of individuals' own experiences over time and also resonates with religion scholar Michelle Lelwica's findings; see, e.g., *Starving for Salvation: The Spiritual Dimension of Eating Problems Among American Girls and Women* (Oxford, 1999), *Shameful Bodies* (Bloomsbury Academic, 2017), and *The Religion of Thinness* (Gurze, 2009). Thus, I will foreground misguided moralism's understanding of eating disorders while acknowledging that this may not be the experience of everyone who struggles with them.

development of eating disorders and the role of relationship in recovery, offering resonant implications for treating eating disorders in a social media age.

ESTABLISHING THE PROBLEM: EATING DISORDERS TODAY

Misguided moralism's role in eating disorders makes clear that the lived reality of struggling with an eating disorder encompasses more than traditional medical considerations and treatment protocols.[12] Less than 6 percent of people who struggle with an eating disorder are medically underweight, and the global prevalence of eating disorders between 2000 and 2018 has increased from 3.5 to 7.8 percent; eating disorder diagnosis rates during the Covid-19 pandemic rose at unprecedented rates and in severity among young people, and have continued to rise.[13] A *New York Times* article indicates that "across the board, the pandemic exacerbated eating disorders, including typical and atypical anorexia, through increased isolation, heightened anxiety, and disrupted routines. Hospitals and outpatient clinics in the United States and abroad reported the number of consultations and admissions doubling and tripling during Covid-19 lockdowns, and many providers are still overbooked."[14] Eating disorders are the second-most fatal psychiatric illness, recently surpassed by opiate

---

[12] In this article I will use eating disorders as a blanket term to encompass both formal eating disorder diagnoses like anorexia nervosa, bulimia nervosa, or OSFED (other specified feeding or eating disorder), as well as disordered eating. OSFED is an official eating disorder classification, encompassing eating disorders that do not meet specifications for other diagnoses (anorexia nervosa, bulimia nervosa, etc.) and according to the Deloitte Access Economics study, is responsible for 33 percent of eating disorder deaths and 39.5 percent of eating disorder diagnoses in men and 44.2 percent in women. Disordered eating refers to sub-clinical pathology that does not meet official eating disorder criteria, is often accompanied by increased anxiety due to a lack of a clear diagnosis, and can be an intermediary step on the way to the development of an eating disorder. The reason for the combination of these terms throughout the essay is not only to avoid mentioning all three terms each time they are invoked, but because I believe that the manner in which moral theology can be responsive to the struggles of people with eating disorders can also be helpful to those with disordered eating.

[13] "General Eating Disorder Statistics," National Association of Anorexia Nervosa and Associated Disorders, anad.org/eating-disorder-statistic/. See also Marie Galmiche, Pierre Déchelotte, Grégory Lambert, and Marie P. Tavolacci, "Prevalence of Eating Disorders over the 2008–2018 Period: A Systematic Literature Review," *The American Journal of Clinical Nutrition* 105, no. 9 (1 May 2019): 1408; Debra K. Katzman, "The COVID-19 Pandemic and Eating Disorders: A Wake-Up Call for the Future of Eating Disorders Among Adolescents and Young Adults," *Journal of Adolescent Health* 69, no. 4 (October 2021): 535.

[14] Kate Siber, "'You Don't Look Anorexic,'" *New York Times*, October 18, 2022.

addiction.[15] Nine percent of the American population (28.8 million people) will have an eating disorder in their lifetime.[16] About 8.6 percent of women who have eating disorders will struggle with their eating disorder for the duration of their life; 4.7 percent of men's eating disorders will prevail for their lifetime.[17] Twenty-two percent of children and adolescents globally will struggle with disordered eating, meaning that they struggle with symptoms of eating disorders that impact their well-being, but do not meet the frequency or severity thresholds of eating disorder diagnoses.[18]

The origins of an individual's eating disorders are personal and complicated. The National Eating Disorder Association's (NEDA's) review of current eating disorder literature identifies nineteen risk factors for eating disorder development. NEDA identifies risk factors as "a complex combination of biological, psychological, and sociocultural factors that converge and set off an individual's predisposed genetic vulnerability" to eating disorders.[19] These three elements—biology (i.e., Type 1 diabetes), psychology (i.e., perfectionism or high conscientiousness), and sociology (i.e., media exposure) each account for particular aspects of risk for developing eating disorders. An independent 2015 research review argues that it is likely that both "psychological and environmental factors interact with and influence" biological factors like genetic risk to create eating pathologies.[20] While an individual may have specific genes or psychological conditions that predispose them to developing an eating disorder (both of which can be influenced by the environment), they are also influenced by the culture around them.

---

[15] "General Eating Disorder Statistics," National Association of Anorexia Nervosa and Associated Disorders.
[16] Deloitte Access Economics, *The Social and Economic Cost of Eating Disorders in the United States of America: A Report for the Strategic Training Initiative for the Prevention of Eating Disorders and the Academy for Eating Disorders*, June 2020, 23, www.hsph.harvard.edu/striped/report-economic-costs-of-eating-disorders/.
[17] Deloitte Access Economics, *The Social and Economic Cost of Eating Disorders*, iv.
[18] José Francisco López-Gil, Antonio García-Hermoso, Lee Smith, et al., "Global Proportion of Disordered Eating in Children and Adolescents: A Systematic Review and Meta-analysis," *JAMA Pediatrics* 117, no. 4 (February 2023): 366, doi.org/10.1001/jamapediatrics.2022.5848.f. This study excluded data prior to 1999, studies that included participants with prior mental or physical disorders, and COVID-19 studies.
[19] National Eating Disorder Association, "Risk Factors," www.nationaleatingdisorders.org/risk-factors.
[20] Kristen M. Culbert, Sarah E. Racine, and Kelly L. Klump, "Research Review: What We Have Learned About the Causes of Eating Disorders—A Synthesis of Sociocultural, Psychological, and Biological Research," *Journal of Child Psychology and Psychiatry* 56, no. 11 (November 2015): 1157, doi.org/10.1111/jcpp.12441.

Western European cultural beauty standards convince women and girls that their worth is tied to their beauty; the onslaught of edited, perfect pictures on social media perpetuate the feminine thin-ideal. The feminine thin-ideal is part of contemporary Western beauty standards that reflect an unhealthy level of thinness for women. Models who represent the paragon of beauty in fashion, advertisements, and on social media are extremely thin, and images are often edited to make them appear even smaller than they are in real life. These ideals have a particular effect on young girls; by the age of eight, girls are knowledgeable about weight loss and different modes of achieving that aim. Forty to sixty percent of elementary-age girls communicated concern about weighing too much in 2000; one can only imagine the spike in that number since the proliferation of smartphones.[21] A more recent study (2019) on thin-ideal internalization indicates that it "is one of the few identified risk factors with sufficient empirical evidence to support its proposed role as a causal risk factor for disordered eating" and that high degrees of thin-ideal internalization can negatively affect recovery and predict higher likelihood of relapse in eating-disorder recovery.[22] In sum, many women and girls feel they are not thin or beautiful enough, and eating-disorder behaviors or restrictive diets become part of the process they engage as they try to earn goodness through thinness. This claim is particularly important in light of the manner in which social media is affecting eating disorder development to a hitherto unfathomable degree.[23]

The standard approach to addressing eating disorders is through medical means. The American Psychiatric Association's current standards for treating eating disorders focus on maintaining or reaching a particular weight and addressing eating disorder symptoms. For anorexia nervosa, this includes setting individualized goals for weight gain and establishing a target weight; psychotherapy to address a number of issues, including restoring one's weight and addressing psychological disturbances like fear of weight gain; and for adolescents or emerging adults, treatment which is family-based and

---

[21] Ellen A. Schur, Mary Sanders, and Hans Steiner, "Body Dissatisfaction and Dieting in Young Children," *The International Journal of Eating Disorders* 27, no. 1 (Jan., 2000): 78.

[22] Lauren M. Schaefer, Natasha L. Burke, and J. Kevin Thompson, "Thin-Ideal Internalization: How Much is Too Much?," *Eating and Weight Disorders* 24, no. 5 (2019): 933. Emphasis added.

[23] Culbert's work, cited above in footnote no. 20, identifies a number of thinness variables (i.e., media exposure, thin-pressures, the internalization of the thin-ideal) which have attained "risk status" for eating disorder and disordered eating symptoms.

includes caregiver education.²⁴ In cases of bulimia nervosa, the APA recommends cognitive-behavioral therapy (CBT), often coupled with a serotonin reuptake inhibitor, in the context of family-based treatment in relevant situations.²⁵ Binge-eating disorder treatments include CBT or interpersonal therapy, in individual or group settings, accompanied by the prescription of an antidepressant based on client preference or when patients do not respond to psychotherapy alone.²⁶ In severe cases, or when these eating disorder treatment therapies are proving ineffective, hospitalization is often recommended. Day treatment programs in the hospital may also be necessary; this includes multiple hours of medical care, therapy, structured eating or nutritional information sessions several days a week.²⁷ If residential treatment is necessary, an individual may live at a treatment facility if long-term care provides the best opportunity for recovery or multiple hospital stays have not resulted in mental or physical health improvements.²⁸ Ongoing health treatment while in the hospital or long-term care is also required in some cases. Such cases include incidences of electrolyte imbalances, heart problems, digestion challenges or lack of nutrient absorption, dental issues, amenorrhea, osteoporosis, stunted growth, or co-morbid mental health conditions.²⁹ Standard treatment protocols focus on the body: controlling symptoms, improving habitual behaviors through psychotherapy, and attaining a healthy goal weight.

The goal of the medical field's treatment protocols is to improve the patient's health. The means by which this end is pursued includes addressing symptoms, weight, and mental well-being, which reflect the tools and resources that medical field possesses. While this treatment protocol may include some exploration of an eating disorder's roots or the human person as a spiritual-social being, such focus will largely depend on the therapist or therapeutic approach. Theologically, this possible omission of the person's spiritual and

---

[24] Catherine Crone, Laura J. Fochtmann, Evelyn Attia, et al. "The American Psychiatric Association Practice Guideline for the Treatment of Patients with Eating Disorders," *American Journal of Psychiatry* 180, no. 2 (February 2023): 168, psychiatryonline.org/doi/10.1176/appi.ajp.23180001.
[25] Crone, Fochtmann, Attia, et al., "The American Psychiatric Association Practice Guideline," 168.
[26] Crone, Fochtmann, Attia, et al., "The American Psychiatric Association Practice Guideline," 168.
[27] Mayo Clinic, "Eating Disorder Treatment: Know Your Options," www.mayoclinic.org/diseases-conditions/eating-disorders/in-depth/eating-disorder-treatment/art-20046234#:~:text=It%20usually%20includes%20a%20mix,disorder%20causes%20or%20makes%20worse.
[28] Mayo Clinic, "Eating Disorder Treatment."
[29] Mayo Clinic, "Eating Disorder Treatment."

social dimension ignores a fundamental component of human existence.

In place of a medical approach that considers the human person as a patient with symptoms, or a moral approach that focuses on a rules-based asceticism, *Veritatis Splendor* offers a moral-theological vision that invites all people, including those who struggle with eating disorders, into relationship with Christ and the church. This invitation affirms the dignity of the human person, offers a way out of social isolation, and leads to newfound interior peace and the possibility of healing in one's relationship with food, eating, and ultimately themselves.

FRAMING MISGUIDED MORALISM: *VERITATIS SPLENDOR*'S CHRISTOCENTRIC ETHICS

John Paul II's *Veritatis Splendor* offers five contributions to exploring eating disorders theologically: treatment of moral theology as an encounter with Jesus; humanity as *imago Dei*; the role of grace; the communal nature of moral theology; and the place of interdisciplinary work in moral theology today. Some of these insights necessitate nuance in their application thirty years after their initial articulation, but all of them can shape a moral theological response to eating disorders.

The encyclical opens with the encounter between the rich young man and Jesus in Matthew's Gospel. Opening an encyclical on moral theology with a biblical meditation reveals that for John Paul II, moral theology's starting place is encounter and relationship with Christ "since Christian morality consists, in the simplicity of the Gospel, in *following Jesus Christ,* in abandoning oneself to him, in letting oneself be transformed by his grace and renewed by his mercy, gifts which come to us in the living communion of his Church" (*Veritatis Splendor*, no. 119). The prioritization of relationship is not only communicated by the encyclical but modeled by Jesus's response to the rich young man's queries about how to gain eternal life. Jesus makes clear that relationship with him, not just following the Law, is necessary and thereby establishes that "the decisive answer to every one of man's questions, his religious and moral questions in particular, is given by Jesus Christ, or rather is Jesus Christ himself" (no. 2). While relationship is primary, it does not replace the need for obedience or revoke the Law. Rather, God is at the very heart of the Law. John Berkman comments that "while the commandments are conditions for full life in Christ, and indeed shape us and form us into such a life, they do not constitute the core of discipleship."[30] "*Jesus himself is the living 'fulfillment' of the Law* inasmuch as he fulfills its authentic meaning by the total gift of himself: *he himself becomes a living and personal Law*, who invites people to follow him" (no. 15) so that he can extend grace through the Spirit to others so that they can participate in his life and love. *Veritatis Splendor*'s sense of morality as coming through relationship emphasizes that humanity cannot reach God on its own. Human effort can neither attain the Good nor fulfill the Law. Fulfillment is extended through grace, as divine gift; it cannot be attained or earned (see no. 11). Christ becomes not only the moral compass and source of answers, but the font of a thriving relationship whereby one's Christian obligation is not fulfilled by an account of scrupulous rule-following. Something much more profound and transformative is at hand: a relationship which inspires one to act out of love, a love given first in relationship such that it orders the person to the good of Christ Himself. John Paul II affirms that the source of morality is a person—Christ—in whom the commandments are fulfilled.

Locating morality within a person instead of a set of rules inspires "within him [the rich young man] new questions about moral good" that in turn enkindle a desire in him to draw close to Christ (see no. 8). Moral theology's heartbeat is encounter with Christ, out of which flows insights and precepts about right and wrong in the context of relationship with a God whose love motivated the Incarnation. Ángel Rodríguez Luño's work supports this insight; he notes that *Veritatis Splendor*'s beginning with a biblical meditation frames relationship with Christ as the goal and means of moral discernment. It offers the person of Christ as a concrete model and relationship with him as the process by which one is orientated to the Christian way, a process which includes the church and is guided by the Holy Spirit.[31] Encounter and relationship with Christ contain the answers to humanity's deepest and most pressing questions. The encyclical also

---

[30] John Berkman, "Truth and Martyrdom: The Structure of Discipleship in *Veritatis Splendor*," *New Blackfriars* 75, no. 887 (November 1994): 535.

[31] Ángel Rodríguez Luño, "El significado de la *Veritatis Splendor* para la teología moral," *Scripta Theologica* 55, no. 1 (March 2023): 105, doi.org/10.15581/006.55.1.101-126. The author's paraphrased translation above is taken from this line: "La lectura del capítulo I, que es fundamentalmente una meditación bíblica, deja la clara impresión de que la vía cristiana tiene un modelo y una orientación muy concreta: Jesús, con sus enseñanzas y sus actitudes, y la Iglesia, que goza de la asistencia del Espíritu Santo para interpretar y aplicar a lo largo de la historia y de todas las circunstancias lo que de Jesús se nos ha transmitido." In the quote above, Luño also notes the connection between Christ and the church, a connection which is resonant given this essay's observations on the role of relationship and community in eating disorder recovery.

claims that questions about morality, intentionally or not, compel a person to approach Christ with their queries.

> In the young man, whom Matthew's Gospel does not name, we can recognize every person who, consciously or not, *approaches Christ the Redeemer of man and questions him about morality*. For the young man, the *question* is not so much about rules to be followed, but *about the full meaning of life*. . . . This question is ultimately an appeal to the absolute Good which attracts us and beckons us; it is an echo of a call from God who is the origin and goal of man's life. (no. 7)

Because the encyclical begins with a biblical meditation, the reader is positioned to hear the echo of God's call in the person of Christ as they read. In so doing, the reader not only intellectually encounters the Truth of Christ in the moral guidelines laid out in *Veritatis Splendor*, but also is—perhaps even primarily—encouraged to encounter Truth as a person.

Veritatis Splendor's vision of the human person is rooted in the identity of the person as *imago Dei*. The encyclical presents morality as the humans' response to their existence as images of God in light of their loving Creator's divine revelation. This conception of the human person as beautiful and inherently good is particularly responsive to the challenges of those struggling with eating disorders. The vision of the human person as *imago Dei* echoes the truth that their beauty and dignity reflect God's glory. Citing Ephesians, *Veritatis Splendor* points readers toward their ultimate purpose as living "*for the praise of God's glory*" such that each action reflects the splendor of divine glory (see no. 10). *Veritatis Splendor* quotes Saint Ambrose, whose words remind humanity of how their beauty echoes God's glory: "Know, then, O beautiful soul, that you are *the image of God*. Know that you are *the glory of God* (1 Cor 11:7). Hear how you are his glory. . . . Know then, O man, your greatness, and be vigilant" (no. 10). *Veritatis Splendor* understands moral theology through the scriptural vision of humanity's relationship with God and the dignity and glory this offers. One's actions should align with "what man is" in accord with divine revelation and serve to draw one more deeply into divine love (see no. 10). "*The moral life presents itself as the response* due to the many gratuitous initiatives taken by God out of love for man. It is a response of love" such that the moral life, "caught up in the gratuitousness of God's love, is called to reflect his glory" (no. 10). Morality is humanity's response as images of God to their loving Creator's self-revelation. *Veritatis Splendor*'s theological anthropology reveals the human person's reflection of God's image which impresses inherent value on their existence as a result of the dignity, beauty, and goodness God's image imparts.

Christ offers not only a personal, living Law that meets persons where they are, but also extends the grace which helps them enter into relationship and choose the good. When the young man asks Jesus what he needs to do to attain eternal life, he realizes that "he is incapable of taking the next step by himself alone" (no. 17). The next step requires the right use of human freedom by which one accedes to divine grace. The "still uncertain and fragile journey" *Veritatis Splendor* describes for those who strive to live out the fullness of Christ's commandments is enabled by grace. This grace enables people "to possess the full freedom of the children of God (see Rom 8:21) and thus to live [their] moral life in a way worthy of [their] sublime vocation" (no. 18) as children of God.[32]

The human inability to earn goodness in the context of relationship with Christ is central not only to theology broadly in order to avoid Pelagianism, but also to those struggling with a sense of misguided moralism. "This is not a matter only of disposing oneself to hear a teaching and obediently accepting a commandment. More radically, it involves *holding fast to the very person of Jesus*, partaking of his life and his destiny, sharing in his free and loving obedience to the will of the Father" (no. 19). Grace is the means by which one becomes good, and is central to relationship with and life in Jesus. "To imitate and live out the love of Christ is not possible for man by his own strength alone. He becomes capable of this love only by virtue of a gift received, not earned" (no. 22). The gift of grace enables true virtue—both in a Christian sense, and in terms of the misguided moralism with which many people with eating disorders struggle. Grace can only be imparted as a gift, not earned; virtue is only possible with grace, not by willpower alone. This paradox of grace, in which one's ardent desire to be good leads one to radical reliance on God, not self, is responsive to misguided moralism's challenges.[33]

---

[32] This does not mean that grace is a recovery strategy, or that grace instantly heals. The working of grace is mysterious; the process of recovering from eating disorders is difficult and often non-linear. For more on the relationship between grace and recovery (in this case, addiction), see Andrew Kim's "Newness of Life and Grace-Enabled Recovery from the Sin of Addiction," *Journal of Moral Theology* 10, Special Issue no. 1 (2021): 124–142.

[33] How one conceives of eating disorders is fundamental to this conversation. Addiction studies approaches addiction through two models: the disease and the moral model. The disease model conceives of addiction as a disease, meaning it is biologically and genetically grounded. Subsequently, it tends to allot less (or no) agency to the individual who struggles with addiction. The moral model believes the agent to have complete control over their addiction; they simply lack the resolve or will to stop engaging in it. I believe the truth lies somewhere between these, taking into account the biological and environmental factors that can foster the development of an eating disorder while ensuring that the individual retains agency and can take responsibility for the choices over which they have control. For further insight into

In his exploration of grace's role in addiction recovery, Andrew Kim writes that Christ's grace "can go where others cannot. He can enter into the cemetery of the . . . soul in a way no one else can and encounter the inward man afflicted, crying out . . . and there not only comfort him but also heal his mind and return him to his family to tell of all the Lord has done for him."[34] Christ gives grace; he is also the one who accompanies each individual in their struggles with eating disorders, disordered eating, or body dissatisfaction. The gift of divine grace conforms the individual to Christ. "*Following Christ* is not an outward imitation, since it touches man at the very depths of his being. Being a follower of Christ means *being conformed to him* who became a servant even to giving himself on the Cross (see Phil 2:5–8). Christ dwells by faith in the heart of the believer (see Eph 3:17), and thus the disciple is conformed to the Lord. This is the *effect of grace*, of the active presence of the Holy Spirit in us" (no. 21) as the disciple seeks the transformation of heart and mind as the fruit of their relationship with Christ. Relationship is not just a means to an end, but a gift in itself. It enables the human person to know themselves in a new way, with the dignity that accompanies being made in God's image. It also orders them toward flourishing, which contrasts with eating-disorder behaviors' short-sightedness and promises of false fulfillment. Grace's effect on the mind, body, and spirit is not a consideration in medical treatments or anthropological understandings of eating disorders. Tending to the spirit as well as the body-and-spirit as an integrated whole is central to eating disorder recovery, and something *Veritatis Splendor* emphasizes that moral theology can offer to the field of bioethics and traditional medical approaches to conceiving of and treating eating disorders.

Veritatis Splendor makes clear that moral theology is not just about the individual's relationship with God; loving one's neighbor is required in order to love God well. This claim is rooted in the commandments: "The commandments thus represent the basic condition for love of neighbor; at the same time they are the proof of that love" (no. 13) and "both the Old and the New Testaments explicitly affirm that *without love of neighbor,* made concrete in keeping the commandments, *genuine love for God is not possible*" (no. 14). Love of God and love of neighbor require and are proof of one another; inevitably, enacting this truth places one in the matrix of community.

---

this topic, the first chapter of my dissertation discusses these models and their relevance to developing a Catholic moral theological response to eating disorders; see Megan Heeder, "The Beauty of a Good Appetite in a Social Media Age" (PhD diss., Marquette University, 2024).

[34] Andrew Kim, "Newness of Life and Grace-Enabled Recovery," 136.

Veritatis Splendor consistently conceives of society's influence as pernicious. In one of the opening paragraphs, the encyclical warns that within the Christian community, moral teachings of the church are coming into question; the root of this dissent is outside currents of thought that decouple freedom and truth (see no. 4). It critiques currents of modern thought that exalt freedom as an absolute to the extent that it becomes a source of values, deriding modern thought that takes place in a "widely dechristianized culture" (see nos. 32, 88). According to *Veritatis Splendor* the Christian is not only at risk of being badly formed by their environment, but he or she can also negatively influence others' relationship to truth. This occurs when one makes his or her "own weakness the criterion of the truth about the good, so that he can feel self-justified, without even the need to have recourse to God and his mercy" because "an attitude of this sort corrupts the morality of society as a whole" (no. 104). *Veritatis Splendor*'s concerns mirror O'Connor and Esterik's assertion that a realistic perspective on health "would recognize that health is broadly social, not narrowly individual," and that the "domain of personal health over which the individual has direct control is very small when compared to heredity, culture, environment, and chance."[35] The faith in healthy living that people possess today functions as "a new religion, in which we worship ourselves, attribute good health to our devoutness, and view illness as just punishment for those who have not yet seen the Way."[36] Self-worship, kindled by currents of modern thought about the self, conscience, truth, or what it is to be beautiful, bears no good fruit.

Veritatis Splendor's warning about the negative effects of environmental influence does not account for the possibility of its inverse effect: the healing people can positively inspire in others. Sharing one's own struggles might help someone choose to pursue recovery or begin a relationship of accompaniment on another's recovery journey. The encyclical's treatment of community spends little time on community's positive influence, something Berkman's commentary on paragraphs 90–93 adds:

> Of course, there is a place for moral rules, but if we wish to answer faithfully Jesus's call to "Come, follow me," we require guidance more fundamental than knowledge of rules, and a wisdom beyond rules outlined by moral theologians. This guidance and wisdom is to be found in Christians who have journeyed most faithfully, who have

---

[35] O'Connor and Esterik, "De-Medicalizing Anorexia," 8.
[36] Marshall H. Becker, "A Medical Sociologist Looks at Health Promotion," *Journal of Health and Social Behavior* 34, no. 1 (1993): 5, quoted in O'Connor and Esterik, "De-Medicalizing Anorexia," 8.

best embodied the faith in their lives, and it is they to whom Christians first turn for guidance. It is in God's faithful people, the body of Christ, that we see Christ in action.[37]

The encyclical makes clear that the members of the Body of the Christ are called to be part of this journey: "In a positive way, the Church seeks, with great love, to help all the faithful to form a moral conscience which will make judgments and lead to decisions in accordance with the truth" (no. 85), but little time is spent in the encyclical discussing the ways the Body of Christ can inspire healing and wholeness in its members beyond resisting outside (i.e., negative) influences. The encyclical could have offered a more robust and positive framework for community's influence in order to develop concrete insights on how relationships within the church can do more than resist the perniciousness of modern thought.

Finally I note that the encyclical also points to the human longing for truth which drives the desire to know, and the possibilities this desire opens for work between fields. "In the depths of [the human] heart there always remains a yearning for absolute truth and a thirst to attain full knowledge of it. This is eloquently proved by man's tireless search for knowledge in all fields. . . . The development of science and technology . . . spurs us on to face the most painful and decisive of struggles, those of the heart and the moral conscience" (no. 1). Paragraph 32 of *Veritatis Splendor* critiques what can be seen in some of these fields and modern moral systems which uphold "being at peace with oneself" as the highest moral good. In the context of eating disorders, however, integrated sense of self—in which the self is not at war with itself, pulling the person between unhealthy eating habits and the desire to leave their shackles behind—reflects a sense of peace which is healthy. Paragraphs 46–50 discuss the ways human freedom is understood in and through the body, not over and against it. This discussion reflects the sense of freedom, and interior peace, a healthy relationship with one's self, eating, and food helps facilitate. *Veritatis Splendor* rightly critiques systems in which the self becomes the arbiter of truth, wherein freedom is exalted to the "extent that it becomes an absolute, which would then be the source of values" (no. 32). This explicitly critiques the adoption of "radically subjective conception[s] of moral judgement[s]" like the system of misguided moralism O'Connor and Esterick articulate, in which persons strive to earn goodness through thinness (no. 32). The response to this suffering is the person of Christ, and "Jesus's conversation with the rich young man continues, in a sense, *in every period of history, including our own*" (no. 25).

---

[37] Berkman, "Truth and Martyrdom," 538.

As part of its caution to avoid making the self the arbiter of truth, *Veritatis Splendor* offers a detailed discussion of conscience and its role in the moral life. Space does not permit a detailed analysis of this topic, relevant though it is to interdisciplinary work, but it must be mentioned that thinking theologically about conscience in relationship to eating disorders is tricky, especially in light of misguided moralism. Without guidance, under the influence of ideas about thinness that elide it with goodness, people may be guided by their conscience to avoid healthy choices. Many people with eating disorders or body dissatisfaction feel immense guilt and shame for what is healthy and well-moderated eating; others feel guilty and shameful for engaging in unhealthy habits like binging and purging, but in their current state have limited freedom to choose otherwise. Reforming one's conscience and navigating the shame a misshapen conscience imparts will likely require therapy, time, and grace. Thinking theologically about conscience in regard to eating disorders, therefore, should be done in a way which does not increase shame or correlate goodness with thinness or base one's fundamental value with the success they have in avoiding unhealthy eating habits.

Veritatis Splendor's presentation of moral theology as located within the person of Christ is one of the enduring fruits of the encyclical's contributions to moral theology. It is particularly responsive to the challenges of those struggling with eating disorders, especially in light of misguided moralism's insights into the way in which many people struggling with eating disorders think about the moral dimension of food and eating and the role of relationships in recovery. In the article's subsequent parts, I explore how conceiving of moral theology as located in the person of Christ can help heal the wounds of misguided moralism and then analyze the power of relationship with Christ and the church within eating disorder recovery, especially in light of the isolating effects of social media.

THE ROLE OF RELATIONSHIPS IN RECOVERY

Veritatis Splendor places relationship at the core of moral theology. Beginning with the rich young man's relationship with Christ, the encyclical proceeds to consider the relationship with one's neighbor as part of genuine love for God. Relationship with God—something often experienced through relationship with others—is a means for grace's mediation. *Veritatis Splendor*'s focus on relationship is particularly resonant in regards to the complex nature of eating disorder development and healing. Eating disorders do not develop or heal in a vacuum; as indicated in this article's first part, they are social undertakings. Today's culture, like that of thirty years ago, must be converted and healed—especially in light of how distorted people's relationships with themselves, their bodies, and food have become. Yet *Veritatis Splendor* acknowledges that a culture's impact on people is not determinative; while all people exist within a culture, they are "not exhaustively defined by that same culture. Moreover, the very progress of culture demonstrated that there is something in man which transcends those cultures" (no. 53). While today's culture of thinness and beauty is not suited to human flourishing or growth in virtue, its presence does not necessarily mean that people will develop eating disorders.[38] The inherently social nature of the human person means that community is tied up in personal transformation, and vice-versa. Transformation toward virtue within the context of relationship is part of both attaining eternal life and enacting one's love for God. Despite cultural forces that encourage individualism, humans remain unfulfilled without entering into relationship with others.

Research on the role of relationality in eating disorders illuminates this truth. A 2004 study indicates that women tend to isolate themselves when they are struggling with an eating disorder. Their social withdrawal, "combined with irrational thinking and the need for control, exacerbated the severity of the eating disorders. In the same study, the women shared that the acceptance of a relationship with a loved one was essential to their recovery because it provided unconditional love, support, trust, and hope."[39] Acts of reconnection, close relationships, articulations of support, empathetic friends, and compassion are proven to improve recovery outcomes.[40] Lack of understanding from others, especially family, can likewise hinder recovery, and shut down avenues for communication.[41]

The role of relationships in recovery is also leveraged in eating disorder support groups. Instead of teaching specific skills that help participants recover, they provide "a sense of shared identity for those living with eating disorders, as well as [increase] a person's mental capacity to protect his/her own well-being."[42] They are a space where people in recovery can express themselves, and the group strives to create a culture that protects participants from bias and stigma while they are in that community.[43] Family therapy is another mode of treatment that addresses relationship in eating disorder recovery. It teaches skills required for communication, conflict-management, and

---

[38] See Daniel Daly's *The Structures of Virtue and Vice* (Georgetown University Press, 2021) for a framework for understanding and responding to structures of vice and ways to foster the development of social structures that encourage virtue.
[39] Dina Wientge, "The Power of Relationship in Eating Disorder Recovery," *Social Work Today*, www.socialworktoday.com/archive/exc_0419_2.shtml.
[40] Wientge, "The Power of Relationship."
[41] Wientge, "The Power of Relationship."
[42] Wientge, "The Power of Relationship."
[43] Wientge, "The Power of Relationship."

tolerating difficult emotions for the person in recovery and their family.[44] These skills are needed for both the individual in recovery and their family; supporting someone in eating disorder recovery is difficult and can consume caregivers. Family members may struggle with feelings of guilt, shame, frustration, sadness, fear, anger, and other emotions. In addition to family therapy, those who serve as primary support for people with eating disorders (family, spouses, close friends, etc.) can benefit from the formation of community with others who have a loved one struggling with an eating disorder. Such groups provide space to share challenges and feelings, and skill-based training in these support groups can improve outcomes for caretakers or friends and those for whom they care.[45]

The relational frame of *Veritatis Splendor* helps moral theology recognize the perils of a lack of community or relationships in eating disorder recovery. In particular, relationship with Christ orients the person to *"the full meaning of life* . . . [with] . . . an appeal to the absolute Good which attracts us and beckons us; it is an echo of a call from God who is the origin and goal of man's life" (no. 7). Misguided moralism provides one way of understanding how the pursuit of goodness through thinness is part of eating disorders and can become the full meaning of life for those with eating disorders. However, the goodness for which humans long can, *Veritatis Splendor* indicates, only be found in the Goodness that is God. Disrupting a paradigm of right and wrong by framing morality primarily in terms of relationship with Christ is responsive to misguided moralism's perils. A Christocentric ethic stands in opposition to a rote system of rule-following detached from the strikingly personal nature of revelation. God's goodness offers the full meaning of life that persons seek—their flourishing and fulfillment in relationship, not in achieving a particular weight or body shape. It offers the internal transformation sought in recovery instead of the external transformation sought by extreme dieting or eating disorder behaviors. Relationship with Christ also provides the unconditional love, support, trust, and hope which can be transformative for those recovering from an eating disorder. Knowing God as a God of love who desires nothing more than relationship with God's creation—humankind—helps one understand one's self as existing fundamentally in relationship. Relationships with others, especially in the context of Christian friendship or the church, can also be loving sources of empathy, compassion, and support on the road to recovery. They are pivotal reminders of one's worth beyond numbers on a scale or other cultural measures of goodness—like thinness, fitness, or success in eating healthily. Eating disorders are not a moral

---

[44] Wientge, "The Power of Relationship."
[45] Wientge, "The Power of Relationship."

problem for an individual alone, to be solved by individual moral action (though moral agency plays an important role in the recovery process), but rather require the support and accompaniment of others as well as the transformation of cultural forces that encourage harmful attitudes toward food, eating, and the body.

Social media is radically influencing connection and relationships. After Covid-19, studies arose which considered the effects of social media on loneliness. One group of researchers found that those who use social media in order to maintain relationships—that is, to connect and facilitate social contact—feel lonelier than those who use social media for other purposes.[46] The reality that those who turn to social media for connection experience more loneliness than their peers is especially concerning for those struggling with eating disorders. Research on connection amongst those with eating disorders suggests that they have smaller social networks and struggle to engage socially with others, and they report a greater awareness of the role of social support and interaction as a result of their recovery process.[47] Social media use seems to be a risk factor for increasing a sense of loneliness, and perhaps constricting one's social circles as a result—something which could be particularly perilous for those with or at risk for developing eating disorders.[48] This also seems true given the positive role developing social skills and a social network can have on adolescents' eating disorder recovery.[49] Time spent on social media continues to increase for these populations; during the Covid-19 pandemic, teenagers experienced higher rates of eating disorders and spent more time on social media.[50] Data from 2023 establishes that 51 percent of teenage girls spend at least four hours on social media each

---

[46] Tore Bonsaksen, Mary Ruffolo, Daicia Price, et al., "Associations Between Social Media Use and Loneliness in a Cross-National Population: Do Motives for Social Media Use Matter?," *Health Psychology and Behavioral Medicine* 11, no. 1 (January 2023): 9, doi.org/10.1080/21642850.2022.2158089.

[47] Krisna Patel, Kate Tchanturia, and Amy Harrison, "An Exploration of Social Functioning in Young People with Eating Disorders: A Qualitative Study," *PLoS One* 11, no. 7 (July 2016): 1.

[48] See the *Wall Street Journal*'s podcast series "The Facebook Files" (www.wsj.com/articles/the-facebook-files-a-podcast-series-11631744702) for internal information on the connection between mental health outcomes and Instagram use in adolescents, which reinforces this assertion.

[49] Patel, Tchanturia, and Harrison, "An Exploration of Social Functioning," 1.

[50] Raphaël Dufort Rouleau, Carmen Beauregard, and Vincent Beaudry, "A Rise in Social Media Use in Adolescents During the COVID-19 Pandemic: The French Validation of the Bergen Social Media Addiction Scale in a Canadian Cohort," *BMC Psychology* 11, no. 92 (2023): 6.

day while older teens spend up to 5.8 hours daily on it.[51] Social media not only contributes to isolation, but also encourages those who use it to compare themselves to unrealistic ideals, portrayed through edited images and seemingly-normal accounts actually run by influencers paid by their sponsors to depict reality in a particular way.[52] The sense of dissatisfaction with one's self or life that results, these product-sponsors hope, will motivate viewers to buy their product to help them "keep up with the Joneses" and achieve the effortless happiness or transformation featured on the accounts they see online.

Veritatis Splendor's invocation of the *Catechism* responds to the challenges social media introduces, calling for temperance to be exercised such that human dignity is respected and economic gain not reign supreme. Part of what the seventh commandment forbids is disregard for people's dignity, "buying or selling or exchanging them like merchandise. Reducing persons by violence to use-value or a source of profit is a sin against their dignity as persons and their fundamental rights" (no. 100). In this excerpt, one hears echoes of the manner in which social media and Western culture encourage people to see themselves as a product to hone, improve, and even market through tasteful pictures, engaging reels, or carefree TikToks. The feminine thin ideal's influence echoes through these multiple media. The work of theologian Beth Haile is helpful to consider here; she reflects on how St. Thomas Aquinas's virtue ethics, especially the virtues of temperance and prudence, might respond to its effects. She encourages readers to consider the process of connaturality by which one comes to love what is presented as favorable, and to respond by being judicious in what one sees and consumes. Haile pushes back against the idea that knowing thin-ideal images portray something edited, unrealistic, and unhealthy is enough to resist their influence, or to curb one's desire to attain what they portray.[53] Knowledge of a problem is not always enough.

---

[51] Johnathan Rothwell, "Teens Spend Average of 4.8 Hours on Social Media Per Day," *Gallup*, October 13, 2023, news.gallup.com/poll/512576/teens-spend-average-hours-social-media-per-day.aspx.

[52] Researchers find it hard to tease out whether people struggling with mental health spend more time online to try to alleviate this, or whether spending time on social media increases their struggles with mental health. However, a recent study indicates that when participants engaged in more problematic social media use, their depressive symptoms and loneliness increased, and poor baseline mental health did not predict higher rates of problematic social media use (Holly Shannon, Katie Bush, Cecelia Shvetz, et al., "Longitudinal Problematic Social Media Use in Students and its Association with Negative Mental Health Outcomes," *Psychology Research and Behavior Management* 17, no. 8 [April 2024]: 1551–1560).

[53] Beth Haile, "A Good Appetite: A Thomistic Approach to the Study of Eating Disorders and Body Dissatisfaction in American Women" (PhD diss., Boston College, 2011), 158.

Haile advocates for a conversion that is not merely intellectual, but reforms the appetite through temperance—which, in her estimation, leads the individual to the conclusion that she should avoid looking at thin-ideal images. For example, a woman might:

> look at such magazines and feel a twinge of desire: "If only I looked like that." Upon rationally recognizing that one's desires are out of line with what one knows rationally ("That woman is too skinny!"), the temperate course of action would be to avert one's eyes, to look at something else. In such a way, one can begin to retrain the appetite to desire those things which one knows to be rationally desirable, healthy, and virtuous. By avoiding thin ideal images in popular media, one can conceivably, at least to some degree, resist the internalization process by which one becomes conformed to these images and subsequently experiences greater body dissatisfaction and eating disorder symptomatology.[54]

Haile's work was revolutionary when it was published, and her insights into connaturality and the role of the virtues are rich. She also acknowledges that there is a limit to the extent an individual can abstain from thin-ideal images. However, she wrote her dissertation in the context of a world without social media's current influence, or the power algorithms, in determining advertisement content. Haile notes the need for reform, and the role of grace in helping one become connatural with divine things by perfecting one's "appetites and capacities and directing them ultimately towards their ultimate goal."[55] While her work is compelling and beautiful, in a social media age, her advice is both helpful and limited. One should be prudent in curating the accounts one follows on social media to eliminate those that frequently feature thin-ideal images, dubious nutritional advice, fad diets, or the assumption that all women need and want to lose weight. The effects of social media algorithms and marketing are such that one cannot moderate the advertisements one sees to the degree Haile suggests, nor moderate the content suggested for viewing based on one's age, sex, and previous engagement history. Even forgoing social media altogether would not eliminate the presence of images or advertisements online.

There is a limit to the way prior work in virtue ethics in this area can now be conducted. While objectively good, cultivating prudence and temperance are not enough to thwart the thin ideal's pervasive presence on social media or Internet. In her final chapter, Haile concludes that women are longing for something to fill the hollowness which exists inside them. She suggests that their hunger can be filled

---

[54] Haile, "A Good Appetite," 183–184.
[55] Haile, "A Good Appetite," 199.

by rightly-ordered asceticism, prayer, and worship, naming "the practices of the church as a sort of antidote towards the practices characteristic of women with eating disorders."[56] The grace these practices impart turns reason and will "to focus on the highest things, and to love material and bodily goods in a way conducive to the pursuit of the higher spiritual goods which ultimately lead to happiness (beatitude)," affirming and carrying forward *Veritatis Splendor*'s emphasis on the role of the church in the world thirty years ago while simultaneously foregrounding its importance of an encounter and relationship with Christ.[57]

In addition to complicating the role virtue ethics can have in helping women and girls recover from eating disorders and body dissatisfaction, the digital age presents another risk to people struggling with eating disorders. Online communities exist that are sustained by social media and support people in their pursuit of eating disorder behaviors. These are known as pro-anorexia (pro-ana), pro-bulimia (pro-mia), and thinspiration communities, which encourage their members to continue their eating disorders. In these spaces people can post and others can offer tips on how to hide behaviors from parents and friends, or share extreme diets or purging techniques. They can also post pictures ("thinspiration") as inspiration for others (i.e., "see how thin you, too, can be?") and track their "progress" in weight-loss that brings them closer to the thin-ideal in the context of a community. These groups began in the early-2000s, and are particularly perilous for young people because they promote eating disorders as a lifestyle choice (not an illness), and offer a sense of belonging and community which can make it difficult for those who participate in these communities to leave.[58] They exist on Tumblr, YouTube, Instagram, TikTok, X (formerly known as Twitter), Discord, Snapchat, and Pinterest as well as in private-access communities and chats. There is also growing concern about developments in AI surrounding information access, image creation, and the ability to develop personalized restrictive diet plans or form a plan to develop unhealthy behavior patterns. It could be argued that these "communities" lack a sense of relationship which compels an individual toward virtue, enabling instead the pursuit of short-term fulfillment which in time results in bodily and self-harm. Authentic community ordered to movement toward the good is central to eating disorder recovery.

---

[56] Haile, "A Good Appetite," 268.
[57] Haile, "A Good Appetite," 269.
[58] Lucy Osler and Joel Krueger, "ProAna Worlds: Affectivity and Echo Chambers Online," *Topoi* 41, no. 5 (2022): 888.

Veritatis Splendor's focus on relationship with Jesus can serve to remind people struggling with eating disorders of their fundamental identity. Persons are made to be in relationship with one another, as they image a relational, Trinitarian God; when one feels lonely and disconnected, lacking life-giving relationships, it is natural to search out a balm for this emptiness. This truth makes sense of the frustration some young people report when they acknowledge that using social media often makes them feel more disconnected from others, yet they use it constantly because they struggle to make real-life authentic connections.[59] In an American culture becoming increasingly individualistic and with young people moving away from their families at higher rates than earlier generations, turning to online connection and community to try to remain in touch and fill a relational void makes sense. *Veritatis Splendor* reminds its readers of the relationship that is most primary to their being: their connection to Christ, whose Incarnation was the result of love and established a radical way of being known by God. This God seeks connection with each person through prayer, the Eucharist, and myriad other moments of daily grace. Being reminded of this fundamental love, presence, and relationship is a balm for the challenges of isolation and loneliness experienced by many in contemporary times. The church and ecclesial culture can respond to what is lacking in contemporary culture, and what young people search for as they turn to social media. Relationship with Christ and others—in particular relationships with others in Christ—can help orient those struggling with eating disorders to their own goodness and worthiness, independent of their weight, body shape, or whether they succeeded in eating "well" that day or not. These relationships can both be part of the healing those who struggle seek, and help challenge the narrative that thinner is better and that our bodies always stand in need of improvement. Parishes and small Catholic communities can respond to this need by fostering opportunities for authentic community—teenagers discovering who they are, young people as they navigate new communities, young parents, empty-nesters, and the elderly who are often forgotten—that helps create disciples and push back against the shame and loneliness those who struggle with eating disorders frequently experience.[60]

---

[59] This paradox often plays out in my college classrooms; students feel compelled to use their cell phones, scrolling social media or texting, until the minute class begins. They desire to use their phone during class breaks and prefer to sit silently in their seats rather than talk to their classmates. Yet, they also write about being lonely on campus and struggling to know how to connect with and reach out to others, both in and outside the classroom.

[60] An astute peer reviewer pointed out the robust possibilities of how membership within the Body of Christ community can be responsive to the ills of eating

Conclusion

Veritatis Splendor places relationship with Christ at the center of moral theology, responding to the needs and struggles of persons with eating disorders. In recovery in particular, the unconditional love, support, trust, and hope people with eating disorders name as their greatest relational needs are found to be perfect in Christ. He offers grace that can help people overcome challenges that willpower alone cannot surmount, and the relational frame *Veritatis Splendor* puts forth responds to the misguided moralist tendency to try to earn goodness. In the context of graced relationships, earning goodness is simply not possible. Reliance on Christ to overcome what is lacking in us is the way of spiritual progress, and echoes some of the truths those in recovery discover in their reliance on others for support and assistance. Relationship with Christ also calls the human person into community with others, in particular the community of the church. This reality also reinforces the church's call to provide conditions and structures for the creation of authentic community, wherein accompaniment and support can take place and God's healing grace can flow into the diverse wounds of the members of the Body of Christ.

The encyclical also notes the gift that moral theology can offer to research in the behavioral sciences, echoed by this article's engagement of other eating disorder related fields. Moral theology's faithfulness "to the supernatural sense of the faith, takes into account first and foremost the spiritual dimension of the human heart and its vocation to divine love" (no. 112). Considering persons as more than just bodies and minds and attending to them as ensouled beings in light of other disciplines' work is essential to moral theology. It also enriches the scholarship done in other fields, such as developing an approach to understanding and treating eating disorders that takes seriously the soul of the person involved, and their relational needs as persons made in God's image. This can improve treatment outcomes and enrich work done in the medical and bioethical fields on eating disorder diagnosis, treatment, and recovery.

For those struggling with eating disorders, the encyclical's conclusion offers two resonant reminders. First is "the joy of forgiveness" (no. 112) God offers to those who fail. Forgiveness is something people who struggle with eating disorders must learn to frequently extend to themselves on the road to recovery; recovery is not linear and often contains regressions. It can be difficult for people

---

disorders—including the role of that Body's connection to the mystical tradition, disability theology, and the theological themes of mercy, grace, and forgiveness. These are riches I hope to explore in a future publication

in recovery to extend such forgiveness to themselves, especially because many people with eating disorders have perfectionistic tendencies.[61] This makes recovery's nonlinear nature difficult for them. God's constant offer of mercy and forgiveness can be a model for the way in which they will have to learn to be merciful with themselves as they recover. The second reminder, found in the encyclical's closing paragraph, is that intellectual conclusions will never fulfill the human person. Instead, it is "only the Cross and the glory of the Risen One [that] can grant peace to [one's] conscience and salvation to [one's] life" (no. 120). Out of the cross of Christ comes the resurrection's hope, offered to those who find themselves in the depths of suffering. The resurrection does not take place without the cross, however. Christ's Incarnation means that he knows human suffering well and is present with each person who endures it. With Christ's accompaniment, presence, and relationship, each person has reason to hope in Christ's glory, and know that because of grace, attaining goodness and wholeness is not wholly reliant upon their effort. Christ's glory comes after His suffering, and so there is reason to hope—even in moments that might seem hopeless in light of the weakness of the human condition. For Christ's is the only hope that does not disappoint.[62]

Megan Heeder, PhD, is assistant professor of theology at the University of Scranton. Her research interests include the development of a theological approach to eating disorders informed by virtue ethics as well as theological aesthetics' capacity to redeem contemporary ideals of beauty. Her vocation as a theologian is inspired by a desire to translate the wisdom and riches of the Catholic intellectual tradition into a medium that responds to contemporary challenges and impacts both the intellects and hearts of her students and those who engage with her scholarship.

---

[61] Rose Stackpole, Danyelle Greene, Elizabeth Bills, and Sarah J. Egan, "The Association Between Eating Disorders and Perfectionism in Adults: A Systematic Review and Meta-analysis," *Eating Behaviors* 53 (August 2023), doi.org/10.1016/j.eatbeh.2023.101769.

[62] I would like to extend my heartfelt thanks to M. Therese Lysaught and the reviewers who made excellent structural changes to the original draft of this article and offered fresh insights that opened up avenues to beautiful theological explorations. Thank you very much for your time, expertise, and the opportunity to think with you; this article is better for your contributions.

www.ingramcontent.com/pod-product-compliance
Lightning Source LLC
Chambersburg PA
CBHW072023240426
43667CB00044B/2258